W9-ATA-983

A Guest at the Feast

Essays

Colm Tóibín

SCRIBNER

New York   London   Toronto   Sydney   New Delhi

Scribner

An Imprint of Simon & Schuster, Inc.

1230 Avenue of the Americas

New York, NY 10020

Copyright © 2023 by Colm Tóibín

All rights reserved, including the right to reproduce this book
or portions thereof in any form whatsoever. For information, address
Scribner Subsidiary Rights Department,
1230 Avenue of the Americas, New York, NY 10020.

First Scribner hardcover edition January 2023

SCRIBNER and design are registered trademarks of The Gale Group, Inc.,
used under license by Simon & Schuster, Inc., the publisher of this work.

For information about special discounts for bulk purchases,
please contact Simon & Schuster Special Sales at 1-866-506-1949
or business@simonandschuster.com.

The Simon & Schuster Speakers Bureau can bring authors to
your live event. For more information or to book an event, contact the
Simon & Schuster Speakers Bureau at 1-866-248-3049
or visit our website at www.simonspeakers.com.

Interior design by Kyle Kabel

Manufactured in the United States of America

1   3   5   7   9   10   8   6   4   2

Library of Congress Cataloging-in-Publication Data is available.

ISBN 978-1-4767-8520-2
ISBN 978-1-4767-8522-6 (ebook)

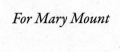

For Mary Mount

Contents

PART THREE

EPILOGUE

PART ONE

Cancer: My Part in Its Downfall

London Review of Books · 2019

It all started with my balls. I was in southern California and my right ball was slightly sore. At the beginning I thought the pain might be caused by the heavy keys in the right-hand pocket of my trousers banging against my testicle as I walked along the street. So I moved the keys into my jacket pocket. The pain stayed for a while and then it went away and then it came back. I was doing readings every day, selling my melancholy stories to the people of Orange County and places south. I wondered, some days, if there might be a doctor in the audience who, if I made a suitable announcement at the end of the reading, could make this pain in my right testicle go away. But I didn't want to make a fuss.

When the readings were done, I went to LA and ignored my balls. Then I went to London and looked them up on the internet. It was clear what I had. The right testicle was painful but not swollen. But the veins around it had decided to swell up a bit. The internet made clear what this condition was called:

A hydrocele is a type of swelling in the scrotum that occurs when fluid collects in the thin sheath surrounding a testicle . . . Older boys and adult men can develop a hydrocele due to inflammation or injury within the scrotum.

A hydrocele usually isn't painful or harmful and might not need any treatment . . . Adult men with a hydrocele might experience discomfort from the heaviness of a swollen scrotum. Pain generally increases with the size of the inflammation . . . A hydrocele might be associated with an underlying testicular condition that can cause serious complications, including infection or tumor. Either might reduce sperm production or function.

I wrote stuff during the day and then attended a few parties and wandered in galleries in London and went about my business in the pretty sure knowledge that I had a hydrocele. Had I been sure how to pronounce it, I might even have started to boast about it. Sometimes, however, my ball was really sore, and the swelling became more significant. One evening, I made my way to one of the London hospitals and was put in the line for accident and emergency. They took blood samples and a urine sample. When a doctor finally saw me, because she was a woman and it involved my balls, she had to have a nurse with her while she was inspecting me. As the doctor looked at my testicles, the nurse looked at me or at the doctor. I looked at the nurse or at the floor.

The doctor said there was nothing in the blood or the urine that pointed towards a clear diagnosis. For that, I would have to get an ultrasound; the hospital would contact me to arrange that. She didn't think it was cancer, she said, as there was no sign of a lump anywhere. So that was good news. The bad news was that the pain in my right ball grew more annoying. I managed to make an appointment with a urologist in Dublin and flew home one morning in late June. As soon as he examined me, the Dublin urologist seemed concerned, though he said nothing. He arranged some blood tests and an ultrasound, telling me that, unlike with kidneys and livers, a biopsy on a ball is rarely a great idea.

The ultrasound was done by two young guys filled with kindness and sympathy. Fully aware that taking your trousers and underpants down and lying flat on your back and then having some sort of gel poured on your junk before a type of prod begins to zoom around the outside of your balls is no fun, they outdid each other in being nice to me. When they had performed their magic, they told me they would have to go further and this meant that the little towel they had put over my dick, such as it is, would have to be removed. "I know this is shaming for you," one of them said. I sat up, rested on my elbows, and looked at him. "When you get to my age," I told him, "nothing is shaming."

It was decided that I should go on various antibiotics for a week and then they would see what to do. In that week, the swollen veins disappeared, but the ball itself got harder and bigger. When I came for the next appointment, the urologist asked me if I was fasting. I hadn't bothered to have breakfast so I told him truthfully and innocently that I was. "In that case," he said, "I can fit you in today."

I knew what he meant; he meant to remove my ball. I went home and packed a small suitcase and presented myself at the hospital. As the afternoon waned, dressed in a gown with no back, I was wheeled down the corridors. Soon, with the help of the anesthetist, I was fast asleep. This was just as well, since during the time that followed, the urologist, with efficiency and speed and skill, removed my right testicle.

As I recovered in my hospital bed, I was told that it would take a week for a laboratory to report back on the intricacies and inner workings of what had been removed. I also got a CT scan so that my insides could be examined by another group of doctors. I was asked if I had a problem with being told the result on the phone rather than waiting for an appointment. I said I had no trouble with the phone.

A week later the phone rang and I was told that I had a cancer of the testicles that had spread to a lymph node and to one lung. Instead of seeing the urologist, I would now need to see an oncologist. For a few days I comforted myself by pretending that, because of my abiding interest in the mysteries and niceties of Being, I had to see an ontologist. Nobody except one of my fellow Irish novelists thought this was funny. The oncologist showed me the scan of my insides on his computer. At first I could not work out from what angle these images had been taken. Then I understood that the scan was a sort of carpaccio of the middle and lower parts of my torso, a slice of the inside of the self. While I saw some well-known organs clearly, the cancer as it appeared on the screen was nothing more than a smudge, a few faint grains. If the doctor had not pointed them out to me, I would have given myself a clean bill of health and gone to play tennis.

To get rid of this cancer, the oncologist told me, I would need chemotherapy. Four weeklong sessions of it, with a break of two weeks between each session. He told me I could stay in the hospital while getting the chemo, which seemed sensible. If something went badly wrong in the middle of the night, I thought, I would be in the belly of the whale rather than at home wondering what to do. "It's curable," he said, his voice low and reassuring, his tone modest and reserved. "We have not lost anyone to it yet."

I had looked the whole business up on the internet and was concerned that the chemo would cause deafness and also a thing called "chemo brain," when a patient starts not to be able to remember things after treatment. The oncologist directed me to a nurse who arranged for me to have a hearing test so that they would have a baseline from which to judge, should there be any deterioration. She was less sure about "chemo brain." Her response was the sort I became accustomed to over the coming months: it depends on the person, it's hard to predict, everyone is different. As Mrs. Cadwallader in *Middlemarch* says, "Everything depends on the constitution: some people make fat, some blood, and some bile."

The nurse noted a great number of details about me before asking me if I drank much alcohol. I thought it wise to respond that I was sober in all my habits, a quiet-living person. The nurse did not seem fully reassured by this. And then she told me that people who drank a good bit of alcohol found chemo easier, since chemo was, like alcohol, a sort of distilled liquid with a poisonous edge that could change your mood and cause you aches and pains and generally damage your system. The more alcohol you had drunk in your lifetime, the less shock chemo would be to your system. In Ireland, there are people who have taken a pledge not to drink ever; they are often members of the Pioneer Total Abstinence Association of the Sacred Heart, founded in 1898. When I was growing up they were simply called Pioneers. You don't hear much about them now, except in the deepest countryside. Nonetheless, the young nurse now invoked their presence. "Among those who have chemo," she said wistfully, "it is the Pioneers who suffer most."

Both she and the oncologist were oddly unalarming. They spoke calmly and sympathetically. Neither of them was interested in spelling out all the terrible things that could happen. They made the future sound manageable and bearable. It was arranged that I would present myself in the hospital the following Sunday afternoon. The Irish poet Patrick Kavanagh has a poem called "The Hospital," which begins: "A year ago I fell in love with the functional ward / Of a chest hospital." This did not happen to me, but it was surprising how quickly the routines of the hospital became comforting and absorbing. They had a way of filling the day, which was long. It was hard to sleep because of the intravenous steroids that were part of the treatment. On one of the first nights, something started to bang and clash in my head. It was not made up of words, but it was like words, or like sentences; it possessed the shape of a sentence or two that were violently seeking an outlet. Every so often, there would be a break and a single word that had nothing to do with anything would suddenly emerge.

All this happened in the silence of my head, but it was like sound, and loud sound. I supposed it was the unconscious taking an opportunity to make itself heard, or perhaps it was what happened if you began to go stark raving mad. When I called the nurse and told her about it, she offered me a sleeping pill. I took it and fell asleep. The next night I had a notebook ready to write down any sentences and words that might come banging into my head, but nothing happened. I never got that strange visitation again. Soon I got into a routine. A sleeping pill every night gave me rest from about 1 to 5 a.m. I woke knowing it wouldn't be long before I heard noises in the corridor; a nurse would check my blood pressure and take my temperature. Then someone—often a very glamorous Asian woman—would visit to take blood that would go to the laboratory. Then—usually between 6:30 and 7 a.m.—the oncologist would arrive, turn on the light, and ask me in a soft voice how I was. Early on, I decided that unless I was fully falling apart, I would tell him I was well. I enjoyed adding that there were "no issues." I had never used the word "issues" before. I had heard it used most memorably by an English novelist at a foreign literary festival when he told his publisher that he "had issues" with his bedroom. Now I could use it every morning if I wanted. It was one of the small compensations for having cancer.

On one of those mornings in that first week, the oncologist told me that a more recent scan had shown a tumor on the liver as well; this meant that the chemotherapy would have to stick rigidly to schedule. In other words, there could be no more than two weeks between each five-day session. He said all this very calmly. After his visit, breakfast came, and the newspapers. Sometimes, I had a drip putting water in my system through the night. And then steroids in the morning, and something else too to stop nausea. All this before the holy ceremony of chemo, also known as the juice.

Two senior nurses would arrive in the room with the chemo on a trolley. They would ask me my name and my date of birth. They would check the number on my wristband. Then one nurse would read out the details of the chemo to the other. This would be done with such seriousness and sense of somber occasion that, the first time, I presumed there would be some response from me when the first drops of liquid went coursing through my veins. Maybe I would shake all over or let out an unmerciful cry. (I later learned that another nurse was waiting outside the room in case I had a bad reaction to the juice.) Instead, nothing happened, nothing at all. The juice was neither cold nor hot. It caused no pain. I wondered if all the talk about it wasn't exaggerated. Instead of shaking all over, I read the newspapers. I listened to the radio. I had my lunch. When the chemo finished, I had a shower and put on my dressing gown and slippers and did a tour of the hospital corridors to see if anything was going on.

In those first five days, I also read a long and difficult novel. When I went home, it looked as if there was going to be no problem. I was able to go to the supermarket, and go up and down the stairs in the house. They had given me anti-nausea pills so that not once in all the time I was on chemo or afterwards did I have any desire to vomit or suffer any stomach problems. The steroid pills, however, were more difficult. Once I'd taken them in the morning, I could feel them grinding away inside me all day. In the early evening, they gave me a sort of energy that dissolved quickly enough but also meant that I could not sleep without sleeping pills, and the pills only guaranteed sleep for four hours.

I lay on the sofa in the house in Dublin and thought about things. I read a bit, but not much. I found that I had no interest in listening to music. For the next three months, I would not need to shave. My eyebrows would thin out but not disappear. The hair on my head would more or less go. The hair on the rest of my body remained in place until towards the end of the chemo, when it disappeared. It took a long time to grow back. In that first week after chemo I lost any desire to eat or drink, and I lost all sense of taste. Instead, my sense of smell became acute. For the next few months, on the street, I could smell everyone's perfume or aftershave or deodorant. It grew to be confusing and surprising. In the house, when I was upstairs, I could smell any food in the kitchen even when there was nothing cooking. I could smell the soot in the chimney.

I wanted to be on my own in the house in those two weeks between chemo sessions. Friends offered to come and stay, or look in every morning, and Hedi, my boyfriend, wanted to come from LA, but I found the possibility of company oddly alarming. It was easier just to lie on the sofa, my head propped up, and think about nothing but have a friend bringing drinks of water or checking to see whether I was still alive. It wasn't as though I was enjoying a period of inwardness and introspection. There was no inner self to examine or get in touch with. There was a surface self and all it could do was stare straight ahead. Over the months, I got used to a few friends who came regularly, and looked forward to their visits in the evenings. But I needed, for the most part, to spend the days alone. People often talk about their "battle" or "fight" against cancer. It was really hard to know what this meant. I was sure that the nurses and doctors were involved in some battles, as were the cleaners and the kitchen staff, but I just lay there not thinking much. All I really wanted to do was fall asleep and not wake up until it was over.

What I never want to hear again is the screeching of seagulls. Dublin, I discovered as I lay on that sofa for much of July and August and September and October and November, is awash with them. They peak in early August and fade somewhat by late October. They would sail towards the house in groups and start to shriek in the upper air. Then they would move lower and shriek some more. They are scavengers and they love the fact that the center of Dublin has so many new restaurants. They get fat on garbage.

As soon as there was the faintest glimmer of sun in the eastern sky, the gulls began their ghastly cries, and they went on screaming even after night had fallen. Even worse, they would breed. Their progeny found rooftops, where they perched, seeming to be immobile, but moving an inch or two back and forth on their horrible little webbed feet. All summer, they did this incessantly over my bedroom; they made their irritating noises against the slate through the night until I came to believe that they and their parents had been sent by some force of darkness to mock me.

Not being able to taste brings with it dreams of tasting. On days when I was at my worst and could be cheered up by nothing, I imagined a large grilled lobster and then I thought about a boiled lobster. And then I dreamed of a steak cut into strips and marinated and then put into the pan to fry. The strange thing about this is that in the normal course of events, I wouldn't know marinade from Toilet Duck. But now, in this time of chemo, it was much on my mind. Food had no taste, none at all, but it had texture and it had color. Sometimes, I was sure I wanted something—a duck breast, for example, or a piece of fruit, or some yogurt—only to find when it was in front of me that I didn't want it at all. I liked really thin, cheap, white sliced bread. I found that I had an interest in making a sandwich with plenty of butter and two grilled rashers. I can't think why I could eat this when I could eat nothing else. I could also eat a sandwich of tinned salmon. A few times I made a big fry-up and added a small tin of baked beans. I ate it all down, even though it could have been sawdust or deadly poison. A few times I gorged on a banana sandwich. I could not drink water. Since I had no taste, my mouth treated it as a foreign object. No other drink was better.

Often, especially early on, I went online to explore my ailment. There are chat rooms where people with cancer share their experiences. For many of them, after a week of chemo, the two weeks afterwards came with much variety. Bad side effects one week; better the next week. But I felt the same way all the time. The internet also mentioned a difficult operation that could take up to eight hours for people like me, whose cancer had spread to a lymph node. When I brought this up with the oncologist, he said he hoped that we wouldn't have to do it.

In the end, I found nothing on the internet that was of any use to me. Except ginger ale. One patient in a chat room said in passing that when he or she could not drink anything, they found they could drink ginger ale. Ginger ale saved his or her life, or at least his or her kidneys. I tried it and it was better than anything else but still not easy to swallow. Then I asked one of the nurses if she had a solution and she said that I should add elderflower cordial to the ginger ale. That became my drink of choice. Food was much harder. Since I was not hungry and could not taste, I could go a long time without food. I went from 175 pounds down to 145. My waist went from 36 to 30. Since all my trousers started to fall down, I had to buy some new ones.

Because I didn't have to shave, I didn't examine myself in the mirror. This was a mistake, since it allowed me to believe that I resembled a normal person. The illusion was broken one day when I was coming out of a pharmacy with a small bag of drugs and needed to get to the hospital for a test. I hailed a taxi and it stopped. As I was about to open the door to sit in the front passenger seat, the driver saw me close up and spotted the pharmacy bag. He quickly drove away. Since there is a methadone clinic for heroin addicts close by, he must have thought that I posed some sort of risk to him or his taxi. In any case, he did me the great favor of making me realize that I looked like a bad Egon Schiele drawing.

After the first five days of chemo, I began to get sores in my mouth. Each day they got worse. When I went for a blood test, it was discovered that some of the cell counts were very low. The hospital phoned and asked if I was all right. When I showed my mouth to a nurse and a doctor I was given some liquid morphine—which I liked—and was told that this problem could be prevented next time by having an injection of some high-tech material that created white cells in some very modern and artificial way.

When my friend Catriona Crowe inspected my house at the beginning of the chemo regime she declared that it would not do. On the floors or on cluttered surfaces there were many items that had lingered there for years. Old keys, old underpants, old Chinese takeaways, old banana skins, half-finished short stories written out in longhand in notebooks, beginnings of novels, books, pamphlets, old mandarin oranges, old apple cores, condoms still living in hope. Catriona made clear that this would all have to go; the house would have to be made hospital-clean. No dishes could be left in the sink. Food would be thrown out when it had reached its sell-by date. The inner reaches of the fridge would be cleared of dried-up food. Smelly socks were not to be left on the floor in the kitchen. Since I did not have a washing machine, bags of stuff had to be sent to the launderette, all of whose machines, it seemed, were now working full-time for me.

Catriona phoned every morning and came most days with news of the wider world and often with food she thought might be palatable. She was judging the Irish Theatre Awards at the same time. As she dropped by on her way back from a performance, I loved asking her if there had been a big crowd at the play. This was what you did in Enniscorthy, where I'm from. If anyone has been out anywhere—at mass, a football match, downtown, in Dublin, to the pub—you asked them: "Was there a big crowd?" When other friends came to visit, they could also be asked if there had been a big crowd at any event they had attended. Once the steroids kicked in, I could talk and pay attention. I don't know why asking about the "big crowd" gave me such satisfaction. The answers tended to be generally the same.

In that first two-week period after chemo, a pattern established itself. I would wake early to the sound of the seagulls and lie there as the room brightened. I would then call my boyfriend and we would talk on the phone. Then I would take some pills and open the curtains and get back into bed, often half-listening to the radio. Then I would turn off the radio and lie in bed for a few hours without thinking. Then I would decide to get up. The rest of the day would be spent on the sofa. It was not merely that the chemo left me brain-dead so that as time went on I could not even read; the effect of the drug darkened the mind or filled it with something hard and severe and relentless. It was like pain or a sort of anguish, but those words don't really cover it. Everything that normally kept the day going, and the mind, was reduced to almost zero. I couldn't think. All I could do sometimes was concentrate on getting through the next five minutes because contemplating any longer stretch of time under the pressure of the chemo and the steroids (and perhaps some other drug) was too hard. At about six o'clock in the evening I would feel OK for a while, but by nine or so a real lassitude had set in again. When I decided to go to bed I would find that the decision made no difference. Two hours later I would still be lying on the sofa. I spent the time staring straight ahead. No watching films; no TV; no radio; no books; no magazines or journals. No memories; no thoughts; no plans for the future. Nothing.

Each day passed like this in pure blankness, punctured by pangs of depression that were close to unbearable and that made going back into the hospital for the second five days of chemo easy. I liked packing my case and getting a taxi across town and settling down in the familiar space of the cancer ward. In the hospital, my mouth became an object of some interest, but otherwise it was the same routine: intravenous water overnight, then steroids and anti-nausea drugs and then the juice itself. And then a shower, a walk around the hospital and visitors and then a few hours lying there and then some sleep.

The day after my second week of chemo ended I went back to the hospital and got an injection in my stomach. It felt like nothing. I looked through the list of possible side effects, but without concentration. This treatment was going to be good; it was going to produce or provoke into being essential white cells. That was a Saturday. A week later, at about six in the morning, I was woken by the most excruciating pain in my pelvic area. It felt like something throbbing; with each throb the pain was more intense until it felt that it could not get worse and then it did and did again. And then it died down only to start again. White cells are made in bone marrow: it felt as though the cells were being produced too fast and were getting ready to crack the bone. I called the hospital and spoke to a nurse. Taking note of what I said, she asked me if I could come to the hospital, if someone could drive me over. I reminded her that the pope was in Dublin. He would be appearing the next day in the city, which was now divided in two for security reasons. A car would not get through. The nurse said she would call me back in ten minutes.

In those ten minutes, as the pain became so intense that I actually believed I was going to have a baby, I imagined appealing to the pope to let me through. I would apologize for all the rude things I have said about him. I would take back the assertion that he doesn't mean a word he says. I would withdraw my view that at least we knew where we were with the previous two. With Bergoglio, no one knows where they are. I would tell him that I was sorry I had said this and would promise to be even more emphatically and eternally sorry if he let me through. This kept me busy as the throbbing pain grew more and more unbearable. Finally, the nurse called back and told me to get the oral morphine I had used before. She told me exactly how much I could take. If the pain was still there in an hour, she said, I was to call back.

I drank the morphine and lay back. Then I called my boyfriend. I took him through the pain as it rose and fell. Soon, we got talking about other things, our conversation peppered with high screams from me. The pain continued for almost an hour. I was ready to phone the hospital again. Eventually, however, it began to die down until, without my noticing exactly when, it disappeared. What it left in its wake was one stoned man. I spent the weekend looking at the pope on my laptop. I was both high and low and sorry I had not had that encounter with him in the middle of Dublin. I had, in fact, got tickets for his event in Phoenix Park, thinking that I might be well enough to trudge across the city and stand in the park while he preached to us all.

Slowly, as the chemo went on, things got worse. There were a few hours, especially in the early evening, that were almost OK, but the rest of the time was grim. There was no pain again, just increasing weakness, continued lack of appetite and growing depression. Nonetheless, the hospital was still filled with distractions and things that amused me. I liked everybody there and that helped. It was the time at home that was hard. One morning, a few days after I had finished the third week of chemo, I knew that I couldn't go on. It was difficult to stand and I could no longer leave the house. I hadn't eaten anything for three days. I was determined, however, to follow the agreed schedule, which included a blood test the next day. If there were any real problem the blood test would show what it was. But I found myself sitting in the middle of a room in real distress. It wasn't just the lack of energy, or the inability to think, or the sense of some vast shadow wandering in my head: it was much more active and present than that. I tried my five-minute trick. I imagined that this would last only for five minutes. All I had to do was concentrate on the next five minutes, keeping at bay the certain knowledge that there would be many such five minutes and that would include today, all day.

In the end I phoned the hospital. The nurse could not have been kinder, but since there was no pain, no precise problem, she did not seem to know what to say. Feeling bad was part of chemo, so the fact that I felt bad was not news. Eventually, it was clear that I really couldn't explain what I felt and we ended the conversation. A few minutes later, she called back and said I should come over to the hospital and pack some things with a view to staying for a few days. Up to now, admission to the hospital had been quick and simple. This time it was slow and cumbersome. Waiting there in the middle of all the bustle and busyness was difficult. I tried to get someone's attention so that I could let them know that I really needed a bed now. My problem remained that I had no pain, no obvious dire predicament. When they finally told me I could go to the ward, I found that I couldn't walk and needed my wheelie suitcase to lean on as I made my way along. When I was spotted doing this, they told me to wait for a wheelchair, but I was too cranky, too desperate to find a bed. I remember a nurse whom I didn't know coming with a list of questions. They included a query about my bowels. Had they moved that day? In hindsight, this seems like a perfectly normal question. At the time, I thought it was funny and I told the poor bewildered nurse that I believed the question to be rather too personal. In fact, I said, I could not think of anything more personal. Then I gave in and told her that, as far as I was aware, my bowels had not moved that day.

I'd got it into my head that the last five-day session of chemo was going to be easier to tolerate. My body was getting used to this poison, I thought, though I had no evidence at all for this conclusion. One day I tried it out on one of the most senior nurses. She looked at me skeptically. Once more, the chemo as it went into the veins could easily have been a relaxant. It was all peaceful. On that last Friday, as the last bag of juice emptied out and the cannula was removed from my arm, I felt like a free man. All we would have to do now was wait a few weeks for another scan to see how much of the cancer was still there and how much had gone.

One night the following week as I tried to go to bed, I knew that I was worse than I had ever been. It was like mixing a major hangover with a major flu. I had not been able to sleep for a few nights in a row and I still was not eating. Lying down brought no relief. In the middle of the night I knew that I could not go on like this. At about seven in the morning, I phoned the hospital. The same problem arose: I was not in pain. I had no complaint that had a name. It took a while before the nurse said that I should come to the hospital. They would find a bed for me at some point.

It was clear to me and to everyone at the hospital that I looked awful, but I began to think that maybe this was standard, something all the medical people had seen before. The next day, however, a doctor and nurse came to see me and assured me that lots of blood tests were going to be done. One of these tests showed that my neutrophil count was very low. When I asked the doctor if it could be lower he shook his head. When I asked how it might go up, he said blood transfusions might help and then it might rise of its own accord, now that there was no more chemo. I would have to have my temperature taken every half hour, he said, including through the night. If it went over a certain point, a big dose of antibiotics was waiting for me. My platelets were also down, he said, and would have to be watched too.

It was in the middle of the night two days later that the nurse, having taken my temperature, whispered: "It has spiked." Quickly, quietly, she left the room and returned with liquid antibiotics that I was to take intravenously. That meant that I was grounded in the hospital for about a week. I could look at the newspapers in the morning and see visitors, but I still had no desire to read or listen to music. One day a friend came in with a bottle of apple juice from his orchard. I was still living on ginger ale mixed with concentrate of elderflower and whatever scraps of food I could manage to eat. When he had left, I was about to put the apple juice aside when it struck me that I should try some. I found that I could taste it. Not fully, but enough. Over the next few days I found that I could taste blueberries and lemon juice, but not orange juice, not strawberries, not raspberries.

Slowly, very slowly, the blood counts started to go up. Once the antibiotics were over, I thought I would be able to go home, but I was told I would have to wait until there was a real upward trend. One Sunday at about four in the afternoon I was feeling especially unhappy. Catriona was in the US; Hedi was in LA. It occurred to me out of the blue that I should tell the nurses I wanted to go home. When I tried this, I was told that going home on a Sunday was unusual but not unheard of and that my request would be put to the oncologist. After a while, the nurse returned to say that I could go home if I wanted. I could leave this very second, if I wanted to, as long as I knew to call if I had the slightest problem.

My problem, not so slight, was that I couldn't really walk. I had been disguising this in the hospital, going to the bathroom only when there was no one around, leaning against walls, moving cautiously, sitting on a plastic chair to have a shower. Now I sat down on the floor of the room and tried to pack a suitcase. Then I sat on a chair and attempted to dress myself. I found that since the suitcase had four wheels, I could lean on it and, bent almost double, move along. I knew, however, that if I passed the nurses' station using this method someone would notice and wonder if I was really fit to go home. I remembered that there was another corridor that led to a smaller lift. I made my way furtively down that corridor and then, via the lift, to a corridor below, where I met a nurse from my ward returning from her break. Having taken one look at me, she stood back. "Are you all right?" she asked. When I told her that I was perfect, I watched as she assessed the moment and concluded that she should wish me well and walk on.

I finally arrived at the lobby, where I got to sit down, feeling that I would never have the strength to get up again. I looked around in the vain hope that I would see someone I knew. After a long wait, I edged towards the door, keeping close to the wall. Once out on the street, I nodded to the taxi driver who was first in the queue. He came and helped me into the car. When I told him where my suitcase was, he went into the lobby and fetched it. Then he drove me home and helped me into the house.

There were many people I could have phoned, but most of them, I felt, would take the view that I should be in the hospital. Also I didn't want to disturb people on a Sunday evening. I lay on the sofa, where I battled against cancer once more by lying there staring straight ahead. I had such great resistance to thought that I didn't even worry. Past midnight, I went to bed. In the morning, I saw that I had no food and no fluids in the house. I got up and took my steroids and dressed. I found walking to the supermarket at the bottom of the street quite easy. I put what I needed in my basket. When the basket was almost full, as I stood in one of the aisles, I realized that again I could not walk. If I tried to move, my knees would buckle. I supported myself against the shelves until a man, I supposed a manager, approached. I asked him for a chair and a glass of water. I didn't actually want a glass of water but I thought the request would make me sound more plausible. When I was sitting comfortably, I asked him if he could get someone to take my basket to the checkout and then bring my purchases back to me so I could pay. I tried to look like someone who would not spend the day annoying him.

I managed to leave the supermarket with my groceries and cross the road, but once at the bottom of my own street, I knew I could go no farther. I sat down on the steps of an office building. I had, of course, come out without a phone. Anyone passing would think I was part of the city's homeless crisis. I didn't feel I could safely stand up. It wasn't cold. If I remained here all day, I thought, something would be bound to happen. I studied the busy office people going by. If I was to accost one of them, I thought, I would have to get it right the first time. It would be too much to have to sit here as person after person ignored pleas for assistance. When I saw a tall, sporty-looking guy in a suit come towards me, I caught his eye and told him what the problem was and pointed to my house at the top of the street. I could stand up, I said, but I would probably need help walking and would need to rest along the way. This guy, who was South African, agreed to help. He was very cheerful. He thought my bag of groceries a bit ambitious. We stopped a few times when I needed to sit down on the steps of buildings. He deposited me, like a little frail old lady, at my door.

After a few days, when my walking had improved, the hospital called to say that it was time to do another CT scan. First I had to do some blood tests. These made it clear that I needed to get water intravenously, so I went into hospital for a few days. The CT scan people were cool, but they couldn't understand why I didn't want a needle in my left arm. The reason was simple: many, many needles had gone in there, including cannulas, which allowed for the chemo to go into the veins. Most people who work in hospitals don't know how to put in cannulas. Nurses tend to be better at it than doctors. What doctors lack in skill, they make up for in confidence. The younger they are, the more certain they become that they know how to put in a cannula. This means that they tend to put the needle in where it least needs to go, and they put it in badly. Often, they have to do it two or three times. In my hospital, there was one nurse who could put in a cannula sweetly, simply, painlessly, perfectly. But she could be busy. Nonetheless, I asked for her when I thought she might be free. In the meantime, my left arm felt like a Francis Bacon painting.

The CT scanners must have thought I was someone who liked making a racket. When they stuck the needle into me, I started to yelp. I yelped my way through the little tunnel as my insides were scanned. I yelped as the scan returned me to civilization. I yelped more loudly as they took the needle out. The scan, despite all my yelping, turned out to be good, with much of the cancer having disappeared. I did not need any more chemo for the moment, but I would have to be checked regularly. I was on parole. The news coincided with the arrival of my boyfriend from LA. I couldn't drink alcohol; I still had no appetite for food; I was skinny and miserable and bald; I couldn't sleep; I found walking hard; I had only one ball. But there really was nothing to complain about.

A week or so earlier, I had begun to work with a physiotherapist. He brought news from the outside world. He went to Vegas on his holidays. He and his girlfriend enjoyed going to restaurants. This meant that I could ask him: Was there a big crowd in Vegas? Was there a big crowd in Fallon & Byrne? He made me sit on a chair and then stand up, and do this twenty times. He made me walk up the stairs without touching the banisters and do this twenty times. He had lines of tough material, like the stuff that makes balloons, that I had to stretch out with my arms. He had many more exercises. He made me walk for miles. I felt better after sessions with him.

Now, as I prepared to leave hospital for what I hoped was the final time, the physio was going to work with me so that I could, by Christmas, have some of the characteristics of a real person. And when I got home, my boyfriend was going to be there and we could talk and make jokes or sit opposite each other on the sofa. I could watch him reading a book while pretending to read one too. We could watch a movie, like ordinary people. An hour after I got home, when the phone rang, I recognized the number. It was the hospital. Could I repack my suitcase and come back over, they asked. And do it now, without any delay at all?

The scan, on closer examination, had revealed blood clots. I needed injections to thin my blood and I needed to stay in the hospital while this was being done. That evening my boyfriend and Catriona came to see me. And then they went to dinner together. I would have liked to go with them. This was one of the five or six things I would like to have done last year and didn't: a friend's wedding in Glasgow; the pope in Phoenix Park; Patricia Bardon in Mahler's Second Symphony at the National Concert Hall in Dublin; the Wexford Opera Festival. As I lay there, however, I could not take the blood clots seriously. I knew that they were potentially dangerous, but that knowledge still didn't make me worry. In bed, I identified the difference between cancer and blood clots. In a tennis match, blood clots would be all smashes, aces, double faults and disputes with the umpire. Cancer would be steadier and stealthier, keeping calm on match points, returning the ball accurately—low cross-court strokes—rather than hitting big winners. In literature, blood clots were Christopher Marlowe, violent, restless, brilliant, while the cancer would be Shakespeare, coming in many guises, dependable, sly, fully memorable. In painting, the blood clots would be Jackson Pollock, the cancer Barnett Newman. In Tory politics, Boris Johnson would be a blood clot; William Whitelaw, if anyone remembers him, the cancer. In Dublin, Malahide is a blood clot, Monkstown the cancer. In Europe, Macron is a blood clot, Merkel the cancer. In other words, instead of battling cancer I was becoming foolishly respectful of it. Like Shakespeare, Newman, Whitelaw, Monkstown and Merkel, it would not respond well to being underestimated.

A rumor spread in the hospital that a doctor who knew about blood clots would visit me later in the day. Only he could decide whether I went home or not. He had the same name as a character in Wallace Stevens's "Notes Toward a Supreme Fiction," who was also referred to as "major man." By this time I was confronting the fact that I was slowly going mad, and that this wasn't helped by the steroids and the lack of sleep and the general excitement about going home and seeing my boyfriend. In bed, I began to whisper "major man" as Catholics in a similar state might call out the name of Jesus or his mother. I also prepared a joke to tell this doctor so that he might accept my urge to go home. Preparation was important, as I can't really tell jokes. I just don't know how. I can try to tell them, but they come out skewed and flat and somewhat sad.

When the doctor arrived, I worried, at first, that I had started the joke too quickly. It was about Randolph Churchill having a tumor removed and the tumor turning out to be benign and Evelyn Waugh saying that they had removed the only part of Randolph that wasn't malignant. The doctor laughed. He seemed like a good-humored guy. He checked that I would be able to inject myself in the stomach every night with some blood-thinning agent. He told me not to take any long-haul flights for the moment. He suggested I see him before Christmas. And then he told me I could go home.

This time I marched proudly if rather slowly past the nurses' station, thanking them for all their kindness and care. I got a taxi home. Soon, I would watch my boyfriend having his dinner and then we would light a fire and lie on the sofa. In the morning, there would be physiotherapy. In the meantime, I went to the bathroom and looked at the scarecrow in the mirror. I hardly knew what to say to him. "Was there a big crowd at the hospital?" I whispered.

"One less now they've let you out," he replied sourly. It would take a while before his hair and his eyebrows showed signs that they might grow again. It would take him even longer to get used to having only one sad, lonely ball. They used to complete each other's sentences, those balls, they were so close, but now the surviving testicle has to get used to the change. It has to realize that the time of two balls has passed. The age of one ball has been set in motion.

A Guest at the Feast

Penguin · 2011

There were no artists in the town, but there were rumors and the odd mention of a writer and a painter who had been born in Enniscorthy and had left. My uncle had written poetry in both Irish and English and he had died in his early twenties of tuberculosis. He was the youngest of my father's family and left behind an afterglow that was strong enough when I was growing up—he had died fifteen years before I was born—that I took his name as my confirmation name. He was the cleverest of them all, they said, and the funniest.

My mother wrote poetry too in the years before her marriage; some of the poems were published in the local paper, and one, which she often quoted, was reprinted in one of the Dublin papers; others were published in a small, short-lived and cheaply printed periodical that my father also worked on.

In the 1930s, each county had two or three university scholarships. My father studied at University College Dublin on one of these scholarships, having come first in the county, and returned then to the town to work as a teacher. My mother was seven years younger. She saw him for the first time as he rode his bicycle past her mother's huckster shop on Court Street on his way to give a Latin grind to a woman called Nancy Connolly. Her father pointed him out and she remembered going out to the footpath in front of the shop to look at him. She was thirteen then, and within a year, on the death of her father, would leave school to go to work, and this would make her hungry all her life for books and learning and impressed by anyone who had access to them. In 1946 she married him, the man on the bicycle who knew Latin.

The plaque to my father is on the left-hand side of the door, and the plaque to Fr. Joseph Ranson with whom he founded the museum is on the right-hand side. I put both of them into my novel *The Heather Blazing* in the years when they worked at making Enniscorthy Castle into a museum. I am not quite sure how much I imagined and how much I remember. But I remember fragments, I suppose; none of it made any sense then, it didn't need to, it was complete and perfect and fascinating. It seemed natural that a model threshing machine should rest on a table in a room where a copy of the execution warrant of Mary, Queen of Scots hung on the wall. There was a room full of old carriages, one of them owned by the poet Moira O'Neill, the mother of the novelist Molly Keane. There was a backstairs that was wooden and an older stone stairs and from the battlements you could see the entire town.

Upstairs there was a 1916 Room, with a postcard on display that my grandfather sent to my father from Frongoch Prison in Wales, where he was interned after the 1916 Rising. My father could have been only two or three years old, and the postcard addressed him as Big Fellow. I remember that he didn't want this side of the card displayed because his students already had one nickname for him— "The Boss"—and he didn't want them to have another.

Behind this was the 1798 Room with pikes and maps of how our side had escaped through Needham's Gap. Old ghosts walked freely in the castle wondering, I imagine, if they should let the queen know what dreadful use the building had fallen into. I remember discovering the dungeon, cut into the rock in the very bowels of the castle. It was airless and dark with a smell of damp and mold. Soon, they put a light down there and distempered the walls, leaving a space for the etching that someone who was imprisoned here had made in the wall, a crudely drawn figure with armor and a sword.

Some Tudor adventurers stayed in this building. In 1581 a lease of the friary and castle was granted to Edmund Spenser. In 1594 there is an entry in the diary of the Lord Deputy, dated December 17: "Sir William Clark and Mr Briskett went to Enniscorthy to the Lady Wallop's for Christmas." Mr. Briskett was the poet Lodowick Bryskett, an intimate friend of Spenser's, whose most famous poem was written on the death of Sir Philip Sidney. Bryskett owned property along the river. Lady Wallop was the wife of Sir Henry Wallop, who came to Ireland in 1579 as treasurer of war for the Elizabethan administration. He made a fortune from the forests that stretched away to the north and west of Enniscorthy. In one of his several petitions for further rewards for his services, he wrote: "I presume I have deserved favour in greater measure for having planted at Enniscorthy, among so wild and barbarous a people." In the 1960s, as we, the descendants of the wild and barbarous, played around the castle, we were led to believe that the word "wallop" had entered the language courtesy of Sir Henry and his violent disposition. "There is no way to daunt these people but by the edge of the sword," he wrote in 1581.

I have never seen a building with the same small, squat, determined shape as Enniscorthy Castle. How could they ever have imagined that we would, someday, have their castle as the museum for things we deem important. (Sweet Slaney run softly.) But this is literary, a game you can play with history, and I feel no real connection with it, as I feel no connection with 1798 other than as an event in the past that was regularly commemorated. 1916, the War of Independence and the Civil War are much closer, more real and genuine.

The Roches, who sold the castle to the museum (I remember the figure of £1,100, but I could only have been five or six at the time of the sale), also sold their gardens, and the Castle Ballroom (it has since gone through several name changes) was built on the site. I know that the Roches had a tennis court and a daughter called Betty because once upon a time one of the more unmannerly natives of the town was invited to play tennis with Betty and began the game by roaring down the court, "Balls to you, Miss Betty," or so it was reported.

Dodo Roche, the last of the Roches to lodge in the castle, went to live with her maid on the Mill Park Road. She was extremely polite and worked for the blind. In the old days, local people pulled Roche wedding carriages through the streets, but now the castle was ours, and visitors wrote their names in the Visitors' Book before they went to look at all the exhibits. And if you wanted something that your parents could not afford, someone always said to you: "Who do you think we are, the Roches of the castle?"

In 2008, while I was staying with my friends Patrick McGrath and Maria Aitken on the island of Ibiza, we were visited by Maria's nephew and a friend of his called Limo. They were very polite and well-educated young Englishmen. In the course of the conversation, I realized that Limo is Lord Lymington, after whom Lymington House and Lymington Road (also called the Back Road) in Enniscorthy are called. He is a Wallop. I inquired if I could ask him a question. Very politely he agreed that I could. "Do you own Enniscorthy?" I asked, knowing that many of the ground rents remain in the family's hands, or did until recently. He thought for a moment. "Oh yes, we do," he said. "Or we did."

The hill that overlooks Enniscorthy, Vinegar Hill, is famed in song and story; it was the last stand of the rebels in 1798. It stood across the valley from our house. I was told how the English tortured the rebels and their associates by giving them a "pitch cap," pouring boiling tar on their heads and then pulling the hardened tar off. As a small boy, I imagined the English pulling the very tops of their heads off and staring inside at the strange, soupy, viscous mixture that made up the brain.

As we passed through the town of Tullow, north along the Slaney Valley, my father would point at a shop whose owners (or rather, whose owners' ancestors) had betrayed a rebel priest, Fr. Murphy. He said that you could never go into that shop. I often wondered why those people did not change their name, or set up shop in some other town.

> At Vinegar Hill, o'er the pleasant Slaney,
> Our heroes vainly stood back to back,
> And the Yeos at Tullow took Father Murphy
> And burned his body upon the rack.

My father believed that every boy should be at the Christian Brothers by the age of seven, even if this meant skipping whole years with the nuns. Thus I found myself aged seven, raw and unprepared, standing in front of a small surly Kerryman called Tommy Brick, whose habits were known to all. He lived in digs and he played bridge and he walked through the town in long strides with his hands in his pockets.

For recreation in the classroom, while his charges were doing a composition in Irish or in English, he would pick his nose and make a ball of what he found there and then flick it at random towards us seven-year-olds. You kept one eye on your composition and one eye on Tommy and you learned to duck his flying snots and this was, in many ways, more useful for later life than the Irish or the English composition.

Since my father had two degrees and had won scholarships and written articles, everyone presumed that I would have to be smart too. But once when a visiting teacher and friend of my father's came to the class and noticed me, I watched the teacher telling him with great solemnity that I was, in the phrase of the time, "no good." And it was true. I lived in a permanent state of dreamy distance from things. Even still, if someone gives me directions, I find I have nodded and given every indication that I am following and thanked them. But I have not been listening. I haven't a clue what they have just said.

So it was with Tommy Brick and Brother Curtin and Mr. Dunne and Brother McInerney and Brother Carbery, each of whom I suffered under for a year. I never listened and I never did anything but the bare minimum at home. Tommy Brick and Brother Carbery used a leather strap to see if it might wake me up. Brother Curtin tried a long stick, Brother McInerney a short one. Mr. Dunne used the back and the front of his hand. None of it worked. I couldn't listen. I would try to listen and then something would occur to me, something quite banal and useless would detain me while every other boy sat quietly listening and afterwards could do the sums or the grammar.

There were only two things I could do and these merely made matters worse for me. I could do mental arithmetic faster than any other boy, except a chap called John McCann, who had a speech impediment that was even worse than mine. I only stammered over certain hard consonant sounds. He stammered over everything. Both of us could multiply 15 by 202 much faster than anyone else.

Both of us could add 15 to 47 and then divide that by 17 and include the decimal points. The teacher became bored asking us so once we put our hands up we were left alone. In any case, because of our stammers, it took us both an age to come out with the answer and this didn't seem to please.

I could also give smart answers. I could say something that would make the whole class laugh. None of the teachers minded this much or noticed but it drove poor Mr. Dunne out of his mind.

"Here you are now," he would say, "with your smart answers, your funny remarks and you haven't a brain in your head."

And then his tone would grow ominous.

"And I'll wipe the grin off your face, I'll get that smirk off your face."

Tommy Brick would lose his temper and roar in his Kerry accent (we were in Wexford on the other side of the country): "Christ Almighty, ye drive me up the walls!" Sometimes, to my delight, he would put the f-word before the word "walls." He looked as though he meant it. Brother Curtin had no temper but was a terrible stickler for spelling. He wore too much hair oil. Brother McInerney was a morning grouch. But it was with Brother Carbery the real problems arose.

Brother Carbery was my teacher for the final year in what was called national school, which I left when I was twelve. This year was important because if you did badly you got put into the B class in secondary school, and no one from my breed, seed or generation had ever been in a B class. Boys from poor parts of the town got put into the B class and boys from the country from small farms got put into the B class. Brother Carbery understood the social humiliation of the B class and he constantly informed me and my classmates that the B class was my destination.

My parents lived in a world of their own, and since these were the days when teachers and parents kept miles away from each other, they had no idea of the looming threat of the B class. (My father, as far as I knew, did not teach much in the B class.) They thought that I should, like the rest of my siblings, try for a scholarship. Since Brother Carbery was training the brightest boys in the class for a scholarship, they told me to join his special class. This meant I was going to have to go to him and ask him. My stammer became much worse. I waited for days until we were all writing an Irish composition (we were always writing Irish compositions) and he was marking copybooks and I approached him. He was a strange man; he merely nodded coldly and said you know the time and the place.

He waited for a few days before he picked on me. Nouns in the Irish language come in declensions, and he had been explaining the most recondite of these declensions. He knew that I did not know a declension from a hole in the wall. He began by asking me to form a simple genitive, which I couldn't do properly, and then each question he asked became more complex. Each time I failed to answer he would find someone who knew. Eventually, he told me to go home.

My mother pounced on me as soon as I arrived home. Why was I not at the scholarship class? I told her Brother Carbery put me out. She went and found my father, who said that these declensions were very difficult and he didn't even teach them himself until the final years of secondary school. My mother got into a rage. The last time she had done this was when a teacher, a colleague and friend of my father's, a more feared teacher called Chick Walshe, hit my older brother across the face. She wrote him a vicious anonymous letter. She was proud of the fact that this had quietened him, and that he had blamed another woman whom my mother did not especially like, confiding to my father the identity of the imagined culprit. She often asked my brother to report any further outbreaks to her.

Now she went and got her hair done and put on her best high heels and set out for the monastery. For days afterwards, she gave anyone who called a vivid account of her interview with Brother Carbery. She told him first of all that she had no interest in anything he had to say, she was here to talk and not to listen. And she was here to tell him that if I didn't get a scholarship, declensions or no declensions, she would blame him personally and write to the head of the Christian Brothers in Ireland about him.

It was deliciously unfair. Brother Carbery stood up to her first, she said, but then suddenly, out of the blue, he said he was sorry, he apologized to her, and thereafter peace broke out. He brought her tea. From then on, I sat in the scholarship class, immune from difficult questions about declensions, and immune indeed from the scholarship as well. Soon, Brother Carbery was coming to visit our house, finding times, I noticed, when he thought my father might not be there. We used to hide upstairs during his visits and fight over who would answer the door to him. And send someone down to listen outside the door to what my mother and the Christian Brother could possibly be talking about. He obviously enjoyed being shouted at, one of my relatives said, and he's back for more. There are men like that, she told me, but I did not believe her. We watched him walk calmly down the street after his visit. My mother, in the kitchen, smiling to herself, refused to say why Brother Carbery continued to come to the house. It was all a mystery.

I remember when they came to the town. They were not like other Traveller families of the time who would come to the door begging, the women wrapped in old rugs, often carrying a child. Unlike other Travellers, this couple and their children wanted to settle, and they did not deal in horses or scrap, and they did not seem to have an extended family.

The woman's face was strong and open. There was a peculiar charm and kindness in the way she greeted you in the street, no matter who you were, even if you were a child. She smiled at you without wanting anything in return as she moved up and down John Street, Court Street, Rafter Street. She often had her children with her, and sometimes her husband. They drank a bit around the pubs. I cannot remember whether this woman begged sometimes or not, but it did not affect her popularity. She was liked and admired for settling and for sending her children to school.

Years later one of her sons, the eldest I think, had got into trouble with the cops. Anyway, he was taken to Dublin and he started a jail sentence. I had been too long away from the town and I couldn't place him, but he must have been one of the small children who followed his mother through the streets.

Then finally he was released. On a Saturday night/Sunday morning soon after he came home, he had a row with his father, or so it was reported, and he ran through the town, breaking shop windows. He did not break the windows at random: he broke the windows of the big stores, and the more unpleasant, uppity shops. He spared the smaller shops, or the shops owned by pleasant, nice shopkeepers. He knew the town like a sociologist; he must have watched it as a small boy arriving with his mother and father and developed a sharp sense of which shopkeepers deserved to have their windows broken and which did not.

In his book on the painter Tony O'Malley, Brian Fallon wrote:

> In a country town, everybody knows you and your family, or at least knows about you; every death or birth is a kind of communal event, and there is a certain sense of an enveloping cocoon of fatalism, of a preordained round ending in the local churchyard. It is a difficult thing to put into words, but it is felt by everyone and permeates the small, tight world; and though the town itself may be left behind, you are marked in certain ways for life.

O'Malley spent some years in the early 1950s in Enniscorthy, where he worked as a bank clerk. He did drawings all the time, walking out at weekends to quiet places near the town. He painted

Vinegar Hill and the Turret Rocks, but his work from that period often centers on places that were not famously picturesque. When he was transferred to another town, he left a suitcase of drawings behind in Hayes's boarding house on Court Street. He forgot about them until one day thirty years later, when an exhibition of his work was on in Gorey, he was walking through Enniscorthy and he met one of the Hayes family who reminded him that his suitcase was still in the attic.

There were drawings he had done of the hill behind Keating's house in Ballyconnigar on the Wexford coast, and they are of interest because the hill has disappeared with the erosion. I imagine him doing these drawings on one of those wonderful warm Sundays when a crowd had come down from Enniscorthy to the strand at Ballyconnigar with the river that changes its course each spring. And farmers with their wives and children sat uneasily on the strand in dull suits staring out to sea.

Our family stayed in a hut here one summer, and as boarders in Keating's another year (where we got ham twice a day), and later in Curracloe, which was nearer Wexford and was more cosmopolitan and exciting. (It had a hotel and two shops and Dublin people and is perfectly described in John Banville's novel *The Sea*.)

But in earlier years until I was seven or eight our Morris Minor—registration number ZR 92—turned left at the ball alley on the road between Blackwater and the sea and ended in what was called Ballyconnigar Upper, but was locally called Cush. Beams from two lighthouses shone in the windows at nights: the Blackwater Lightship and Tuskar Rock, which was more powerful. And there were black insects called clocks that scuttled across the cement floor in the mornings.

Each year new steps had to be cut into the damp marl of the cliff so that "the bathers," as the locals called us, could make our way down to the strand. The soil was weak and it was easy each year for the winter to eat into the cliff. Where once there had been fields now there was thin air. It was getting worse each year and was a great topic of conversation for all visitors.

There was a Dublin woman living up the road from us and it was said that one of the local women didn't like her and could make her cows shit directly outside the Dublin woman's door.

All along this stretch of the Wexford coast there was an elaborate network of lanes, rutted, with thick bushes and briars on the ditches, and all of them led somewhere, to remote holdings, whitewashed houses with red galvanized roofs, and a sheepdog barking as you approached.

One day in the late 1960s, I found three forbidden books on top of my mother's wardrobe, three novels that had been banned by the Irish censorship board: John McGahern's *The Dark*, Edna O'Brien's *The Country Girls* and John Updike's *Couples*. I cannot imagine my father reading these books, but I can imagine my mother and one or two of her friends, Catholic women in a provincial town who desperately sought a window onto the wider world, exchanging them, discussing them and hiding them from the children.

This, then, was samizdat Irish-style where women in a small town who were curious about the outside world would learn to recognize one another and would exchange forbidden texts that dealt with sexuality and adultery.

In 1971 when I was sixteen, I won a book token in an essay competition and was allowed to travel from my Catholic diocesan boarding school to Dublin to collect the award and spend the book token. I have a vivid memory of being stopped by two priests when I arrived back and being asked to show them the books I had bought. I proudly produced Jean-Paul Sartre's *The Age of Reason*, Kafka's *The Trial* and Hemingway's *The Sun Also Rises*. One of the priests said that he didn't like Kafka, he was too dark, and the other suggested that I should write an essay on the books when I had read them. They nodded and went off. It didn't occur to them to confiscate the books or worry about their influence.

In five or six years we had moved in Ireland from the censoring of serious books for adults to the wide availability of paperbacks. Reading, suddenly, was to be encouraged for all. The censorship law was reformed in 1967, but the attitudes seemed to change overnight. My mother and her friends were brought up in a conservative, insecure state; in their forties they found themselves living in another place altogether, a world where everything once held dear was questioned and undermined, where Irish television and the Irish newspapers and even elements within the Irish Catholic church encouraged the open discussion of things that had been closed when they were growing up.

In my novel *The Blackwater Lightship* I tried to dramatize a moment in my mother's life that seems to me still mysterious and unfathomable. My mother's mother believed that when someone in the family was ready to die, loud knocks would come to the door at night and the women in the family would hear these knocks. I remember my mother saying that she heard them the night before her mother died. That was 1960. And then she said that she had never heard the knocks since. This meant that when my father died in 1967 she didn't hear them. And she implied, when she talked about the knocks, that it was something that belonged to an old belief system, something that had passed.

Thus, sometime between 1960 and 1967 in Ireland, my mother ceased to believe in magic, or something that was very like magic. There was no point in asking her what date she stopped believing this, or if she had really ever believed. Nothing in this story was precise like that, or easy to pin down. I am not sure what a sociologist could do with this, or an anthropologist even, but I know as a novelist that I was brought up in a house where books were important enough to be dangerous and that I witnessed a dramatic change happening to the beliefs and attitudes of the generation before mine. This was a great unsettling, Ireland's opening itself to the outside world.

Sometimes an announcement would be made that we were going to Wexford town. Clean socks, a good pullover, combed hair. For me, even still, Wexford town is a most exotic place. It had a Woolworth's and a bookshop and a long main street. At a certain age I was allowed to go off on my own and meet the family later back at the car. Ice cream, photographs of film stars, sweets, an orange drink that you could see bubbling in a Perspex box. Woolworth's was fascinating. But mainly it was the sense of elsewhere, or being away from our own town, if only for a few hours, that made the town of Wexford so wonderful.

Wexford town has a strange beauty in the washed light of the early winter. It is not hard to imagine that boats once sailed from here to Buenos Aires, that in the early years of the last century the long quays of Wexford were busy with trade and traffic. That is all over now; the harbor has silted up. But the town still looks like a medieval port town, and the atmosphere of Wexford is full of the rich mixtures that the harbor and the fertile hinterland combined to make. The town got its name from the Vikings, and clearly remained an important center of trade, but its tone was set by the Normans. Half the names of the people are Norman, and in the plainness of the architecture, there is a Norman austerity. The other elements include not only the Gaelic, but the English and Huguenot.

Thus three writers from the town—John Banville, Billy Roche, Eoin Colfer—have surnames that are Huguenot and Norman but backgrounds that are mixed. Roche's work is full of the sadness of the town; history for him has enough associations in just one generation. He has a way of placing a halo around ordinary speech, finding a common phrase and making it sound like a poetic moment of truth. Banville's Wexford, which appears sporadically in his work, could be a light-filled town on the sea anywhere in the northern hemisphere. In *Mephisto*, Wexford could be a Hanseatic town. Banville is concerned to clarify and illuminate and make more mysterious the central matters of order and chaos, memory and imagination, language, truth and logic. Roche presents a Wexford full of talk, he is interested in spiritual topography; Banville's tone is much grander.

The train journey along the Slaney River between Enniscorthy and Wexford remains for me the most moving and resonant landscape anywhere in the world. In that silvery still afternoon light, for several miles you see no roads and hardly any buildings, just trees and the calm strong river.

All of us have a landscape of the soul, places whose contours and resonances are etched into us and haunt us. If we ever became ghosts, these are the places to which we would return. There is a small single-lane bridge along that stretch of the Slaney called Edermine Bridge; it spans the river at its loneliest and most mysterious. If you stop for one second and look north, you can see the spire of Pugin's cathedral at Enniscorthy rising over the other buildings of the town and the brown-green water below you cutting deep into the sandy soil, moving slowly towards Wexford and the sea.

It is 1971 in Wexford and I am sixteen. Those of us at St. Peter's College boarding school who want to go to the dress rehearsal of the opera have to assemble every afternoon before study to listen to a recording of the opera and have the story explained. I have a clear memory of the stereo record player being rigged up and the light from the sea shining through the long windows and the old broken-down desks and the chipped wood of the wainscotting and the peeled paint. I have no memory of the music, however. Not a note from those afternoons has lingered in my memory, not a sound. And nothing of the story. And yet I know that I went there every afternoon for a week.

When my family came to visit, I casually mentioned what we were doing and I told them the name of the opera, *The Pearl Fishers* by Bizet. My mother said that it had the most beautiful love duet in all opera and she tried to hum it, and she told the story of how two men, a tenor and a baritone, were in love with the same woman, and they sang the most beautiful love song in her honor. At home, she said, we had a record of John McCormack singing it. I can still see the record sleeve, blue and silver, and I know that later I listened to it. At the time of the opera, however, I had never paid any attention to it, being too wrapped up in James Taylor, Simon & Garfunkel and Leonard Cohen.

I know that I was upstairs in the balcony during the opera, but I could not have been very far back, because the lighting and the opening scene are still clear in my mind, and the extraordinary precision of the singing is still with me. I know that the soprano was called Christiane Eda-Pierre, but I have no idea of the names of the other soloists. Now, as I write this, the word "motif" comes back to me. In the talks about the opera each afternoon, we were told to watch for motifs, but that did not sink in then as very important. Now, as I sat in the Theatre Royal in Wexford, I recognized the motif that came before the first duet and I was ready for those soaring moments when the two voices merge and move apart and compete and merge again.

*   *   *

I hitchhiked to Gorey, the next town north, in the early 1970s because I saw a news item in the *Enniscorthy Echo* that there was an arts center open there and I wanted to see it. I didn't realize then that art was a way of making shape out of your own concerns. I thought painters lived at a remove from what they painted, and writers invented plots and poets thought of suitable subjects.

Paul Funge was a painter and he ran the arts center in Gorey. I met him on my first day there. He smoked all the time and lacked the solemnity I associated with adults. He had, I would later learn, an extraordinary facility with paint, but what was important for me then was the idea that his work was autobiographical, that it came out of himself, his experiences, what he knew. He was not afraid of that.

There was a lot of talk in Gorey; a lot of people—artists, poets, journalists—came and went. I worked on a poetry broadsheet. I held a spotlight in a production of *Murder in the Cathedral*. I went to the pub with anyone who was free. At first, I didn't drink; I didn't like the taste of alcohol, but then I discovered vodka and white lemonade, and that became my staple diet in Gorey. I learned that if I drank a lot of it I tended to puke, but found that almost immediately I was fine. Once I washed out my mouth and blew my nose I could go back to the bar and drink loads more.

During my second summer hanging around the Gorey Arts Centre, James Liddy arrived from America to edit the poetry broadsheet. He too lacked solemnity and there was a lot of laughter in

French's pub on the main street. I had never heard talk like this before, nor come across such opinions and attitudes. I could sit in the back room of French's and laugh my head off at what was being said, or stare in wonder at a worldview that had not been taught in school.

A few times the two worlds collided. One Sunday night, with a lot of vodka and white lemonade inside me, I ventured out rather late from French's to hitchhike home to Enniscorthy. I got a lift from a law-abiding family who were neighbors, their son was near my age. I tried to say as little as possible. When I spoke, I could hear the vodka in my voice. It was a journey of twenty miles. Before Camolin, thank God, they started up the rosary, Mammy and Daddy doing the first mysteries, then junior and then me. It was a sobering business.

"Don't, whatever you do, leave your bike out there." The voice of the draper's wife, Mrs. Monk Doran, was sharp and authoritative as usual, but now it was agitated as well. It was the Market Square in Enniscorthy in 1967. I was twelve and there was something new, unexpected and exciting happening. When I brought my bicycle into her shop, Mrs. Monk Doran looked as though she had been taken hostage and the town laid siege.

Fleadh Cheoil na hÉireann had come to Enniscorthy. Halls and public spaces all over the town had been reserved for the many competitions in all areas of Irish traditional music from dancing to fiddling to singing in Irish and English. All ages could take part in the competitions. The organizers had left nothing to chance. The town was ready: food, accommodation, parking facilities, toilets, everything was in place.

But something new was going on that no one had prepared for. On Friday of the long June weekend—Monday was a bank holiday—huge numbers of people with scruffy clothes and long hair began to arrive in the town. They did not look like the sort of people who wanted to take part in competitions. It was hard to imagine them waiting their turn to be heard. The men wore jeans, and, what shocked people like Mrs. Monk Doran more than anything, the women wore jeans too. Later, when the Fleadh Cheoil was discussed in our street—and in every street in the town it was discussed for months on end—a neighbor said that for the whole weekend he walked through his own town and he could not tell the difference between the men and the women. They all had long hair, they all wore trousers, they all walked around as though they didn't care about anything. Other neighbors nodded gravely as though nature had been disturbed at its very source.

All that weekend, the long-haired strangers camped on the Bare Meadow. The meadow beside the river was really bare that weekend, our neighbor said, as people on the road above could look down and see those people, men and women, cavorting naked on the grass. In their bare skin. It was a disgrace.

As Friday moved into Saturday, it became clear that the numbers were way above expectations. Many had no tents and nowhere to sleep, so an appeal went out to the townspeople to open their houses to the visitors.

Property owners in the town were nice, quiet people. They had seen this new generation on television, but they never expected to see them in the flesh, and they certainly didn't want them in their houses. Their main interest that Saturday was to stop the town's own young people from being contaminated by this free-for-all, so once I had made my purchase, Mrs. Monk Doran instructed me to go home and stay at home. And when I arrived home, it was announced that all children were banned from going downtown. The Fleadh Cheoil was going to happen in our absence.

That evening, at about seven o'clock, I had an idea. My father was in the Castle Museum, and I could tell my mother and all adults who stopped me that I was going there to help him on his express instructions. This was a lie and it worked. And when I arrived in the museum, my father realized that he could not send me home unaccompanied. He told me that I was to stay by his side.

When the museum closed, I walked through the town with him.

Streets that were normally quiet and dull, streets where nothing happened day after day, these streets were now alive with drunken groups linking arms and pushing their way forward, yelping and shouting. On corners, lone singers roared out songs, accompanied by banjo or guitar. There was a huge crowd outside Billy Stamp's public house in the Market Square; some of them were sitting on the ground, they all had bottles or glasses, and they were all laughing and talking in a way that was new to me. There was nothing cautious or watchful about them, and a few couples were kissing passionately. Some of the men had big beards as well as long hair.

My father knew and I knew that he should have taken me home. But I also knew he didn't want to. Both of us were too excited to go home: Enniscorthy was being transformed from a small provincial town into a center of depravity, hilarity and loose living. My father took me to Peter Hayes's pub.

We stayed there until the early hours. I was fed bottles of fizzy orange while my father and various friends of his drank pints of Guinness and watched the comings and goings of this brave new world, young men and women in a massive state of abandon. When these outsiders sang, they threw their heads back, they sang as though the world depended on it. A few times that night in Peter Hayes's pub on Court Street in Enniscorthy, I witnessed an awed silence as one of the visitors sang or played. They were totally weird but, slowly, as the night wore on, my father and his friends began to get used to them. I remember before we left, a woman with long hair came in selling pigs' feet. And years later, when I would tell people that I was from Enniscorthy, they would often laugh and say that they had the time of their lives in that town during Fleadh Cheoil na hÉireann in 1967. It was, for them, the summer of love.

"A student! A student!" she repeated as though it was the word for a wild animal. "I don't know. Will you want to have beer parties?" She peered at me. I needed the flat and I would have promised anything: I insisted that there would be no beer parties. She looked at me again. She was old and her sight was not good. She was unsure; she would have preferred a civil servant. The last tenant had been a doctor. I assured her that I was a quiet fellow from the country and I would be no trouble. I tried to look innocent. The rent, I remember, was three pounds a week. The room was at the back of the house and overlooked a long garden and the empty space where the Harcourt Street train line used to run. There was a huge fireplace, an enormous sofa, a single bed, a table and some chairs, and there was a gas cooker and a sink in the corner. It was so quiet it might have been in the middle of the country. I could, the landlady said, leave my bicycle in the hall. The flat was mine.

Up to this I had lived near University College Dublin at Belfield in the southern suburbs. Now I was living in the center of Dublin. I could use the National Library, which Stephen Dedalus and James Joyce and W. B. Yeats had used, rather than the modern library at Belfield.

Most days I walked down Earlsfort Terrace, past the old university that would later become the National Concert Hall, and I crossed St. Stephen's Green. Here was the real world full of old ladies on their way to the Country Shop for morning coffee and men in suits on their way to meetings. In the main hall of the National Library on Kildare Street the porters checked your bag in case you were carrying a bomb or a sharp instrument, but in those days—this was the autumn of 1974—they did not check your credentials: they presumed that you were doing serious research and treated you accordingly.

You signed your name in the big old book as soon as you went into the magnificent round room of the library. You found a table, making sure that the light worked, and you set about ordering your books from the library's vast store. I don't think that I had ever been as happy as during those first months in the National Library.

I read what I could find about the Dublin book trade in the reign of Charles II. I worked on another paper about the idea of the past in Restoration England. I looked around me a lot and I regularly went out for a smoke.

In those days the College of Art was sandwiched between the National Library and the Dáil and the art students were as exotic and colorful as jungle birds. They were either very tall or very small; they had either very long hair or very short hair; some of the boys looked like girls and vice versa. The readers in the National Library, on the other hand, were a dull-looking lot dressed in faded tweeds. The art students seemed to have made their own clothes, or bought them secondhand. They were perfect in every way. I wished I was an art student.

It was the time before most of the pubs in the center of Dublin were taken over by young people. In Kehoe's public house on South Anne Street, where you could go when the library closed, there were old people and middle-aged people as well as students, and it was the same in O'Neill's on Suffolk Street and the Scotch House on Burgh Quay, and these pubs became part of my life now that I lived in the city center. Captain America's on Grafton Street was all the rage; it was more expensive than the Coffee Inn on South Anne Street or Gaj's restaurant on Baggot Street. You could only go there if someone else was paying, or you had plenty of money, or you had drink taken and thus had thrown caution to the wind.

On Thursday nights as I wandered back up towards Hatch Street I could check to see if there was a new film ready to open in the small cinema that later became the Irish Film Theatre. I saw most of the Bergman films there and I believed in their northern gloom and deep seriousness as I believed in nothing else. When the real winter came, I had coal delivered, carried through the basement and emptied out from sacks into a shed in the backyard. I felt responsible and adult and organized, like a child playing house.

There was a city to explore. Behind Hatch Street was Harcourt Terrace: I was fascinated by the row of Regency-style houses there, uniform in a way that was unique in Dublin. Except for parts of Fitzwilliam Square and Merrion Square and the new housing estates in the suburbs, the city seemed to have been built house by house, each a different size and shape, as though they wanted nothing to do with one another. These stately, grand houses in Harcourt Terrace around the corner from my lodgings were all painted the same color.

Opposite them, beside the police station, was the office of the film censor. He had cut a crucial scene out of Fellini's *Amarcord* when it was shown in the Academy Cinema and he had banned *Last Tango in Paris*. I wondered what he was doing in there all day.

One Saturday I found Camden Street. Up to this I had never checked what was beyond Harcourt Street; I had done my shopping in Baggot Street. My city was a Dublin of new office blocks beside Georgian and Victorian buildings, and shops that were like monuments such as the Eblana bookshop on Grafton Street, Smyth's on the Green, Mitchell's wine shop on Kildare Street and Wigmore's the optician. Most of the shops on Camden Street, on the other hand, had a provisional, ramshackle air, and they were much busier and less formal than any of the shops on Baggot Street. There were no supermarkets. This was more like a village than a city: people looked at you as though they knew you.

It was the beginning of the gentrification of the area between Camden Street and Clanbrassil Street. Here, once more, were rows of houses built at the same time in the same style. I don't know why I found this notion so satisfying: a city streetscape as something planned and shared. As spring gave way to summer you could wander in these streets and watch the young married couples decorate what had once been lower-middle-class and artisan houses in the style of various glossy magazines. Dividing walls were knocked down; new walls painted white; house plants everywhere; abstract paintings over the mantelpiece; floors stained and varnished. A new design-conscious middle class was emerging in the city. Beside them, old-fashioned and resolute, lived people born in the area, who sat in the pubs on Camden Street bewildered at decimalization and rising prices and the new lives and lifestyles coming into shape around them.

When I remember the view from Camden Street towards the Dublin Mountains, I remember the light, raked and liquid, and the constantly changing sky and the biting wind that could last into April. I had never lived in any other city then. So I don't think I noticed the light at the time, or thought that there was anything strange about white billowy clouds racing across the sky on a summer's day, and even the wind must have seemed normal. This was the world as far as I was concerned.

In June, the university closed, but I did not have exams until September. No matter how hard I planned to study, I spent more time out of the National Library, wandering the streets, awestruck by the city, than at my desk. And afterwards, when the bell rang in the vast shadowy reading room, and the last few diligent readers gathered up their books and papers and turned off their lights, there was still an hour or two of pub life. You could sit on the ground outside Doheny & Nesbitt's on Baggot Street with your pint beside you and your pullover around your shoulders and wonder what you were going to do when the exams were over or, more important, where you were going to go when the pubs closed. The city was glamorous, exciting, full of possibilities.

In those years I used to go to the Stag's Head, which is hidden behind Dame Street. On weeknights the bar would be half-empty. I remember it, however, at its most stately and shadowy and beautiful on Saturday mornings in the winter and spring.

One Saturday morning in that pub in the spring of 1975 I found myself sitting close to an old man who was small and wizened, with skin like parchment and lines deeply etched into his forehead; he was wearing poor clothes. There was an air of hunger about him, not only of the body but of the soul, not unusual in Dublin pubs in those years. The man studied me in disapproving fits and starts before he moved closer. I had a book with me and he asked me about the book. At first, I thought he was slightly mad or drunk, and, as he began to talk, I realized that he could not hear very well. I also discovered that he knew a great deal about books. And as he made a few sour and pointed remarks about writers, for a second he could have been a figure out of Flann O'Brien or even out of *Ulysses*. His eyes took me in fiercely. He asked me to buy him a drink, but nothing more than a glass of Guinness.

At some point he inquired if I had ever managed to get a copy of John McGahern's *The Dark*. I said I had one in my flat. He tensed to listen. Slowly, I realized that he believed that the book was still banned. (It had been banned on publication ten years earlier.) I told him that the ban had been lifted and the book was in paperback now in every bookshop. He expressed great surprise, once he understood, and the expression on his face turned almost tender; he said that he would love to read the book. Could I get him a copy? And there was something, he said, he could give me in return. He asked me where I lived. He would like to deliver it to me, he said. I became uneasy.

He wanted to know then if I liked twentieth-century music and I said that I had heard some Bruckner and Bartók but Mahler was really as far as I had got. He ignored me, or did not hear me, as he mentioned Delius and Vaughan Williams. By this time, I was uncomfortable with the intensity of his tone and wondered how I had so quickly and easily got myself into a position where I might have to meet him again or have him call to the flat. Nonetheless, he was oddly funny and sharp-witted and I was interested in his strange bursts of enthusiasm and warmth and immense interest in things. I told him slowly that I would see him in the pub at the same time the following week and would bring a copy of *The Dark* with me; he expressed satisfaction at this. He did not want another drink. He said he had to go. I noticed as he left how small and frail and shabby he was.

I have just looked him up in Henry Boylan's *A Dictionary of Irish Biography*, where the entry under his name gets eighteen lines. His name was Frederick May. He was in his mid-sixties when I met him that day; he had another decade to live. I would sometimes see him over the next while at classical concerts in the city turning his face from the orchestra in fierce concentration and some pain. He seemed to hear better if he turned away. "In later years," the dictionary says, "he suffered from a form of tinnitus."

In Mark Fitzgerald's essay on May, published in the *Journal of the Society for Musicology in Ireland*, vol. 14 (2018–19), he writes: "Much of May's output—consisting of chamber works, songs, theatre music, orchestral pieces and numerous arrangements— remains generally unknown, unperformed and in some cases in un-performable condition."

Fitzgerald emphasizes that it is unclear how long Frederick May stayed in Vienna, where he went to study in 1933, and uncertain precisely with whom he studied. He quotes from an article May wrote in 1975 about Alban Berg's *Wozzeck*:

When I travelled to Vienna in 1933 as a student from the Royal College of Music in order to learn more about composition, I was looking forward with eager anticipation to attending more than one performance of *Wozzeck* at the Vienna State Opera. However, I reckoned without the composer's compatriot Chancellor Engelbert Dollfüss, who banned the work as being decadent, and unfit for human consumption. I had passionately desired to be present at a performance of it all during my adult life, but even the fall of Fascism and the restoration of something approaching civilization left my wishes unfulfilled for many long years. When I saw it was to be revived at Covent Garden this spring, I knew it was a case of "now or never" and Friday, April 11th, will always remain as a red-letter day in my memory . . . Infusing it as he did with his own deep compassion and love for suffering humanity, [Berg] produced a work that bids fair to outlast all the changes of fashion, a work that will come to be acknowledged by succeeding generations as one of the glories of the 20th century.

From this article, it is clear that around the time I met him May was in a fit state to travel to London to hear an opera. But most of the time, he was living in a Dublin nursing home, run by the Little Sisters of the Poor at Sybil Hill in Raheny.

A week after our first meeting I turned up at the Stag's Head with the book and Frederick May came with an LP under his arm that had just been released by Claddagh Records. He gave me the record and I gave him the book. It was a new recording by the Aeolian Quartet of his string quartet. He did not want me to look at it for too long and became gruff when I expressed surprise and gratitude when I found out that he was the composer. His work was forgotten, he said, and now this had come out. It wasn't much, he said.

He asked me to put it away when I began to read the piece by the novelist James Plunkett in the sleeve notes. We had a drink and he arranged to call at the flat during the week, by which time he would have read the book and I would have listened to the record.

The music, when I put the record on, shocked me with its assurance, its edge. May had finished it when he came back to Dublin from Vienna in 1936. He was twenty-five then, and knew, it seems, that he was facing progressive deafness. I was amazed by the ringing confidence of the opening of the first movement, the swirling and passionate repetitions, the pulling back, the retiring into quietness, the driven sense of anguish, hidden and then exposed and emphasized.

I have the CD now of a recording made in 1996 by the Vanbrugh Quartet; the notes say that it was more than a decade after its composition before May's quartet "came to public attention." It was an early work, according to the writer, "and therefore is untainted by the increasing embitterment he felt on his later return to Ireland."

There is not a single Irish sound in the whole string quartet. Or maybe every sound is Irish. Maybe the unforgettable ending of the last movement, slow and plaintive, unwilling to finish, coming back again and again to a haunting melody, which is half offered and then withdrawn and hinted at and then lifted to an extraordinary pitch of beauty, maybe that is Irish. But I don't think so; it is too easy to make claims like that.

Maybe it is more true to say that the tone of helplessness and sadness in this music was enriched by May's knowledge that he was doomed by illness and that his own creative life would not be continuous. In 1958, in a broadcast, he said:

I have often felt myself to be like a rock on the seashore that is covered over by the incoming tide every so often, but when the tide withdraws again, it is left once more desolate and forsaken.

ometimes one may ask oneself in moments of depression whether it would not be better never to have been given any creative gift at all than only to have been granted an unserviceable kind of half-gift, so variable, so uncertain and so capricious.

I imagine him, having studied with Vaughan Williams in London, living in an attic room in an old house in the center of Vienna, having come to sup at the tilted table of Berg and Schoenberg. He was our Adrian Leverkühn, homosexual, talented, deeply melancholy, ready to wash his bones clean of Ireland, its damp prejudices, its insularity and its misery. I imagine him too, like Vienna itself, only half aware of the danger he was in and the fate he would meet.

He came to my flat and talked about the McGahern book, which he loved. It was hard to have a conversation with him, he would turn his head to the side in pained frustration because he could not hear properly. He invited me to come to the sound archives of the national Irish radio station RTÉ to hear his song cycle *Songs from Prison*, based on a setting of poems by Ernst Toller and Erich Stadlen, which had been recorded by the station years earlier by the baritone Austin Gaffney but never been released.

I found the songs hard. I remember May's face more than anything, the pale skin drawn tight over his cheekbones, the eyes darting about, as he tried to listen to music he had composed more than thirty years earlier. His last composition, or the last that is mentioned in anything written about him, was a nine-minute mood piece for chamber orchestra called *Sunlight and Shadow* from 1955, the year I was born.

After his death in 1985 I heard three things about him that stayed in my mind. In the first story, the nuns discovered in 1981 that May had been made a member of Aosdána, an academy of artists set up by the Irish state, and thus could be looked after financially to some extent, if he should need money. The nuns were worried. He was settled in their home, they said. They made clear to one of the architects of Aosdána that the composer in their care would be better not knowing about the money.

In the second story, May was a stray guest who was making a nuisance of himself in the house of the Irish-language writer Máirtín Ó Cadhain in Dublin sometime in the late 1950s. He was drunk, I was told, and wouldn't go home and played the tin whistle in the late hours. Eventually, he was put into a taxi. The driver was told to deposit him in a certain house in Rathmines and given a large tip to ensure that May was to be left inside the house despite the protests of the owner, a man called Ernest Blythe who would, no doubt, appear in his pajamas and insist that he had no connection with May and May had no right to come into his house.

The dictionary of biography says that May "was director of the Abbey Theatre orchestra for fifteen years," and this explains that last story and the next. May's boss at the theatre was Ernest Blythe, of whose legacy as a politician (he was a minister in the first Free State government) or a theater manager (he ran the Abbey from 1941 to 1967) it is hard to speak well, and who was also a bully. Blythe made Freddie May's life a misery. It is easy to imagine the contempt May must have felt for the theater orchestra and the terrible plays the Abbey put on in those years. He was drinking. Dublin was a prison.

His work was not performed. He was going deaf and he must have been going out of his mind with other frustrations. Blythe picked on him.

And Frederick May simply told everybody that he would wait and he would live to dance on Blythe's grave. And dance he would, he assured them all.

The same dictionary says that Blythe lived until February 1975, which is close to the time when I met Frederick May. May attended Blythe's funeral, I was later told, and he stood among the mourners at the graveside and he watched the coffin being lowered with much pomp into the ground, for Blythe had been a patriot.

And then May waited. He moved among the gravestones as the others left the graveyard. He bided his time. And when the grave had been filled and the gravediggers were out of sight and his tormentor lay well beyond tormenting him, he stood on the fresh clay, alone as light fell, and he did a dance on the grave of Ernest Blythe as he had promised, before anyone else got the chance. And then he walked down to the pub where he found company who had been at the funeral and he told them proudly of what he had done.

Frederick May's string quartet has the stark passion that usually you find only in last work, in Beckett's last prose pieces, for example, or in some passages from *Finnegans Wake*, or in some of Yeats's last poems. It is hard to believe that May wrote it when he was twenty-five. And hard to believe also that he did not know that this would be his last substantial work as well as his first. In an undated letter, he wrote to the composer Brian Boydell about the quartet:

It was written at a time when I believed that my ear trouble would give me little further prospect of any creative activity, and consequently I was in a state of inner tension. Of course, as you know yourself, musical themes & ideas generate their own logic & certainly I wasn't thinking along these lines the whole time, but that was the general basis.

In any case, the old man who came up to me in the Stag's Head in 1975, the broken dancer with his sour wit, was responsible for one of the most exquisite contributions to Irish beauty that has ever been made.

I am in my mother's bedroom. It is September 9, 2000, the morning after she has died. This room is as she had left it when she was suddenly taken to hospital. She was seventy-nine. I am trying to recapture her; I am trying to imagine what these last years of her life have been like.

Some of the furniture is new to me; some pieces were not there when I was growing up, but the wardrobe in the corner near the window where I found the banned books has always been there.

My mother left school at fourteen. For her last two years there she had a teacher, a nun, Sister Catherine, who had a profound effect on her. She loved the poetry she learned from Sister Catherine in those two years, loved reciting as she moved about the house: Shelley, Matthew Arnold, Tennyson, Browning, the early Yeats. And when she was in her twenties a touring theater came to the town regularly and did Shakespeare, and those performances of *Hamlet* and *King Lear* and especially *Othello* meant the world to her. She learned long speeches from Shakespeare and recited them to herself in the kitchen.

My mother's hunger for books and her lack of a formal education gave her a sort of freedom that is mostly lost now in the developed world. Soon after my father died in 1967, the Irish censorship laws were relaxed, and paperback books, even ones about sex, became freely available. And in the thirty years that followed, my mother devoured books without much idea that there was a canon, and with a taste that was confident and unpredictable.

For example, none of Joyce interested her: the early work was too dreary, she thought, and the later work too obscure. She paid no attention to the later Yeats. But when she discovered Wallace Stevens, she got years of pleasure from him, she loved the luxury of his language, his uplifted tone, and she didn't mind at all when she failed to understand a line. And this led her to Eliot, but to *The Waste Land* rather than *Four Quartets*, which she found too abstract. She learned "Death by Water" by heart.

She lived in a town of six thousand people. She had no one to talk to about poetry; no one she knew was reading the way she was. So she kept her garden, she played bridge and Scrabble, she went on outings with her friends. She did, as James Merrill said about Elizabeth Bishop, a lifelong impersonation of an ordinary woman. But, in the meantime, she was discovering Robert Lowell and Sylvia Plath and Philip Larkin and R. S. Thomas from anthologies that she bought when she went to Dublin and then from volumes of their work.

Sometime in the 1970s she began to pay attention to fiction. She hated anything she deemed "slow-moving." Dickens, George Eliot, Jane Austen were all slow-moving, not to speak of the Brontës. She liked novels to be "smart," she said. It was impossible to give her a novel, or recommend something to her, because it was hard to tell what, in her book, was "smart" and what was "slow-moving."

Saul Bellow, for her, was the essence of smart. She, a middle-aged, Irish Catholic widow in a provincial town, loved the raunchy bits of Bellow, the sex drive of his heroes delighted her. She loved Bellow's women too, their fleshiness and sensuality. And then she would read the overblown prose of Antoine de Saint-Exupéry and she would love that also. There was no talking to her. Saint-Exupéry led her to Proust. She confined herself to *Swann's Way*, which she read over and over. Was it not slow-moving, I asked? "It is," she said, "but I don't care."

Slowly, then, she built up her own canon. Simone de Beauvoir, especially the nonfiction, was in; Sartre was out. *Buddenbrooks* was in; the rest of Mann was out. Almost all contemporary Irish fiction was out; almost all contemporary Irish poetry was in.

The Americans, she would say, they were the smartest. But she could not believe that I loved Henry James. Yet she talked very little about what she didn't like. She would never use a word like "out" about a book. She remembered a time when books were rare and precious objects, even dangerous objects. She would shake her head and smile and say nothing and then say that she would be happy with just Shakespeare and a few modern poems.

I am in my mother's bedroom on the morning after she has died. On the locker beside her bed is the list of numbers for use in an emergency, headed by the number of the doctor, the hospital, the ambulance service. Her prayer book is here and Catholic pamphlets to help her towards a happy death. She has burned all her diaries, but torn out five or six pages describing a holiday in Spain and the light and the freedom and the happiness. She has left these pages lying there. She has left two notebooks, one from the 1940s, with poems transcribed, and one from recent years with poems cut out from *The Irish Times*. And scattered around on top of this locker, or the other locker, or on the floor, are the books she was reading in the time before she died. Doris Lessing's *Love, Again* has been left half-finished. (Funny, she never mentioned Lessing.) And books by the Irish poet Seán Dunne, who had died a few years earlier, whose poems are elegant and elegiac. And a paperback volume of Hardy's selected poems that looks recently bought with a bookmark on his poems from 1912 about the loss of his wife, which are almost unbearably sad. Now, knowing that she must have read them in her last weeks, it makes me wonder at how brave she must have been. Or maybe not. Maybe the poems shocked her as much as they shock me now.

Everything she read, once she had left the care of Sister Catherine, she discovered for herself. Her private life, her secret self, for the last thirty years of her life, and perhaps for the years before, came from books, from the printed word. She knew nothing about the theories and movements that came and went in her lifetime. She was what most writers long for, and what most of us still write for: the ordinary reader, curious and intelligent and demanding, ready to be moved and changed, and believing still that the written word has all the power to make the deepest imprint on the private self.

*   *   *

I have a memory of a misty day on the strand in Curracloe. It must be the early 1960s. A neighbor is there with her husband. My mother is there and my auntie Maeve. Maybe my father, and certainly two or three others. The adults are sitting on rugs and the children are swimming or playing in the sand. We are not meant to be listening to the adult conversation and if we are noticed doing so we are sent away. It is one of those days when everyone is poised to make a run for it if the mist hardens into rain. We watch the adults watching the clouds.

I don't much like the sea, or the sand, or the other children, but I know that if I sit even on the edge of a rug and draw the slightest attention to myself one of the adults will tell me to go away and play. Nonetheless, I love listening to them and therefore approaching the adult rug stealthily is always worth trying.

My auntie Maeve is reciting poetry. She is sitting up and staring out to sea and her voice has the same stilted, serious and incantatory tone she uses when she is giving out the rosary. All of the others have grown serious, each in different poses, one lying back, one resting on an elbow, one sitting up. My auntie Maeve has tears in her eyes. The poem is long and it rhymes. I wish I could remember what it was.

No one talks when she is finished. I know never to talk when the adults leave silence, because the next thing said is often the most unusual and unexpected. The next thing now is my mother. She is reciting "The Lake Isle of Innisfree." I have heard her doing this before. Her voice is much softer and more dramatic than her rosary voice, but, like Auntie Maeve, she does not take her eyes from the far distance when she recites. And something else too: for both of them reciting these poems evokes a terrible sadness that is far from the light, funny talk they normally have on the strand.

And then Pat Sheehan starts. He is a captain in the army and they have rented a house just beside the Winning Post. He is from Clare so his accent is different. He knows poems that they all seem to know, but they allow him to recite them and join in only at the end of verses. He too stares out to sea when he recites. He recites the words slowly and carefully.

Then the poetry fades, or my memory of it fades, and the scene melts back to ordinary talk. I don't know how long this lasts, but it is broken by my auntie Maeve, who in mid-talk without warning has started to recite another poem. The others all stop and pay attention, but she doesn't seem to mind about the others; she is reciting the poem to herself or to the sea or to some other power and all of the others recognize this and pay special attention. Once more she has tears in her eyes and I cannot stop looking at her.

Recently, I have been going through the photographs that my mother kept beside her bed close to the poems and the missal and the list of important telephone numbers. So many of them were taken on those beaches on the Wexford coast, black and white photographs of moments when she and her sisters and their friends were young or when their children were young. It seems unbelievable that almost all of the adults who sat on that rug that day in Curracloe are dead. They were all as happy that summer, let us suppose, as they ever would be. They were on holidays. At night they went to the bar of the Strand Hotel; during the day they lay on the beach and swam and watched the sky in case the sun might come out once more. The women wore slacks. There was a lot of laughter. They had all known each other for years. And yet, at times, something else came to them, something brought them close to the strangeness and the mystery of things, away from their jokes and their stories and their easy talk and their holiday mood. At times poetry came to them. It came easily and naturally, but when it took over, it was not ordinary. It changed everything, like a new element, or a small opening in the sky. Everything about them then, how they spoke and listened, how they looked out at the gray-blue sea, seemed ready to take it on board, use it and remember it, allow it to offer a swell of resonance and meaning to the moment.

Recently, I went back to St. Peter's for the first time in thirty years. Since 1972, when I left the Catholic boarding school in the southeast of Ireland at the age of seventeen, I have had many dreams about it. One of these dreams is that I have to face exams again with no preparation and no work done. The dream takes me in detail through all my subjects. I know I can probably do the English, because I am a writer, and maybe know more than the examiner. And perhaps in Spanish I could also at least know how to read the paper. And there are certain parts of history I could do. But maths and Irish and geography also have to be done and they are a nightmare, I have prepared nothing. I will probably not be able to answer a single question. I don't wake up screaming, it's not that sort of dream, but I wake feeling uneasy and strange and oddly guilty that I have done no work for my exams. Then I remember that I don't have exams and never will again.

The other dream is set more explicitly in the school building. I am me now, I control my own life, I do what I like every day, I travel a lot. If I don't want to get up in the morning, no one will make me. In the dream, I have to return to St. Peter's College and spend a final year there. I have to forget about traveling and running my own show; instead, I have to fit in with all the other students who are seventeen and eighteen and all male. I have to go and find my bed and learn the timetable and know that this will be my life until the following June.

Strangely, this dream is not a sad dream or a frightening dream. It is comforting. My life will be structured and organized for me. I will have no decisions to make. But when I wake up, I am glad nonetheless that it was just a dream and I don't have to go back to St. Peter's College after all.

There was a new entrance to the school and new buildings where the old gardens used to be, but the minute I walked into the old school building I knew where I was. At the end of a corridor was the library. I had spent hours in this room reading because I did not do sport. Most of the other students thought this was a sort of punishment.

I recognized everything, every change, but it was all paler somehow, as though the colors had been muted, and were less real, less solid. Some things had changed. The darkroom where I had learned photography was gone and the two small oratories where the priests had said mass were also gone.

The big changes were that the priests had now gone, and the school was run by laypeople; the other big change was that the school was no longer a boarding school, it was only for day boys. When I was a student, there were three hundred boarders; now the dormitories are empty and some are derelict. The Department of Education wants to build new extensions to the school as the numbers increase. It is cheaper to build than renovate, so the old classrooms at the front of the buildings will be left there. I thought this was a bit sad as we walked the corridors in search of my class photo from 1972.

It was a relief to drive out of the building back to the town, back to the real world. I suppose old ghosts must linger in those old buildings, but I didn't see any. In the end I felt nothing much and that surprised me more than anything. Maybe over the next thirty years I will develop some new dreams.

There were two houses, one owned by an aunt, my mother's sister, another by an aunt and uncle, on my father's side. Both were on hills in Enniscorthy, each house was part of a terrace of four. They must have been built at the end of the nineteenth century. Both houses had two rooms upstairs and two rooms downstairs and a back kitchen that had been added much later. Munster Hill, where my mother's mother lived with my two aunts, had been built for office workers in the nearby flour mill and was owned by the mill until one of my aunts bought it for a small sum of money in the 1960s.

I do not know for whom the four houses in the other terrace on Bohreen Hill had been built. My father was born in Bohreen Hill and all through my childhood his brother and sister lived there.

Both houses—Munster Hill and Bohreen Hill—require their own archaeologist, someone who would notice that they did not have toilets indoors at the beginning, a student who would find traces of the outdoor toilets at the back of the small concrete yards. This is more obvious in Munster Hill than Bohreen Hill. Someone who would study the extensions that were built, realizing that the bathroom added in Munster Hill halfway between upstairs and downstairs matched the bathrooms of the other houses in the terrace and must have been built by the mill, most probably in the 1950s. It has the look of a more planned extension than many of these additions to such houses.

The extension to Bohreen Hill was added in the early 1960s. It interests me more now because it has not been touched since then. The same lino, the same bathroom furniture, the same glass in the window and light fittings, all this has been gathering a resonance of smells and associations for more than fifty years. It began as bright hope, and now has a sour drabness. It is waiting to be swept away, thrown out on a skip to be replaced by a new set of floor coverings and modern furniture, new colors. It is hard to imagine that it was ever all specially chosen.

The bathroom in this house is on the ground floor, down a short corridor behind the kitchen. There is another door off the corridor to the right that leads to a small room with a window looking onto the yard. This was a room built to hold papers and books. Before it was built, and indeed during all the years afterwards, papers and books spilled over into the two downstairs rooms. These were my uncle's; my aunt longed for the day when they could be contained and did not spread like ivy onto every chair and table surface and on the floor.

In the planning of the room for books and papers and the new bathroom, my aunt grew more ambitious. She wanted two bay windows as well, one in the front of the house where she and her brother sat in the evening, one in the back room where the dining table was. This would mean months of hammering and disruption. For my aunt, it meant the end to the darkness and dinginess of small windows, it meant that the house she was born and brought up in would be suddenly opened to light. For her brother, it meant change and it meant hope invested in interior decoration, which was, he believed, the height of silliness. If the house was good enough for everyone until now, why change it?

She won. It became, in those early years when it shone, not only the house she lived in, but the space she had imagined. It was hard to believe the way it had looked before. I have no memory of those rooms before the bay windows were built, and no memory of the house before the bathroom and the room for books and papers were added. All that I must imagine.

I suppose new wallpaper must have been added as well and allowed to fade. Flowers and birds were the customary design, but nothing too loud. I have no memory of the wallpaper. Even though I have been recently in the house in Bohreen Hill, I still cannot conjure up any wallpaper patterns. I see a pale cream color, or a faded white, a great blankness that oversees the furniture, all of which I remember.

I wonder if they put new doors in when they redecorated Bohreen Hill. My earliest memory of that house is locking myself into the back room by accident, using a key that was in the door. A locksmith or carpenter had to be found. I have no memory of there being keys in the doors of that house after that.

Both houses had narrow staircases with a small landing and then a turn. To the outsider, they might have appeared similar, made from the same plan. But for a small boy there was a very notable difference. The house in Bohreen Hill had a staircase with two very steep steps, steeper than in any other house I had ever been in. You needed help from an adult, or you needed to put your hands on the step above and haul yourself up. The steps of the stairs in Munster Hill were, on the other hand, perfectly normal.

In all the redecorations, the electric votive lamp in front of the picture of the Sacred Heart, which flickered like a sort of under-developed neon, was left in place in both houses.

On the mantelpiece in the back room in the house in Bohreen Hill there was a calendar that had to be changed manually every day, which no one had time to do. So my first job on arrival was to change the date before attending to the small glass ornament that sat beside it. If I shook it and then left it down, cascades of snow fell on the scene inside. And beyond that, perhaps on the mantelpiece too, or on a small table, was a statue of the Virgin, which had been purchased in Lourdes, with a key that, if you turned it, caused the statue to play "The Bells of the Angelus." While you could shake the snow ornament as much as you pleased, the rule was not to turn the key of the statue too hard or force it in any way because it could break.

By this time, my grandmother in Munster Hill had died and one aunt had married, leaving another aunt alone in the house. She was almost twenty years younger than my aunt in Bohreen Hill. She was glamorous and looked marvelous, she loved buying clothes and discussing her wardrobe. The fitting room of a large department store in Dublin was the place of her dreams. She played golf and went to the pictures and still worked in the office of the mill, which moved from the town center in these years to the bottom of Munster Hill, close to the spot where the Urrin River flows into the Slaney.

The books in these two houses told you everything. My aunt in Munster Hill had hardly any books, a large red Bible, a collected Shakespeare, some anthologies of poetry and stray hardbacks and paperbacks that had been assembled by chance. In Bohreen Hill, on the other hand, in the front room downstairs and on the landing at the top of the stairs there were large glass bookcases that contained history books and patriotic books, maybe some Irish novels and poetry, but no Joyce or anything like that, not even any Frank O'Connor or Sean O'Faolain.

This was a serious house where serious things had happened. Munster Hill, when I went there first, was a house of women talking about clothes and holidays. You would get mandarin oranges from a tin with whipped cream, or bananas. In Bohreen Hill, you would get lemonade and biscuits, but there would never be talk of clothes or shopping or golf.

Despite the bay windows and the extension, the past lingered more purposefully in Bohreen Hill. The fact that my grandmother died in the house in Munster Hill made no difference to it, but the knowledge that on Easter Monday 1916 my grandfather had lifted the floorboards of the front bedroom in Bohreen Hill and had taken out some rifles he had hidden there for use in the Rising, this made the house a more serious place. The idea also that my father's younger brother had died of tuberculosis in the house in Bohreen Hill and that it had to be vacated for a week or more after his death by the whole family, while it was disinfected or cleaned or purified, or whatever the word is, this made it a place whose past grew more palpably interesting to me as its décor and its furniture and its knives and plates and glasses did not change, moved gradually from new to old.

In 1967 my aunt in Munster Hill got married. Because she and her husband were popular, they received vast numbers of wedding presents. Myself and my younger brother made our way to Munster Hill every evening to witness the arrival of the presents, many many pairs of sheets and pillowcases, many many sets of towels, some Waterford glass, including a vase, which is in my house in Dublin now, and some sets of cutlery. But it was the big presents that interested us most, a standard lamp, a three-piece suite, a set of small tables, a few sheepskin rugs. The house was transformed by the wedding, not as much by the arrival of a husband, but by the arrival of all the wedding presents.

Slowly, the business of heating began to preoccupy everybody. No one, in the early years, considered oil-fired central heating. It was too expensive to install and to run. My aunt in Munster Hill had an old paraffin oil heater in the kitchen, which must have also been there in my grandmother's time. It was battered, blue-gray in color with a small piece of glass on one side to show that it was lighting. It gave off strong heat and heavy fumes. In the other rooms there were fireplaces, and coal fires were lit in the living room at night and maybe in the early afternoon on a Sunday.

But this was not enough. After great hesitation, a storage heater was put into the back part of the hall of Bohreen Hill, and then, years later, a storage heater in the front room downstairs. There was never any heating upstairs or fires lit upstairs. Also, there were two-bar electric fires in both houses but these were seldom used and much frowned upon as they ate electricity and dried the air.

These were the years of drafts, or when fear of drafts became common, and there were heavy curtains against the doors in Munster Hill to keep drafts out. Work had to be done to avoid rising damp with new techniques that rendered both houses damp-proof. In Munster Hill, my aunt's bedroom at the front of the house upstairs had a high ceiling and it meant the room was cold so she had the ceiling lowered or a false one put in, probably the latter. Then she installed oil-fired central heating, but seldom turned it on, preferring to light coal fires and put on good winter clothes and protect herself, as best she could, against drafts.

There must be a special place for dead furniture, for that paraffin oil heater, for the broken toilet bowl in the disused outdoor toilet, for the dead three-piece suite, for the sagging bed, the ancient mattress, the rusty bath, the handy contraption with a little wheel used to whip fresh cream. There must be also a special place in the mind and the memory for these old things, for the aura of these rooms, but there is not. You are trying to clear things away so the house can be sold. You are trying also to take photographs with your eyes, to transform the grim tension of dead space into something memorable, useful, with meaning. But nothing happens. It is easier, or almost easier, if you sit and close your eyes and let the words come. Try saying it again.

There were two houses. Both were on hills, each house was part of a terrace of four.

There are two other houses, and they both belong to dreams. I was born in one of them and learned to navigate the world in its rooms. This house is on the edge of Enniscorthy; it is part of a housing estate that was built in the late 1930s, called Parnell Avenue, named after the lost leader of the Irish Parliamentary Party, Charles Stewart Parnell. There were twenty-two semidetached houses, set around two fingers of rising ground. Ours was at the top of one of the fingers in a cul-de-sac. The house had a view of Vinegar Hill across the Slaney Valley, the hill that the Irish rebels held for three or four weeks in the summer of 1798 and where the last battle of that rebellion was fought and the rebels were defeated.

A few times each summer we climbed that hill, but it was not the legacy of the rebellion that loomed largest, but the view of the town below, and Parnell Avenue at the edge of it, so toylike and insignificant. And there was a reservoir up there too, with a roar of water underneath the concrete. If you dropped a stone down, having lifted a small metal opening, it seemed as though you dropped it down into the very bowels of the earth itself.

The names of the families who lived in each of those houses in Parnell Avenue, and indeed the faces, and the different ways of walking, or dressing, or smiling, are etched in my mind and will, it seems, never leave now. I do not have to rack my brains or, indeed, think for even a second to summon up those people. Fifty years ago, the names as you came into Parnell Avenue and moved from number 1 to number 22 were as follows: Miller; Browne (soon sold to the Robans); Hanlon; Doyle; Lynch; Mitchell; Grace; Hennessy; us; Hayton; Kelly; McCormack; Martin; Ruth; Duggan; Barry; Crane; Tobin; Doyle (soon sold to Priestly); Maher; Doyle; Mahon.

I can still see old Sergeant Mitchell on a summer Sunday standing at his gate discussing a hurling or football match with Paddy Grace or Sean Lynch, and being joined in a bantering way by Dan McCormack, and all of them excited by some player, some goal scored, or their different loyalties (Mr. Lynch was from Cork), or some new set of possibilities.

I can still see the firelighters made out of twisted paper that Rita McCormack made and often sent over to our house. Or the different sort of front gardens—some tidy with just lawn, others with shrubs, or flower beds, or rosebushes. Seamus Doyle in number 21 had serious rosebushes and spent much of his day tending to them. He was grumpy. He had led the 1916 Rebellion in the town and was sentenced to death afterwards, which was later commuted. I wondered later if being a revolutionary when he was young, or indeed having once been sentenced to death, gave his rose-tending more impetus, or indeed had caused at least some of his grumpiness. He was my brother's godfather. Once—it must have been 1966— President de Valera was driven up in a state car to visit him. We all shook the old blind president's hand.

There were five or six cement steps to our front door, which had a knocker rather than an electric bell. This door was normally painted green. And then inside the door, a long hallway with lino on the floor and a hall table to the left at the foot of the stairs. The kitchen was a continuation of the hallway, like a connecting railway carriage. And there was a back door that led out of the kitchen to a yard where there was a shed where coal and bicycles and garden things were kept.

As with half of the twenty-two houses, there were two rooms to the right of the hallway; the other half had these rooms on the left-hand side of the hallway. The first room, which had a window overlooking the front garden, was called the parlor and was seldom used. This was normal for most of the houses, although the Haytons had a dining room table there, and the Duggans a television. In some of the houses there was almost nothing at all in this front room. It was kept bare and spare. It was for visitors, or Christmas. Ours had bookshelves in two recesses on each side of the tiled fireplace. They were filled mainly with my father's history books. The parlor also had a three-piece suite and a fragile glass case where good china was kept. There was a carpet on the wooden floor. In later years, this room was used for studying, and I wrote my first poems there, but in those early years it was not for children. Once, when new cream and unpatterned wallpaper was put up on the walls of this room, a former pupil of my father's arrived and managed in the course of an evening to rub his hair, which had hair oil on it, against the wallpaper; the effort to remove the stain made it worse. There was much discussion about this.

The back room, as it was called, was where everything happened. It had patterned wallpaper. The room was maybe fifteen feet by fifteen feet and had a cement floor covered in lino. How could a dining room table and seven or eight chairs, a sideboard (could the sideboard have been here too?), a bookcase with my mother's poetry books above a pull-out desk and some drawers, two easy chairs, a fireplace, a hot-press with a copper water cylinder on the left-hand side near the large (or comparatively large) window, another press on the other side of the fireplace where my father's papers were, and eventually a television, my parents themselves, and five children, and even a dog, how could all of these things fit in that room? How could evenings have been spent there by all of us? Wet Sundays?

This house was the space where I learned to talk, to walk, to read, to write. I used it in my novel *The Heather Blazing* as the house of Eamon's childhood; it is also in *The Blackwater Lightship* as the place of Helen and Declan's childhood. It is the house where the novel I am writing now takes place. It comes in dreams; it comes in imaginings. Sacred space; once it was ordinary.

The second dream house was a space I helped dream into being. Most summers for the first ten or eleven years of my life we moved to Cush for a month or more in the summer; the other summers we stayed at Ballyconnigar Lower, also known as Keating's.

Both places were remote, oddly lonely and desolate. I didn't put much thought into that landscape, but when I came to write a chapter of my first novel, *The South*, I found I could conjure it up without any difficulty. It almost came of its own accord, summoned by something I was not fully conscious of. I could get something of its broken and melancholy aura in a chapter of that novel called "The Sea." I wrote about it again in *The Heather Blazing* and again in *The Blackwater Lightship* and again in *Brooklyn*. It is also conjured up in a number of short stories.

For some miles the cliffs are eroding. Each year some land falls into the sea. My godfather's house fell in, and so did Keating's house. I suppose this is an interesting image of time, and a metaphor for what time does. But I am more interested in the exact thing itself— the actual detail of bits of this landscape that I have known for so long falling, dissolving, being washed away, not being there anymore.

I began to want to spend time down there on that stretch of strand that is stony at the edge of the water and sandy then between the stones and the cliff. A place of gentle tides and soft gradients and marly clay and white sand. I went to all the estate agents and eventually found a site with a view of the sea, but far enough back that I would not have to worry about the erosion in my lifetime. I spoke to a friend, Denis Looby, an architect, and he started to draw up plans.

The difference between the detailed plans he drew up and the house itself when finished, so filled with sea light, is the difference between the body and the soul, between musical notation and a song, between the idea for a drawing and the actual drawing itself.

What I learn from this house is simple; it is the lesson of each day. I get up around half nine or ten in the morning and walk into the main room from the bedroom at the side. I have been careful to pull the blinds up before I go to bed. And now I can see sunlight on the sea, or clouds over the sea. And nothing is ever, not even once, the same color or the same texture in the world out there. Each time I walk into the room, sunlight is hitting the sea in a different way; the sea can seem dark gray, or a lighter color, with elements of green or white; there could be one shaft of sharp sunlight hitting it far out to make it look like soft metal; or the sky above could be a hazy blue and the sea below almost dulled by the haze; or it could be brightened by the easy clear morning light. But never in the same way. And each minute, each half-minute, and maybe more often on some days, it all shifts again, the light changes, the tones change, the sunlight is a mere shaft, or a brilliant ray of light, or inky clouds gather. That lovely tension begins between what is settled and unsettled as rain threatens to blow in from over the sea. It is as though the world, for a small time, held its breath, and now is ready to exhale. The wind stops as though to check that no one is following it, and then darts towards the grass in front of the house and then hits the house itself. Rain slants hard against the glass of the window. Most days, when it is blown in by the wind like this, it will not last long.

Sometimes when I walk down to the strand I notice the few new houses. Most of them are built on raised ground. All the old houses,

85

however, are built in dips in the land to protect them from the wind and the rain. The locals do not care about sea views. Some things look exactly the same as they did fifty years ago. But I know that this is an illusion, something deceptive. The grass is not the same grass; it is merely similar; it is merely like the grass that was there before; so too the air, and the view as you turn down the lane that leads down to the cliff. The smell on a summer's day seems not to have changed; and the light itself, the light over the east coast of Ireland at this point in Wexford, oddly gentle, and subtle on most days, is filled for me with images and a confused jumble of memories, and then, on days when I am lucky, something becomes utterly clear, as though already shaped by all the time that has passed.

A Brush with the Law

The Dublin Review · 2007

During the days in 1980 when the High Court considered a constitutional challenge to Ireland's laws against homosexuality, I went down to the Four Courts two or three times. It was before serious journalism had developed in Ireland, and thus the newspapers and RTÉ got their information from a single court reporter and reported merely the bare facts of the hearing. There was no one describing the atmosphere in the court, no one writing about those tiny moments in a hearing that make all the difference.

David Norris was, in my opinion, both the best and the worst person to bring such a case. He was the best in that, as a lecturer in Trinity College Dublin and a person of immense independence of mind, he was in no danger of losing his job or having his position made impossible as a result of the case. But he was the worst in that he seemed, on the face of it, not to have been greatly damaged by the laws in question; he had not served a prison sentence. He appeared

87

to be a happy, well-balanced person living a life of ease and privilege in Ireland. What exactly was his problem?

A courtroom, with its adversarial traditions, was perhaps not the best place to explain that to be gay in a repressive society is to have every moment of your life clouded by what is forbidden and what must be secretive. In George Orwell's *1984*, the most severe punishment for citizens was to forbid them the right to love. To most readers of the book, this seemed a cruelty far-fetched and almost impossible; but for most gay people it was a nightmare we inhabited while pretending, sometimes even to ourselves, that it was nothing, or while telling ourselves that it would not easily change and that it was dangerous to complain. It was best to carry on as though equality for gay people were not a substantial issue worthy of public discussion. The laws forbidding us to love, forbidding us to couple as others do, affected us in ways so deep and basic as to be obvious sometimes only to us, and almost impossible to explain to a senior counsel in the High Court who is being paid to pick holes in an argument and suggest that what the witness is saying should be discounted by the learned judge.

There was an extraordinary moment in the High Court hearing when a liberal priest, a learned fellow himself, gave evidence in favor of David Norris. He suggested ways of interpreting the Bible and the gospels that would not preclude a court in a civilized country, whose ambiguously worded constitution implied certain fundamental rights, from declaring laws against homosexuality to be repugnant to that constitution. It was a subtle argument, and difficult to make, especially under cross-examination. In one moment, under fire, the priest used the word "we," referring to homosexuals. The senior counsel, acting for the state, was a well-known figure at the bar. He stopped, left silence, and then said quietly: "Father, did you say 'we'?" A chilly wind blew through the court, letting us all know how brave David Norris was to bring this case, and how brave this priest was now as he attempted still to make his argument. For days afterwards, the question in all its insinuation, in the ease with which it could be asked, stayed in my mind. I was not surprised when David Norris lost his case in the High Court.

Norris, represented by his counsel Mary Robinson, appealed to the Supreme Court. By the time five judges of that court made their ruling early in 1983, my circumstances had changed. For the High Court hearing I wrote a short piece for *In Dublin* magazine; at the time of the Supreme Court ruling I was, at twenty-seven, editor of *Magill* magazine. *Magill* was owned by Vincent Browne, and Vincent had also been the editor of the magazine until becoming editor of the *Sunday Tribune* in Dublin. In the early days, as Vincent got ready to produce his first issue of the Sunday newspaper and I prepared my first issues of the magazine, we had a number of long discussions that emphasized, at least to me, that there was a wide gap between us. I discovered that Vincent Browne believed in politics in a way that I did not. He believed that the purpose of journalism was to hold those in power to account so that they might become better and more enlightened. He viewed our role and their role through the same lens. I viewed Irish politics as unreformable. I thought it was our job to set up a world apart from politics, to write from a position of total opposition to how power was held and wielded.

A few times, I was genuinely shocked when Vincent mentioned judges whom he admired, and whom he thought *Magill* should write about. I simply did not know that you could admire a judge.

One Friday afternoon in April 1983 Vincent came to the *Magill* offices with papers in his hands. These were the opinions of the Supreme Court judges in the Norris case. Norris had lost again. Vincent was especially appalled by the judgment of the chief justice, Tom O'Higgins, and he wrote an editorial in the *Tribune* against it. He seemed really surprised by it, and we—meaning myself and a few journalists working on *Magill*—were amused at his response. What else did he expect, we asked him. Wisdom? Compassion? He was in the wrong place, we told him, but he was sure that if he wrote enough editorials, and if journalists could make passionate and rational arguments, then change could come, even judges could change. And if not, it was our job to hold them to account. The next issue of *Magill* contained nothing much about the judgment. I did not think it worthy of our comment.

Over the next few months Vincent argued strongly that I should begin to take the Supreme Court seriously; the court thus began to appear on lists of long investigative articles that *Magill* would do in the future. (The private finances of Charles Haughey appeared on these lists too.) Vincent also said that he was worried by the slow pace of change in the law relating to freedom of the press and wondered if it might better come from the courts rather than through legislation. A few times he mentioned how interesting it might be were a case about defamation and libel to go before the Irish Supreme Court. These were matters that preoccupied us at that time, especially as we knew that one serious libel action could badly damage the viability of a magazine like *Magill*. I tended not to speak much when Vincent mentioned the law. He knew more about it than I did.

Towards the end of that year Vincent was approached by the journalist and writer June Levine, who had an interesting story to tell. Vincent thought the story would work better in *Magill* than in the *Sunday Tribune*, as we would be able to devote a lot of space to it. It was the story of the murder of the prostitute Dolores Lynch, whose house had been set on fire. A friend of hers, an ex-prostitute called Lyn Madden, was ready to testify against a man called John Cullen, who had been charged with the crime. The story of Lyn's life in Dublin was disturbing, a portrait of an underworld that had been dealt with only in some sketchy court reports and in the tabloid press. In return for her story, which she was ready to tell to June Levine, Lyn Madden wanted money.

We had to think about this. Lyn Madden was about to put herself in danger because of the evidence she would give in court. Clearly, she would need the money. I had some ethical difficulty with this, but I soon managed to convince myself that it could be justified. Journalists have a funny habit of being able to do that. This was, I thought, a story about which we had a duty to inform our readers. Lyn Madden was an entirely innocent party. She was not asking the magazine to allow her to benefit from a crime she had committed. Nonetheless, it was a gray area. We would not be able to publish unless John Cullen was convicted. The better Lyn's evidence, the more likely that he would be convicted, and the more likely the conviction, the more likely she was to get paid by us. June Levine was adamant that Lyn's motives for giving evidence against John Cullen had nothing to do with money. She would testify no matter what. Lyn believed it was the right thing to do. But she wanted the money as well. I knew the story would sell magazines. I put my qualms aside. We did a deal.

As editor, I was emotionally involved in the story. I saw that June Levine was trying to write it as a news story and I began to work with her to make it read more like a long magazine story in the tradition of Truman Capote. I went to her house each evening to read new drafts of what was becoming a very long and fascinating piece. Slowly, we grew to be friends. I also met Lyn Madden and saw her giving evidence in court. I realized how immensely courageous she was, what an outstanding person she was, and I hoped desperately for the conviction of John Cullen not only to save our story but to save her. The case depended on the jury finding her credible. In the end, late at night, the jury returned with a guilty verdict. Lyn had won. We could publish the article, which would later become a book and was, by any standards, a wonderful piece of writing, a frightening account of the life of a prostitute and a violent pimp in the Dublin we all inhabited.

I knew, as I went back to the office that night, that we were going to sell a lot of magazines. And, as it was coming up to Christmas, the magazine was also going to be full of advertising. This story was going to make us financially secure for the next while. There is nobody more smug than an editor who has a story that he or she believes is not only very significant but will sell like hotcakes in a publication that is fat with advertising. I was going to enjoy Christmas.

The grin was wiped off my face early the following week, however, when a young solicitor arrived in the office, asked for me, and handed me a piece of paper informing me that the High Court had issued an *ex parte* injunction preventing us from publishing the article. I immediately rang our solicitors, who contacted the barrister who read *Magill* for libel, and I rang Vincent. We discovered that there could be a hearing of the case quite soon, but the issue was that John Cullen was appealing his conviction to the Court of Criminal Appeal, a three-judge, non-jury court, and this meant that the case was still *sub judice* even though it had already been widely reported and commented on. The buzz term at the meeting with the lawyers and in our local pub on Merrion Row that night was not "*sub judice*" but "prior restraint." Vincent believed that we should once and for all get a ruling from the High Court against the idea that the courts could ever, on an application, prevent something from being published because of some theoretical damage it might do. Thus we could, if we won, broaden freedom of the press.

As we arrived in the Four Courts, it looked good. The judge, Donal Barrington, not only was blessed with intelligence but was a known liberal. As we stood outside, a funny thing happened. Judge Declan Costello passed by in full judge's regalia, led by his tipstaff, on his way to another hearing. His eyes were on the ground, averted from us all. It was like something from the Inquisition. He looked absurd. I knew that Vincent had been a member of Fine Gael when Declan Costello, as a leading Fine Gael politician, had put forward the idea of the Just Society. "There goes your Just Society," I said to Vincent, but he just scowled, pretending he had not heard.

The judge in our case, despite his intelligence and his reputation as a liberal, did not rule in our favor. He referred to our "exclusive contract" with Lyn Madden and went on to say:

> I have read the article which is a lengthy one. It is written with verve, and is, I am prepared to accept, for the purpose of this application, a serious piece of investigative journalism written about matters which may be thought to be legitimate objects of public interest and concern . . . My own reaction, having read the article, was that, if I were subsequently requested to sit on the Court of Criminal Appeal to hear Mr Cullen's Appeal, I should ask to be disqualified.

The judge went on to admit that judges are trained and "for that reason courts have traditionally taken a less serious view of adverse pre-trial publicity where a case was to be tried by a judge or judges alone than when it was to be tried by a judge sitting with a jury." But then he went on: "Speaking for my own part I think it would be unwise to assume that judges are totally immune from frailties commonly held to afflict jurors." Thus he granted the injunction. The article could not appear.

As we walked back up the river from the Four Courts, all my prejudices against judges and their kind had been confirmed. We had lost. It was my job to find another article for the magazine and soon, as the weekend before production was looming. Magazines like ours could be distributed only on a Thursday. This was December 2. We had planned two issues between now and Christmas to take full advantage of the advertising. Losing one of these issues would be a disaster for us.

Vincent Browne was in a different mood, however. This was what he had been looking for—a chance to appeal and to secure a Supreme Court ruling on an important principle of press freedom. This was how many other important freedoms in Ireland had come, I knew, such as the liberalization of the laws against contraceptives and the allowing of women to sit on juries, to name but two. But I was against appealing. I thought it would be a waste of time. I did not think that the Supreme Court would entertain us for one moment, and this view appeared to be confirmed when we asked how long it would take for an appeal to be heard: we were told that the chief justice himself had said that he would be in no hurry to hear this case. Vincent insisted, however. It was not just our job to publish magazines, he said, but to use a case like this to create a more liberal climate for publication in the future. We sent in a formal application to appeal. To our surprise, the Supreme Court agreed to hear the case four days after the High Court injunction.

Over that weekend we produced two magazines—one to be published if we won, and the other if we lost, both full of advertising. The hearing was on a Tuesday and this meant that we could have the winning or losing magazine out by Thursday. Vincent stayed away from the court. I wonder if he was afraid of seeing any more of his heroes looking ridiculous, but maybe he was just too busy, or, more likely, weary of hanging out with me. He mentioned to a mutual friend—we had only one at the time—that when he spoke I had developed a way of staring at him that profoundly irritated him.

Vincent had done work on American judgments relating to prior restraint and freedom of the press. He handed a large amount of documentation to our lawyers. If looks could kill, then we would have been dead when we arrived armed with all this in the court. The three judges sitting for the hearing—Tom O'Higgins, Anthony Hederman and Niall McCarthy—clearly took a dim view of us, and it appeared as though Rex Mackey SC, representing John Cullen, was going to triumph once more. But then it became obvious that the judges, looking pompous in their wigs and sounding so high and mighty with their posh accents, had a problem. If a mere magazine article could influence them in their consideration of points of law, who were they? Surely they were above being influenced? Our barrister did not raise a single American example. He simply sat down, later explaining to me that he did not want to antagonize the judges once he saw that they were ready to ask poor Rex Mackey if he genuinely believed that they would not be able to carry out their priestly duties just because of an article "written with verve"—Mr. Justice McCarthy with great sarcasm repeated the phrase of his learned High Court colleague.

They then ruled. Chief Justice O'Higgins said: "The Court of Criminal Appeal will be asked to consider pure questions of law relative to the appeal. It cannot be suggested that in considering such questions, publication of this or any number of articles in any number of periodicals would have the slightest effect on the objective consideration of legal arguments." Mr. Justice Hederman agreed, not saying very much. Mr. Justice McCarthy, who had led the attack on Rex Mackey about the dignity of judges, had more to say, including a very interesting sentence: "The courts must be vigilant to protect the citizen, who also has the right to be informed." He continued: "There is no suggestion that the publication of the impugned material would scandalize the Court of Criminal Appeal or undermine, in any sense, the administration of justice or bring it into disrepute." Neither he nor O'Higgins disguised their dislike of the article, McCarthy referring to "chequebook journalism" and O'Higgins saying that "better taste might indicate that articles of this kind should not be published during the currency of legal proceedings involving a citizen." But they lifted the injunction. We had won.

Vincent came up with the idea of putting a big ad in *The Irish Times* showing the cover of the magazine with a strip across it saying: "By Permission of the Supreme Court." It must have driven them crazy. Vincent, to give him his due, thought it was typical of Irish justice that this case, which was a small landmark, should be called *Cullen v. Tóibín* and not *Cullen v. Browne*. He shook his head a number of times and laughed at the sheer unfairness of life. The magazine sold out.

As a result of my first brush with the law, I grew interested in how the Supreme Court functioned. There were at that time six members of the Supreme Court. I began to study their form and background.

First, I found the judgments in the Norris case and read them. In the High Court judgment, which David Norris had appealed to

the Supreme Court, Mr. Justice McWilliams had made a remark
that is at best unfortunate and perhaps does not merit comment.
He was writing about the idea that two women acting alone cannot
commit the act of buggery, and wondering if this fact meant that
the law against buggery thus discriminated against men. He wrote:

> It [buggery] may be performed by either homosexual or hetero-
> sexual men with either men or women. Although it is perfectly
> obvious that such acts will usually be performed between homo-
> sexual males, which is probably what the legislatures had in mind,
> that does not constitute an invidious or arbitrary discrimination
> against homosexual citizens any more than the statutes making
> theft an offense constitute an invidious or arbitrary discrimination
> against congenital kleptomaniacs, supposing there were such a
> group of people.

Mr. Justice McWilliams made reference to rights implied by
Article 40 of the Constitution, including part 1 of section 3, which
reads: "The State guarantees in its laws to respect, and, as far as
practicable, by its laws to defend and vindicate the personal rights of
the citizen." This sentence is clearly open to interpretation; it means
whatever the judge thinks it means. It would seem obvious to me
that it would require a judge to declare the Victorian laws against
homosexual acts between men unconstitutional. What greater
personal right is there, after all, than the right to love? But it might
not seem so to you, or to a judge. And Mr. Justice McWilliams also

had to look at the preamble to the Constitution, which begins: "In the Name of the Most Holy Trinity, from Whom is all authority and to Whom, as our final end, all actions both of men and States must be referred . . ." He referred to the judgment of Mr. Justice Brian Walsh in the *McGee* case (about contraception), which said that rights under Article 40 "are to be related to the laws of God as understood by Christians." He then went on: "[I]t is reasonably clear that current Christian morality in this country does not approve of buggery or of any sexual activity between persons of the same sex."

This was the judgment that the Supreme Court had to consider when it came to it on appeal. The majority judgment of the Supreme Court, written by Chief Justice O'Higgins, was not, in my opinion, the most enlightened in the court's history. I understood now why Vincent Browne had been so concerned about it and I regretted that *Magill* had not published it in full at the time it was delivered. In his judgment, given in April 1983, Chief Justice O'Higgins did not advert to Mr. Justice McWilliams's reference to kleptomania. He wrote instead:

A right to privacy or, as it has been put, a right "to be let alone" can never be absolute. There are many acts done in private which the State is entitled to condemn, whether such be done by an individual on his own or with another. The law has always condemned abortion, incest, suicide attempts, suicide pacts, euthanasia and mercy killing.

These, it appeared, could be equated with two consenting men making love in private. He went on to say that homosexual conduct is

of course, morally wrong, and has been so regarded by mankind throughout the centuries. It cannot be said of it, however, as the plaintiff seeks to say, that no harm is done if it is conducted in private by consenting males. Very serious harm may in fact be involved. Such conduct, although carried on with full consent, may lead a mildly homosexually oriented person into a way of life from which he may never recover.

He summarized his views as follows:

1. Homosexuality has always been condemned in Christian teaching as being morally wrong. It has equally been regarded by society for many centuries as an offence against nature and a very serious crime.

2. Exclusive homosexuality, whether the condition be congenital or acquired, can result in great distress and unhappiness for the individual and can lead to depression, despair and suicide.

3. The homosexually oriented can be importuned into a homosexual lifestyle which can become habitual.

4. Male homosexual conduct has resulted, in other countries, in the spread of all forms of venereal disease and this has now become a significant public-health problem in England.

5. Homosexual conduct can be inimical to marriage and is per se harmful to it as an institution.

The chief justice also wrote (and this was, I imagine, what had most offended Vincent Browne): "I regard the State as having an interest in the general moral wellbeing of the community and as being entitled, where it is practicable to do so, to discourage conduct which is morally wrong and harmful to a way of life and to values which the State wishes to protect."

The two dissenting judgments in the *Norris* case also made for interesting reading. The more trenchant of the two was by Séamus Henchy, who wrote that David Norris had

in a number of subtle and insidiously intrusive and wounding ways . . . been restricted in, or thwarted from, engaging in activities which heterosexuals take for granted as aspects of the necessary expression of their human personality and as ordinary incidents of their citizenship. It is not surprising that the repressive and constricting treatment suffered by the plaintiff affected his psychological health. As an involuntary, chronic and irreversible male homosexual he has been cast unwillingly in a role of furtive living, which has involved traumatic feelings of guilt, shame, ridicule and harassment and countless risks to his career as a university lecturer and to his social life generally. Those risks are not the normal lot of the fornicator, the adulterer, the sexually deviant married couple, the drunkard, the habitual gambler, the practising lesbian, and many other types of people whose propensities and behaviour may be thought to be no less inimical to the upholding of individual moral conduct, or to necessary or desirable standards of public order or morality, or to the needs of a healthy family life, or to social justice, or to other expressed or implied desiderata of the Constitution.

He went on to write about David Norris's refusal to emigrate to a society that was more tolerant, a decision that "had the effect of transforming, to a limited extent, his fear to indignation." Judge Henchy then made, in passing, an uncharacteristically stupid comment about David Norris: "His subsequent public espousal of the cause of male homosexuals in this State may be thought to be tinged with a degree of that affected braggadocio which is said by some to distinguish a gay from a mere homosexual."

Henchy had more serious things to say, however, including an observation that some of the points made about homosexuality and society by the High Court judge (and, indeed, by the chief justice, although he did not name him) had not been derived from evidence given to the court, since the state had not, in fact, defended the case in any substantial way. He was thus implying that the points made by McWilliams and O'Higgins arose from those two gentlemen's private prejudices and had no place in their written judgments.

Where a constitutional challenge depends on expert opinion about the actual or potential effect of questioned statutory provisions, the constitutional point must be ruled on the basis of the facts or opinions as admitted to be correct or as duly found by the judge from the evidence given. Where the evidence given is entirely to one effect, it cannot be rejected.

In this case, the evidence given was entirely to one effect, as "not a single witness was called by the Attorney General to rebut the plaintiff's case that the degree of decriminalization sought by him posed no real threat to public order or morality."

The other dissenting judge, Mr. Justice McCarthy, pondered "the extent" of the right to privacy and of "the right to be let alone" and suggested that the laws as they stood were simply unfair to homosexual men. He must have enjoyed reading out this part of his judgment, worthy of Jonathan Swift:

> If a man wishes to masturbate alone and in private, he may do so. If he and another male adult wish to do so in private, may they not do so? No, each commits an offence under section 11 of the Act of 1885. If a woman wishes to masturbate in private, she does not commit an offence. If two women wish to do so in private, neither of them commits an offence. If a man and a woman wish together to do so in private, not being married to each other, neither of them commits an offence. In such latter circumstances, the act committed by the woman upon the man may be identical with that which another man would commit upon him, save that his partner is a woman.

"In my opinion," he concluded, "a very great burden lies upon those who would question personal rights in order to justify State interference of a most grievous kind (the policeman in the bedroom) in a claim to the right to perform sexual acts or to give expression to sexual desires or needs in private between consenting adults, male or female."

Over the next while I began to read Supreme Court judgments in other cases and meet with some barristers who pointed me towards the most significant of them. The first judge I telephoned was Brian Walsh, who was the most senior judge on the Supreme Court, having been appointed in 1961. He was gruff but friendly on the phone and told me he would see me any time that suited me. He worked mainly from his office at the Law Reform Commission on St. Stephen's Green—he was chairman of the commission and also a judge of the European Court of Human Rights—which was very close to the *Magill* office. During the days before I met him I read some of his judgments, and thus I was aware that he had a most formidable mind. But as I walked across the Green to see him I also had in my head the dissenting judgment he had given in 1981, as a judge on the European Court of Human Rights, in the *Dudgeon* case, the Northern Irish version of the *Norris* case, and knew that he had caught a disease, common it seemed in the Four Courts, of stark raving madness on the question of homosexuality.

> A distinction must be drawn between homosexuals who are such because of some kind of innate instinct or pathological consti-tution judged to be incurable and those whose tendency comes from a lack of normal sexual development or from habit or from experience or from other similar causes but whose tendency is not incurable. So far as the incurable category is concerned, the activities must be regarded as abnormalities or even as handicaps and treated with compassion and tolerance which is required to prevent those persons from being victimized.

Judge Walsh did not have a posh accent, and this distinguished him from most judges and barristers. His tone was direct, he mumbled a good deal. He agreed to go through the many landmark judgments he had made at this meeting and any others I had time for. He mentioned that he had seen me on television arguing with Conor Cruise O'Brien on the Sunday after the extradition to Northern Ireland of Dominic McGlinchey, a leader of the Irish Republican terrorist group the INLA. *Magill* believed that such an extradition should not have taken place on the basis of a mere warrant being presented to the courts; we believed that there ought to have been *prima facie* evidence and that the evidence should have to be closely examined. There was a central question of liberty involved.

I thought that Brian Walsh, who had not been a judge in the extradition case, was going to guide me through the law involved in this, and I was ready to take notes, but when he began to speak, I put my pen down, amazed at what he said, and careful also in case my note-taking would make him more cautious. On St. Patrick's Day that year, 1984, a month or two before we had this conversation, he received a telephone call at home, he said. The caller told him that Dominic McGlinchey had been captured in Clare in a shootout, and that, at a private sitting of the High Court, Donal Barrington had ruled that McGlinchey could not be extradited to the North. Would Brian Walsh be available, the caller asked, to come to the Four Courts that evening and sit on a three-judge Supreme Court to hear an appeal from the state? Walsh told me that the person on the other end of the phone was the chief justice, Tom O'Higgins. Walsh said that he let O'Higgins know that he would certainly be willing to sit on the court, and that he did not believe that McGlinchey should be extradited, but should rather be tried for offenses allegedly committed in the South. He added that if McGlinchey were to be extradited it should not be done in any case until Monday morning; the reasons were historical, he explained. Kevin Barry had been hanged on All Saints' Day, Rory O'Connor and Liam Mellows had been executed on the feast of the Immaculate Conception. Dominic McGlinchey should not be extradited on St. Patrick's Day. O'Higgins, who was in favor of the immediate extradition, did not ring back. The two judges who came to the court with him that night and extradited McGlinchey were Séamus Henchy and Frank Griffin. I was told at the time that of the five judges of the court besides Tom O'Higgins, Henchy and Griffin were considered the two most likely to agree with O'Higgins and make the decision unanimous.

Walsh did not tell me that this information was off the record, and it was apparent as he spoke that he wanted it known, although I knew that I could not name him directly as the source. He was evidently in a rage about having been phoned in this way, which he viewed as highly irregular and I viewed as shocking. Although he did not say so, I understood him to believe that if he had not made his position so clear, he would have been invited to sit on the court. Since I was so surprised at being taken into his confidence in this way, and did not wish to antagonize him by implying a criticism in a question, I did not ask why he had, without hearing the case, offered his view of it so freely to O'Higgins. I felt that it was my job not to speak at all, but to leave the building as quickly as possible before he changed his mind and said I could not print what he had told me. I understood as Walsh spoke that he had actually been asked by the chief justice what his view on the case was, but I did not know that for certain. He could have offered it without being asked. He was not afraid of his own opinions. My shock came at the idea of the chief justice, who supported a particular view, leaving a senior judge off the court after hearing him express the opposing view. Once the chief justice called him, in my opinion, he had to take him, no matter what he said on the phone. Walsh's rage, which came through in his tone and in the set of his jaw as he spoke, arose, I supposed, from this.

There was something wonderful about Walsh in his exile from the Four Courts. He was sharp and fearless, and he spoke about writing his judgments as a novelist might. He understood the importance of what he and the former chief justice Cearbhall Ó Dálaigh had done. They both sought to move the Irish legal system from its British moorings, where parliament was supreme, towards an American system in which a written constitution, which Ireland had had since 1937, contained implied rights as well as stated ones. Thus the courts interpreted the Constitution and these interpretations could override parliament in the name of the people. These two men, and some of their colleagues, were nationalist intellectuals. The more I saw Walsh, the more he reminded me, in his way of remaining serious, almost distant, while also exuding a kind of warmth, of my father and my uncle, my father's older brother, both of whom had been active in Fianna Fáil. I began to take an enormous interest in Walsh's tone, his gestures, his diction, although I knew I would only be writing about his judgments in my article.

In the Ó Dálaigh archives at UCD I found a frank and beautiful letter that Walsh, one of the least emotional people I had ever met, wrote to Cearbhall Ó Dálaigh in August 1972 in reply to Ó Dálaigh's letter about his going to be a judge at the European Court. Ó Dálaigh had said that the Supreme Court under himself and Walsh "had earned the respect and trust of ordinary people." Walsh wrote back:

> I had always looked forward to sitting beside you in the Supreme Court for at least the next ten or eleven years secure in the knowledge that the court would be led with the integrity, regard for principle, and courtesy which made your first decade as C.J. so outstanding and which earned for the court the high respect which I believe it now enjoys. I felt another decade of the Ó Dálaigh court could only be for the everlasting benefit of the country. I cannot at all agree with your reference to your age and temperament and patience. I am only too conscious that on many occasions I have put the last virtue to the test and still did not (apparently) exhaust it. Your departure will be a great personal loss to all of us and to the Bar. I also have the suspicion that the administration may also avail of the opportunity so to adjust the leadership and the personnel of the court to reduce the risk of the court's "initiatives" of the past decade.
>
> There is also something I find it easier to write than to speak. That is to thank you for the pleasure and happiness I have derived for thirty years from your friendship and support both at the Bar

and on the Bench and away from the law. In particular I am conscious of the fact that I joined the Supreme Court on the same day as you became Chief Justice and I shall always regard the eleven years as the most satisfying and valuable years of my professional life. With a Chief Justice of a different and less sympathetic temperament things would have been different. It is now a matter of deep regret to me that our professional paths must now part.

Walsh was, of course, right that the administration, often irritated at the disloyalty and interventionism of the judges, would use this opportunity to appoint more conservative judges and thus marginalize Brian Walsh.

As I worked, I discovered that there were two sorts of eminent barrister and indeed judge in the Four Courts. One sort took a keen interest in the way in which Walsh and Ó Dálaigh, by asking for American precedents and being receptive to using the spirit of the Constitution to extend ideas of liberty, had effected a revolution in Irish law. These barristers and judges tended to be or to have been supporters of the Fianna Fáil party.

The other sort were Fine Gael; they were more interested in talking about individual cases and had no real sense of the overall shape of jurisprudence over the previous twenty-five years. I noticed too that while the Fine Gael people were careful about what they said about Ó Dálaigh, they were united in disliking Walsh and disapproving of Mary Robinson. They disliked Walsh for his interventionist stance as a judge but also for his lack of clubbability. It was hard to imagine Walsh telling amusing anecdotes about the Bar and its more colorful members or discussing his art collection. Some of the attitudes towards him appeared to me to arise from snobbery. He had none of the tones of Belvedere and Gonzaga—two posh Jesuit schools—sacred to many lawyers of the Fine Gael persuasion. The same people disapproved of Mary Robinson because she was foremost among those who had taken full advantage of the Supreme Court's advances in constitutional thinking; she tended to bring high-profile cases relating to personal rights rather than get involved in the day-to-day business of the Bar. I admired her for this, as much as I grew to like Walsh's manner. But I said nothing. I listened carefully to the Fine Gael side, realizing that they had held power in the Four Courts between the foundation of the state and 1961 but had lost it now and were puzzled as to how this had come about.

A number of High Court judges also agreed to see me and two of them in particular—both of Fianna Fáil origin—gave me a great deal of their time and attention and spoke of Ó Dálaigh and Walsh and what they had achieved with a sort of awe. I needed these judges because when I phoned Séamus Henchy he barked at me, making clear that he viewed a request for an interview as an example of considerable cheek. Anthony Hederman was very rude and brusque and said that he would under no circumstances see me. I had no interest in Frank Griffin. That left only two: Niall McCarthy and the chief justice himself, Tom O'Higgins.

Niall McCarthy, when I phoned him, explained that he could not discuss the Supreme Court. I said that he had been involved as a lawyer in so many landmark cases that it would be impossible to write a long piece about the court without his assistance. We agreed to discuss only cases that had occurred before his appointment as a judge. He invited me for lunch in his chambers.

When I arrived, he was in the company of a very eminent barrister whom I knew. They were busy, very busy, they said, composing clerihews. Did I know what a clerihew was? Niall McCarthy of the Supreme Court asked. I told him I did. It was a four-line poem with the name of a person at the beginning.

McCarthy had just composed one he was rather proud of, he said. As he recited it, I wished I could put it into my article, which was 20,000 words long, but with no space for clerihews. *Magill*, when it was serious, was very serious indeed. Thus readers were deprived of a great clerihew:

> Marcel Proust
> Abused
> Everyone he knew
> When he wrote *À la recherche du temps perdu.*

McCarthy proceeded, once I had paid suitable homage to his clerihew and the barrister had left us, to give me a brilliantly cogent version of what had happened in the Supreme Court over the past twenty-five years. He seemed to have particular reverence for Ó Dálaigh and made it clear, by implication, that he did not believe that Tom O'Higgins, the chief justice under whom he now served, had much of a legal brain. The lunch was very good, served, as McCarthy proudly told me, by his tipstaff, a former head waiter at the Royal Hibernian Hotel.

Before I phoned Tom O'Higgins I read many of the judgments he had given over the previous decade. I had expected, because of his Norris judgment and his call to Brian Walsh on St. Patrick's Day 1984 and what was generally said about him, to find an old-fashioned right-wing judge; but his position on the court was much more interesting and complex than that. There were many cases, including cases involving suspects and prisoners, in which his judgments were liberal and humane and far-reaching, and he could not be easily dismissed.

I was surprised at how simple it was to speak to him by phone and how relaxed he was about seeing me. While it was clear that our conversations were to be off the record, he put no other restrictions on their scope or focus. I saw him in his chambers. He spoke about his family and his background in Fine Gael, and managed in the nicest possible way to say very little about the court. I had a feeling that the work of Ó Dálaigh and Walsh did not interest him as much as politics did. He had been a TD and a minister for health and run twice for president, coming within 10,000 votes of defeating Éamon de Valera in 1966.

Over the months as I worked, the shadow of the 1983 abortion referendum, in which the electorate had approved a constitutional amendment establishing that the unborn child had a right to life equal to that of the pregnant woman, loomed large. In the magazine we had been vehemently opposed to the idea of the referendum itself, and to its wording. In that period you judged people by what side they had been on in that debate. I knew, for example, as I sat in the chamber of the High Court judge Rory O'Hanlon, that he had been in favor of the referendum and might even have had a hand in the drafting of the dreadful wording, as indeed Brian Walsh might have had. A year earlier, in my mind, O'Hanlon had been a great demon. Now, as we sat talking, I found him remarkably likable, even more than Brian Walsh. These men reminded me that I was not from Dublin, that I had been brought up in a conservative, nationalist household in provincial Ireland in which the Fianna Fáil party and Ireland were synonymous. My father used to say that you could salute Fine Gael people if you met them, but if you ever voted Fine Gael your right hand would wither off. These men reminded me that my liberalism did not quite belong to me. And, as far as I know, it never occurred to any of them that I was homosexual, both pathological and incurable. I had a great deal in common with them, and slowly out of my conversations with them grew not only an article, but a novel, one in which I would use every part of my own childhood and background and marry it with the way in which these men had managed to change Ireland and keep it the same. Up to then I could only imagine a novel about Fianna Fáil as a comic novel, or a satire, or an angry attack. I had no interest in wasting my time on a book like that. But in those days in the chambers of O'Hanlon or in Walsh's office or during other interviews I began to feel almost tender about my Fianna Fáil background, a background that up to then had been a sort of embarrassment. I began to see how a serious novel about aspects of the party could be written.

One day, as I was sitting in Rory O'Hanlon's chambers, his tip-staff came to say that the jury had returned. They had been out a long time, which was why the judge could see me during working hours. He told me not to move, he would go down to the courtroom and come back soon. I sat alone in the judge's chambers looking out at the river. After about forty-five minutes he came back and removed his wig and gown and sat down to resume our discussion. Almost in passing he remarked on the strangeness of the case he had just heard. "I thought they were going to come back with a manslaughter verdict," he said. "But they decided it was murder." I realized that as I had sat dreaming, he had been sentencing a man to life imprisonment, the mandatory sentence for murder. I realized that only a novel would do justice to justice as it sat in front of me, full of both charm and steel, ready to discuss the law in practice and in theory.

One evening soon afterwards, as I was coming towards the end of my research on the Supreme Court, and indeed of my time as editor of *Magill*, I was sitting in the plush home of a leading Fianna Fáil barrister who was helping me with the article. He had the best memory of all of them and perhaps the sharpest mind. His wife came into the room for a moment and asked us if we had everything we needed. We told her we were fine. She was what we call in Ireland a very nice woman. She smiled and said that she was off to a pro-life meeting. She closed the door. I knew as I walked home that evening that I had my novel now. I could finish *The South* without worry because the next one, *The Heather Blazing*, which would deal with the ambiguous place where poetics and politics meet, a novel in which I could both put myself in and leave myself out, was clearly and firmly in my mind. I had the husband and the wife. My brush with the law had been well worth it.

PART TWO

The Paradoxical Pope

The New Yorker · 1995

Somewhere now, surely, among the College of Cardinals, the stately old men of the Roman Catholic church, there is a Gorbachev in the shadows slouching towards Rome to be born. You watch their stony faces, note their dignified bearing and the richness of their robes, and you think that there must be one among them, cunning and secretive, who is planning a quiet revolution in the Catholic church. It could happen overnight: suddenly, without warning, the Berlin Wall of clerical celibacy could be destroyed; the bans on contraception, on women priests, and on divorced people who have remarried receiving the Eucharist could be overturned. The Catholic obsession with the forbidden fruit of sex could fade away.

Those who want change in the church are waiting for John Paul II to die, because it is clear that there will be no change, and no discussion about change, during the rest of his pontificate. Yet as he grows weaker, the light in his eyes strengthens, and his performances become more powerful and fascinating. I watched the magic in Ireland in 1979, in Rome in 1986, in Poland in 1991, and in Rome again in 1994; his presence lifting the crowd out of itself—his voice, his hunched shoulders, his bulky frame, the set of his stubborn jaw against the softness of his eyes. It is not simply the aura of his office that draws people to him but the mixture of his strength and his sympathy. Also, he was once an actor, and knows about the theater. In Częstochowa, Poland, in 1991, at the shrine of the Black Madonna, he said mass for a million young people. He seemed to emphasize his own frailty as he walked to the altar where he would address the crowd and say mass. We all watched entranced as Wojtyła made his way up the steps. He moved slowly, hesitantly. There was one moment when he looked as though he could go no farther, and when he turned for a second he had that strange melancholy expression that is one of his signature looks, that mixture of bemusement and power. He walked as though he were in a state of reverie and contemplation, and then he turned again and waved, not as a celebrity might wave, but rather as someone briefly distracted, oddly bewildered, with larger things on his mind. This spellbinding mixture of strength and weakness, the power of his office and its burden, worked on the crowd, worked on all of us.

For six hours that night the pope sat at the altar with television lights beaming on him. He sat at first on his throne with his head in his hands, as if he were alone in prayer and contemplation. When he finally spoke, he was funny and welcoming. Later, in his sermon, he was serious. "During this night vigil," he said, "so full of feelings and enthusiasm, I would bring your attention, my dear young friends, boys and girls, to three terms that are our guides: 'I am,' 'I remember,' 'I watch.'" He did not mention sex once, or sin, or church rules; he made no reference to what these young people must or must not do. He did not hector us. His words were suggestive, at times poetic. There was hymn-singing; there were blessings in Latin; a large cross was solemnly carried to the altar.

Twice Wojtyła spent long periods with his hands over his face. The crowd below watched him, fascinated. All the lights were on him. It was hugely dramatic and unexpected, the pope unplugged, as it were. He was giving us an example of what the spiritual life would look like; his message was mysterious and charismatic. If you did not know anything about the religion he represented, you would say that it was one of the most beautiful ever imagined, wonderfully speculative and exotic, good-humored and sweet but also exquisite and exalted. While he lost nothing of his power, the glory of his office, Wojtyła seemed at times almost sad about his own elevated position, suggesting that his real life was the one he spent alone in prayer and contemplation, the one we had seen when he sat without moving, his face covered. He was displaying this rich private life of his to the crowd as the life they could have if they followed him.

The spell was broken somewhat, and a sign of the future offered, by a press conference held the following day at the monastery. All the journalists were told to be there as a very important announcement was to be made. I wondered if John Paul was ready finally to announce that Catholics could use artificial contraception, or that women could be priests, or that he was going to abolish the rule of clerical celibacy, but instead a local journalist told me not to bother going, the conference would merely announce that Danuta, the wife of Lech Wałęsa, had not, despite the rumors, slept in the monastery the previous night, that no woman had ever done so. Scotching these rumors was, for the church in Poland, a matter of the utmost importance, it seemed.

On nights like the one I witnessed in Częstochowa, it was easy to grasp why Catholicism still holds such sway in poorer countries and in the United States, where the number of Catholics is expected to increase to seventy-four million in 2005, as compared with forty-six million in 1966. This man's authority is serious, absorbing, all-embracing, just as the rituals of his church—the moment of transubstantiation, for instance, when the bread and wine become the body and blood of Jesus Christ, or the moment of forgiveness in the confessional—are powerful and unambiguous.

In a recent *Newsday* poll of New Yorkers, 56 percent of Catholics said that they were very happy with the church, 30 percent were moderately happy, and only 12 percent were unhappy. Thomas C. Fox, in his book *Sexuality and Catholicism*, summarizes the views of the American Catholic sociologist and novelist Fr. Andrew Greeley, which are that "Catholics like being Catholic. They especially like the 'sacramentality' of the church," and "the imaginative outlook that views creatures as metaphors for God, as hints of what God is like." Another interesting finding of Greeley's is that 68 percent of America's Catholics, as opposed to 56 percent of non-Catholics, have sex at least once a week and are consistently more sexually active than all others.

Dissent from papal teaching and general dissatisfaction within the Catholic Church, then, centers on issues of sex and gender rather than on those of ritual or sacrament. Fox's book is a definitive account of the tensions that have existed between American Catholics and the Vatican since the Second Vatican Council opened, in 1962. Some of these tensions are based on a fundamental misunderstanding: at times, the pope appears to be the only person who understands that he is under no obligation to listen to anyone; the faithful, however, including members of the Catholic hierarchy, are increasingly frustrated that their voices are not heard.

In October 1979, a year after his election, John Paul II was briefly addressed, in Washington, D.C., by Sister Theresa Kane, who was then the president of the Leadership Conference of Women Religious:

> As women we have heard the powerful message of our church addressing the dignity and reverence for all persons. As women we have pondered these words. Our contemplation leads us to state that the church in its struggle to be faithful to its call for reverence and dignity for all persons must respond by providing the possibility of women as persons being included in all ministries of the church.

The pope, however, made it clear that he would not soften on the issue of women's ordination, and in 1993 he went further, stating that he was speaking "definitively," and insisting, according to Fox, "that Catholics must stop discussing the issue."

But part of John Paul II's appeal is that he offers conciliation as well as condemnation, soft talk in the same breath as old-fashioned, authoritarian rhetoric. His recent letter to women, dated June 29, 1995, admits, "Women's dignity has often been unacknowledged and their prerogatives misrepresented; they have often been relegated to the margins of society and even reduced to servitude . . . And if objective blame, especially in particular historical contexts, has belonged to not just a few members of the church, for this I am truly sorry."

There are moments in *Crossing the Threshold of Hope*, a book of interviews with the pope, in which he displays a practical knowledge of the world that women inhabit. In a section about abortion he says (characteristically emphasizing his points in italics):

> Often *the woman is the victim of male selfishness* . . . precisely when the woman most needs the man's support, he proves to be a cynical egotist, capable of exploiting her affection or weakness, yet stubbornly resistant to any sense of responsibility for his own action . . . The only honest stance, in these cases, *is that of radical solidarity with the woman.*

Jackie Hawkins, the executive editor of the Catholic journal *The Way*, was not impressed by the pope's letter to women. "The approach is one of effusive flattery," she wrote. "Nothing has changed. We are still simply human props of various designs." It is clear now that the issue of women in the church will never be sorted out until Rome yields on the matter of women priests. Fox states the matter decisively in his book: "Approaching the outer edge of the beginning of the twenty-first century, an exclusively male Catholic priesthood is the most painful, most intractable, most divisive, and potentially most damaging issue facing the church."

The dual response that we have come to associate with the pontificate of John Paul II—on the one hand, forbidding debate, and, on the other hand, seeming sympathetic and open—has its reflection in the generally ambiguous response of Catholics to church teaching. During the 1970s, Andrew Greeley reported that the papal encyclical *Humanae Vitae*—issued by Pope Paul VI in 1968—which reaffirmed the ban on the use of artificial contraception, resulted in a dramatic decline in church credibility and in Catholic contributions. One of Greeley's American studies noted that shortly before *Humanae Vitae* was issued, 67 percent of responding priests, who would normally have insisted on a strict interpretation of church rules, said they would not refuse confessional absolution to laypeople practicing birth control; five years after *Humanae Vitae*, that number had increased to 87 percent.

Catholics also have a dual response to the pope's authority. Most Catholics know that the doctrine of papal infallibility was established by Rome itself in the late nineteenth century. Even Catholics who revere the pope know that they are not bound by his every statement. In fact, it is generally accepted among Catholics that the church is capable of changing its position on contraception, on clerical celibacy and on women priests, but not on abortion or divorce or transubstantiation.

In Pope John Paul II's statements and his writings—such as *The Gospel of Life: The Encyclical Letter on Abortion, Euthanasia, and the*

Death Penalty in Today's World or *Crossing the Threshold of Hope*—
both abortion and artificial birth control are seen as aspects of the
same darkness: the "culture of death" in the modern world. Reason
does not interest John Paul II; reason is merely another aspect of
the filthy modern tide. The arguments made against the blanket
ban on abortion are presented with great lucidity in Fox's book.
But they miss the point of John Paul's argument, which is that he is
not open to argument. In *Crossing the Threshold of Hope* he quotes
St. Paul: "Proclaim the word; be persistent whether it is convenient
or inconvenient . . . For the time will come when people will not
tolerate sound doctrine." And he adds, "Unfortunately, don't these
words of the apostle seem to characterize the situation today?"

The pope makes it clear in *The Gospel of Life* that he is not especially impressed by democracy. "Democracy cannot be idolized to
the point of making it a substitute for morality or a panacea for
immorality," he writes. "Fundamentally, democracy is a 'system'
and as such is a means and not an end. Its 'moral' value is not auto-
matic, but depends on conformity to the moral law to which it,
like every other form of human behavior, must be subject." And it
is the pope who, as the head of the church, determines the moral
law for Catholics. In an age of opinion polls and pressure groups,
the church stands apart, viewing its own authority as absolute. For
many educated Catholics, the pope's refusal to listen to his flock is
becoming increasingly infuriating.

In arguments about the future of the church, the subject of John
Paul II's Polishness comes up again and again. It is the first thing that
dissenting Catholics point to when they attempt to come to terms with

the stubbornness and inflexibility of the Vatican. Somehow, people feel, if he were German or Italian or from Africa he would understand the need for change. But the Polish mindset, Catholics who want change will tell you, has known only blinkered authority. Poland did not experience the Reformation or the Enlightenment, and is not fully European or modern—this, the dissenters say, explains why the Polish pope's devotion to the Virgin Mary is so emphatic, and why he will not tolerate discussion, and why, on his journeys, he demands people's love and respect but will not accept their questioning.

Karol Wojtyła was born in 1920 in Wadowice, a town in southern Poland. His father was a patriotic retired army officer. His only brother, Edmund, was born in 1906; a sister died in infancy; his mother died when he was eight. Karol was brought up by his father, in a household without any women but in which his mother's memory was deeply revered. His brother, who was away at medical school while Karol was growing up, died suddenly of scarlet fever in 1932, and in 1941 his father also died suddenly, of a heart attack. Thus, by the age of twenty-one, in a Poland occupied by the Nazis, Karol Wojtyła had lost all his family.

Most Catholic priests became clerical students at the age of seventeen or eighteen, immersing themselves during their formative years in the rituals, teachings and politics of the church to the exclusion of all else, and are looked after materially and financially by the church and their families throughout their lives. Karol Wojtyła's experience was different. In 1940, in order to avoid forced labor, he began working in a quarry near Kraków. In his spare time, he was involved with a theater group in the city, and he wrote poems and plays. In 1942, he decided to study for the priesthood, and joined a secret seminary—the church was under severe pressure from the Nazis, and many members of the clergy died in concentration camps—in the archdiocese of Kraków, but continued to work as a laborer until close to the end of the war. His work during the war, Tad Szulc writes in the most useful biography that has yet appeared in English on the pope's background, "taught him how to suffer in silence and dignity, and instilled in him a habit of absolute discipline, which, as pope, he seeks to impose on an increasingly rebellious church."

Szulc's biography is mostly uncritical of John Paul II in all phases of his life. The author is emphatic about the lack of anti-Semitism in Wojtyła's background, and this view is supported by considerable evidence in speeches and statements made by the pope. In 1991, when the pope visited Wadowice, which is close to Auschwitz, I heard him speak about the Jewish presence and heritage in the town and the tragedy of its disappearance. He has been careful over the years, as Szulc points out, to refer to the Holocaust as the destruction of people whom he viewed as part of his own community, and to distance himself from general Polish anti-Semitism. (In 1936, the Catholic Primate of Poland wrote in a pastoral letter, "There will be the Jewish problem as long as the Jews remain . . . It is a fact that the Jews are fighting against the Catholic church, persisting in free thinking, and are the vanguard of godlessness, Bolshevism, and subversion.")

It is easy to understand John Paul II's stubbornness and his single-mindedness in light of the deaths in his family and the terrors of the Nazi occupation of Poland, but there is another matter to consider in any attempt to understand the nature of his papacy. After the Second World War, with the virtual disappearance of the Jewish population, and the Soviet annexation of western Ukraine, Poland became almost exclusively Catholic. Wojtyła, Szulc writes, "is also identified with the messianic concept of Polish Catholicism, the national idea and religion being inseparable." Poland sees its own martyrdom as an aspect or a symbol of Jesus's martyrdom. Thus the events of Polish history are viewed as part of a struggle between God and Satan. At Easter 1990, six months after the collapse of the Berlin Wall, I noticed that many Catholic churches in Poland placed the national symbol, the crowned eagle, at the center of the altar, as though Easter that year should preeminently commemorate the resurrection of Poland from the dead. In the minds of many Poles, the Polish nation and Catholicism are merely aspects of each other. It would be difficult for anyone rising to prominence within this system to accept that religion is a private matter or that the individual conscience should become a governing factor in Catholicism or that the pope should respond to public opinion and relax rules.

In *Sexuality and Catholicism*, Fox writes, "It is difficult to over-emphasize how important holding the line against artificial birth control has been for Pope John Paul II. During one trip to South Africa, for example, he condemned birth control forty times in ten days of public speeches." Some of this obsession can be explained by his book *Love and Responsibility*, which is based on a course of lectures he delivered at the Catholic University of Lublin in 1957–58, and which was a bestseller in Poland and was translated into several European languages. He goes into great detail about the "sexual urges" (the phrase is his) of men and women and the responsibilities arising from these urges. There is an odd innocence about his tone; homosexuality, for example, with *its* attendant urges, is mentioned only in passing and stamped as a deviation. He writes as though sex and marriage go hand in hand—as they did, perhaps, in Poland in the 1950s, where both Communist and Catholic puritanism kept young people out of harm's way. A stroll around Warsaw or Kraków on a Saturday night, even in the early 1990s—the silence in the streets, the sense that everyone was at home, living quietly, timidly obeying the rules—explains something of John Paul II's views on sex.

How did he become pope, then, having come from such a backwater, isolated from the real world by the Iron Curtain? It must be remembered that the Second Vatican Council gave church intellectuals like Wojtyła an opportunity to shine in Rome; and since Cardinal Wyszyński, Wojtyła's immediate superior, was not especially interested in the matters raised by the council, Wojtyła emerged as the effective head of the Polish church at the council, and made many friends and contacts. In 1967, when he was forty-seven, he was made a cardinal by Paul VI, though at that time there was already one Polish cardinal and thus no urgent need to appoint a second. "Clearly, Paul VI regarded him as a favorite," Szulc writes. Between 1973 and 1975, he had eleven personal audiences with Paul VI. According to Szulc, "He had attained the highest levels of the Holy See in terms of personal influence, prestige, and access all the way to the top, and his network of friends reached deep into the Curia." In February 1976, he was asked to conduct the Roman Curia's Lenten Retreat in the presence of the pope.

From the late 1960s on, Karol Wojtyła traveled widely through-out Europe, the United States, Canada and Australia. Almost everyone who dealt with him at that time attests to his energy—he loved skiing and climbing as he had once loved football—and to his humor, charisma, strength, organizational skills, his popularity with young people and his ability to speak many foreign languages. He was also known, of course, for his diplomacy in dealing with Polish authorities and his concern for the future of the church. It is clear from Szulc's book, and from a biography of John Paul II written by Michael Walsh and published in Britain in 1994, that the cardinals in the conclave that met in the Sistine Chapel in 1978 to elect a successor to John Paul I were deeply divided between two Italian candidates—one viewed as a liberal, the other as a conservative. Karol Wojtyła was not an outsider or an unknown quantity or a dark horse but someone who had worked his way to the very center of power in the church and who came from one of the most Catholic countries in the world. He managed to represent to his colleagues both the sense of hope and renewal that resulted from Vatican II and an older, unreformed, almost medieval Catholicism.

What distinguishes the pope's pontificate is the power of his spirituality, which, despite everything, still manages to inspire Catholics all over the world, and his belief in authority. His *Prayers and Devotions: 365 Daily Meditations* and *Crossing the Threshold of Hope* amply reflect these two aspects of his vision. The latter book takes the form of John Paul II's replies to a series of written questions posed by an Italian journalist, Vittorio Messori. It is hard to think of many people in the world who would tolerate the tone of naked obsequiousness in the questions that Messori puts to the pope. The replies, too, contain their fair share of cliché and banality. They are delivered in full solemnity, lacking the humor and fire of his public appearances.

In 1990 the American bishops wrote in a statement after their national conference, "The Word of God proclaimed to all nations is by nature inclusive, that is, addressed to all peoples, men and women. Consequently, every effort should be made to render the language of biblical translation as inclusive as a faithful translation of the texts permits." The catechism was thereupon translated into what Fox calls "modestly inclusive language," only to be delayed for two years until the Vatican had the text rewritten, using exclusive terms. (God "calls man to seek him, to know him, to love him with all his strength.") A new translation of the Bible, approved by the American bishops, has been suppressed by Rome for similar reasons.

Nothing is being left to chance. The pope and those closest to him are determined to push back the tide of equality and modernity. And this is happening without any lessening of the pope's popularity; the crowds still turn out to see him. In a way, his intractability adds to his appeal: the hard man with the soft voice, who remains fascinated by the world, speaking with divine authority and without any interest in current thinking or pressure groups, prepared to watch but refusing to listen, treating the whole world as though it were Poland in the 1950s, and insisting on the force of tradition and time-honored mystery.

Among the Flutterers

London Review of Books · 2010

In 1993 John McGahern wrote an essay called "The Church and Its Spire," in which he considered his own relationship to the Catholic Church. He made no mention of the fact that he had, in the mid-1960s, been fired from his job as a teacher on the instructions of the Catholic archbishop of Dublin because he had written a novel banned by the Irish censorship board (*The Dark*), and because he had been married in a register office. Instead he wrote about the great gift of being brought up in the Catholic Church: "I have nothing but gratitude for the spiritual remnants of that upbringing, the sense of our origins beyond the bounds of sense, an awareness of mystery and wonderment, grace and sacrament, and the absolute equality of all women and men underneath the sun of heaven. That is all that now remains. Belief as such has long gone."

In considering a future in which the church in Ireland would have no power at all, a future that has, due to the antics of its leadership, very quickly come to pass, McGahern quoted a letter Proust wrote in 1903, at the height of an anticlerical wave that was sweeping through France:

> I can tell you that at Illiers, the small community where two days ago my father presided at the awarding of the school prizes, the *curé* is no longer invited to the distribution of the prizes . . . The pupils are trained to consider the people who associate with him as socially undesirable . . . When I think of all this, it doesn't seem to me right that the old *curé* should no longer be invited to the distribution of the prizes, as representative of something in the village more difficult to define than the social function symbolized by the pharmacist, the retired tobacco-inspector and the optician, but something which is, nevertheless, not unworthy of respect, were it only for the perception of the meaning of the spiritualized beauty of the church spire—pointing upward into the sunset where it loses itself so lovingly in the rose-coloured clouds; and which, all the same, at first sight, to a stranger alighting in the village, looks somehow better, nobler, more dignified, with more meaning behind it, and with, what we need, more love than the other buildings, however sanctioned they may be under the latest laws.

Within fifteen years of McGahern's essay, the power of the church in Ireland has been fatally undermined. A number of reports into the abuse of children by members of the Catholic clergy have found that such abuse was widespread, at times endemic, and that the church authorities failed almost as a matter of policy in their duty to protect children. The bishops in response have learned the language of apology, which they use as often as they can. There are fascinating lapses, however, such as the outburst, at the end of the three-day Irish Episcopal Conference last March, by the bishop of Elphin, Christopher Jones, a member of the Bishops' Liaison Committee for Child Protection, who accused the media of being "unfair and unjust": "Could I just say with all this emphasis on cover-up, the cover-up has gone on for centuries, not just in the church . . . It's going on today in families, in communities, in societies. Why are you singling out the church?"

He continued:

I object to the way the church is being isolated and the focus on the church. We know we've made mistakes. Of course we've made mistakes. But why this huge isolation of the church and this huge focus on cover-up in the church when it has been going on for centuries? It's only now, for the first time ever, that victims have been given a voice to publicly express their pain and their suffering. And, before that, for centuries, no one spoke.

He added that when Freud alluded to the high levels of venereal disease among children, "he had to withdraw it. That's the kind of cover-up that has gone on for centuries."

Such lapses in the new humility were echoed in the Vatican on Easter Sunday this year when Cardinal Sodano dismissed criticism of the child sex abuse scandal in the church as "idle gossip." Or on Palm Sunday in New York when Archbishop Timothy Dolan compared the pope to Jesus, saying he was "now suffering some of the same unjust accusations, shouts of the mob, and scourging at the pillar," and "being daily crowned with thorns by groundless innuendo." Or on Good Friday in the Vatican when Raniero Cantalamessa, preacher to the papal household, told those at St. Peter's Basilica, including the pope himself, that he was thinking about the Jews in this season of Passover and Easter because "they know from experience what it means to be victims of collective violence and also because of this they are quick to recognize the recurring symptoms." He was referring to the "collective violence" of those who have been critical of the church. He went on to quote from a letter written by an unnamed Jewish friend: "I am following with indignation the violent and concentric attacks against the church, the pope and all the faithful by the whole world. The use of stereotypes, the passing from personal responsibility and guilt to a collective guilt, remind me of the more shameful aspects of anti-Semitism."

The idea that the church authorities simply don't understand what is going on was further emphasized when the Vatican last month outlined its opposition to the sexual abuse of minors by members of the clergy and to the ordination of women in the same document, and threatened greater punishment for those who got involved in the latter than in the former. Indeed, the document went further in its unwitting indication of how deep the Catholic hierarchy is in denial. It made a change in the way allegations of sexual abuse would be handled, doubling the statute of limitations from ten years after the victim's eighteenth birthday to twenty years. It is clear that the church still believes that it, more than the civil authorities, has a role in handling such cases, and that its rules about the statute of limitations remain somehow relevant.

The church now has a strange ghostly presence in Irish society. Its hierarchy still meets as though it represents something, including power; and to some extent it does still represent power. Catholic parish priests still control the majority of primary schools: they appoint the teachers and chair the boards of management, despite the fact that in the most recent opinion poll only 28 percent supported their control of schools. Orders of nuns in Ireland still own convents and schools and have control over some major hospitals. This might seem amusing until you need to ask for advice about abortion in one of those hospitals, or seek genetic counseling, or, indeed, try to get promotion as a doctor who has spoken out on these issues. The bishops, priests and nuns are sinking, but have every intention of putting up a struggle before they drown.

The laity too are putting up a struggle. In the United States, the media, including *The New York Times*, have been reporting regularly on cases of abuse and on the church's handling of such cases. They have been reporting that the church protects priests, for example, rather than reporting them to the civil authorities, and that it moves abusers from parish to parish. This reporting has been deeply shocking for the Catholic laity. In her *New York Times* column on March 27, 2010, Maureen Dowd wrote:

> The Catholic church can never recover as long as its Holy Shepherd is seen as a black sheep in the ever-darkening sex abuse scandal.

Now we learn the sickening news that Cardinal Joseph Ratzinger, nicknamed "God's Rottweiler" when he was the church's enforcer on matters of faith and sin, ignored repeated warnings and looked away in the case of the Rev. Lawrence C. Murphy, a Wisconsin priest who molested as many as 200 deaf boys.

The church has been tone deaf and dumb on the scandal for so long that it's shocking, but not surprising, to learn from the *Times*'s Laurie Goodstein that a group of deaf former students spent 30 years trying to get church leaders to pay attention.

On April 6, Dowd, certain that the hierarchy might listen better if criticism of them came from a man rather than a woman, quoted from her "conservative and devout" brother Kevin's views on where the church was going, mentioning that she had learned, "shockingly," that she and her brother "agreed on some things." "Vatican II made me wince," Kevin Dowd wrote:

The church declared casual Friday. All the once-rigid rules left to the whim of the flock. The mass was said in English (rendering useless my carefully learned Latin prayers). Holy days of obligation were optional. There were laypeople on the heretofore sacred ground of the altar—performing the sacraments and worse, handling the Host. The powerful symbolism of the priest turning the Host into the body of Christ cracked like an egg.

In his book *Goodbye, Good Men*, author Michael Rose writes that the liberalized rules set up a takeover of seminaries by homosexuals.

Vatican II liberalized rules but left the most outdated one: celibacy. That vow was put in place originally because the church did not want heirs making claims on money and land. But it ended up shrinking the priest pool and producing the wrong kind of candidates—drawing men confused about their sexuality who put our children in harm's way.

In her column on March 30, Dowd had referred to the efforts to demonize gay priests as a way for the hierarchy to wriggle out of responsibility:

> In an ad in *The Times* on Tuesday, Bill Donohue, the Catholic League president, offered this illumination: "*The Times* continues to editorialize about the 'pedophilia crisis,' when all along it's been a homosexual crisis. Eighty percent of the victims of priestly sexual abuse are male and most of them are post-pubescent. While homosexuality does not cause predatory behavior, and most gay priests are not molesters, most of the molesters have been gay."

This idea was echoed the following month when Cardinal Tarcisio Bertone said it was homosexuality, not celibacy, that was to blame for the child abuse in the church. "Many psychologists and psychiatrists," he said, "have shown that there is no link between celibacy and pedophilia, but many others have shown, and I've been told recently, that there is a relationship between homosexuality and pedophilia. That is the truth. I read it in a document written by psychologists, so that is the problem." (The Vatican distanced itself from the cardinal's remarks.)

It was interesting that Kevin Dowd felt as free as Bill Donohue and Tarcisio Bertone to mention the existence of homosexual priests and seminarians as a problem for the Catholic Church. And interesting too that, he wanted a return to the time before the "takeover" of seminaries by homosexuals; that he deplored the "shrinking" of the "priest pool" that had allowed "men confused about their sexuality" to become priests. How odd that he believed there really was a time when "men confused about their sexuality" did not become priests, when other sorts of men, men not confused in this way, were ordained. He was filled with nostalgia for an earlier church: "The church I grew up in," he wrote, "was black and white, no grays. That's why my father, an Irish immigrant, liked it so much. The chaplain of the Police and Fire Departments told me once: 'Your father was a fierce Catholic, very fierce.'"

The issue of homosexuality and the Catholic Church about which Donohue, Cardinal Bertone and Maureen Dowd's brother are so concerned is not likely to go away in the near future. For the many gay priests in the church it is deeply disturbing and indeed frightening that their sexuality can be so easily associated with rape, sexual cruelty and the abuse of minors, and that there is a view that somehow before they came along the church was just fine, and, indeed, if they could be rooted out, and the church could go back to the "black and white" days, then the problems would dissolve totally.

There are very good reasons why homosexuals have been traditionally attracted to the priesthood. I know these reasons because
I, as someone "confused about my sexuality," had to confront and
entertain the idea that I should join the priesthood. In 1971, aged
almost sixteen, I gave up my Easter break so I could attend a workshop for boys who believed they had a vocation.

Some of the reasons why gay men joined the priesthood are
obvious and simple; others are not. Becoming a priest, first of all,
seemed to solve the problem of not wanting others to know that
you were queer. As a priest, you could be celibate, or unmarried, and
everyone would understand why. It was because you had a vocation;
you had been called by God, had been specially chosen by him. For
other boys, the idea of never having sex with a woman was something
they could not even entertain. For you, such sex was problematic;
thus you had no blueprint for an easy future. The prospect, on the
other hand, of making a vow in holiness never to have sex with a
woman offered you relief. The idea that you might want to have sex
with men, that you might be "that way inclined," as they used to say,
was not even mentioned, not once, during that workshop in which
everything under the sun was discussed.

That you were gay was something you managed to know about
yourself and not know at the same time. This is almost an aspect
of the Catholic religion itself, this business of knowing and not
knowing something all at the same time, keeping an illusion separate
from the truth. We knew that the bread and wine, for example, were
literally and actually changed into the body and blood of Our Lord

Jesus Christ by the priest at mass, and, at the same time, we must have known that this was not the case, that, really, they remained just bread and wine.

The shame an adolescent felt about being gay in those years should not be underestimated; the feeling that you were less than worthy, that if people found out the truth about you they would despise you, went deep into your soul. This was another reason to become a priest. You could change your own powerlessness into power. As a priest, you would be admired and looked up to, you would spend your life—as so many Catholic priests have indeed spent their lives—doing good and being good. And being seen to be good, being needed by the sick and the dying, being wanted to officiate at weddings and baptisms and funerals, saying the sacred words that would mean so much to the congregation, all this would offer you a fulfilled and fulfilling life. Becoming a priest solved not only the outward problem of forbidden and unmentionable sexual urges, but, perhaps more important, offered a solution to the problem of having a shameful identity that lurked in the most profound recesses of the self.

This idea of knowing two things at the same time has been essential to gay people in other ways. Gay people have known that our sexuality was actually, despite what we read or were told, quite normal, quite natural; it was only the world that thought otherwise. While the world's view often ate into the self, there was another part of the self that remained intact, confident, sure. Introspection, the study of the self, for gay people grew to be necessary, fruitful. The struggle between our knowledge and their prejudice meant that a spiritual element in our being—something private, wounded, solitary and self-aware—had cause to come to the fore and seek nourishment in a close relationship to God. This is another reason so many gay men have felt themselves to have a vocation for the priesthood.

Gay liberation made its way, strangely, into the seminaries. I received a letter from the novelist John McGahern in response to my piece about the Ferns Report (see p. 193), describing his visit to an Irish seminary in the 1980s. Since the church was liberalizing at that time, it would not have been unusual for writers to be invited to seminaries to speak. McGahern had no intention of being shocking, or amusing. He spoke about literature, choosing the dullest subject for the seminarians. What he noticed among them, however, was anything but dull; and it surprised him greatly. He saw an immense amount of male fluttering; he listened as young candidates for the priesthood, boys from rural Ireland, attempted Wildean witticisms; he noticed them wearing specially tailored soutanes, moving around one another, excitedly. Here it was, and he was not the only one to witness it: "the takeover of the seminaries by homosexuals."

But this was merely what it looked like. What such a seminary would have looked like a generation or two earlier, or indeed a century or two earlier, was as much an illusion as what my friend witnessed. Before the creation of a post-Stonewall gay identity and the presence of gay role models on television and in the movies, most gay men worked out a strategy, in early adolescence, to do a perfect, lifelong imitation of a straight man, to move around in that gruff, rangy way straight men had invented for themselves. For many homosexuals, the stereotype of the mincing, high-pitched queen was the most frightening idea that ever walked towards them. They hated it and feared it and worked out ways not to look like that themselves, or to be invisible when they did so.

Catholics who grew up in a black-and-white church, and who, like Maureen Dowd's brother, resented the changes made by Vatican II, might have cause to believe that the abuse of minors by priests was a sign of decadence. But they might be wiser to pay attention to the words of Bishop Christopher Jones, when he expressed the view "It's only now, for the first time ever, that victims have been given a voice to publicly express their pain and their suffering."

This new fearlessness on the part of victims is, as Jones would have it, a feature of the age in which we live; it is this same age in which homosexuals have won freedom and celibacy is viewed with suspicion. In many parts of the world now there are gay priests who entered the seminary in good faith, and found self-knowledge and more good faith among the flutterers there. They are either celibate as a conscious, thought-out choice, or they use the gay scene when it suits them. Many of them are open to themselves and, to some extent, to their congregations about their sexuality, which is no longer a poison, but a gift, a way of understanding others, including Christ himself and his apostles, whom the world wished to victimize and marginalize. This poses a serious problem for the Catholic hierarchy, serious enough for them to ignore it, which is one of their skills. It is one of the most notable features of the Catholic Church in the United States.

Homosexuality in the church, however, comes in many guises. It comes in the guise of this new openness, but it also arrives on the newsstands in a time when the press is less afraid to declare sexual activity among Catholic priests in the Vatican, say, a form of hypocrisy. A time, too, when the police are less likely to be subservient. In January this year, for example, the carabinieri in Rome recorded an exchange in which Angelo Balducci, a Gentleman to His Holiness (a name for ushers in the Vatican who are expected to "distinguish themselves for the good of souls and the glory of the name of the Lord"), a man who was also a senior adviser to the Congregation for the Evangelization of Peoples, spoke to a Vatican chorister on the telephone. They discussed a seminarian. Balducci is said to have asked: "Listen, have you spoken with the seminarian by any chance?" The chorister replied that he was "probably at mass or something." Later, the chorister called again to recommend "a colleague, a friend" of the seminarian because the latter was unavailable. He said the colleague is "better, taller, a bit taller than you." Later, he asked: "Can I send [him] around straight away?" and inquired where Balducci was. Balducci replied: "Up at the seminary . . . where the cardinal lives." The chorister replied: "He could get there within half an hour . . . the time it takes to catch a taxi and get there." The transcripts also implied that over a period of around five months in 2008, the chorister procured for Balducci at least ten contacts with, among others, "two black Cuban lads," a former model from Naples and a rugby player from Rome.

In July this year two undercover journalists from the magazine *Panorama*, which is owned by Berlusconi, witnessed priests in Rome having gay sex and visiting gay clubs and bars. John Hooper in *The Guardian* reported that the Diocese of Rome, in response, urged gay clerics to leave both the closet and the priesthood. It said: "Consistency would require that they come into the open" but they "ought not to have become priests." Hooper went on:

> One priest, a Frenchman in his thirties identified as Fr Paul, attended a party at which there were two male prostitutes, then said mass the following morning before driving them to the airport, *Panorama* reported. A photo on its website claimed to show the priest in his dog collar but without his trousers with a gay man who acted as decoy for the magazine. In other shots, priests were shown apparently kissing *Panorama*'s collaborator.
>
> A member of the clergy quoted by the magazine put the proportion of gay priests in the Italian capital at "98 percent." The Rome diocese insisted the vast majority of priests in the city were "models of morality for all," while adding that the number of gay clergymen was "small, but not to be written off as isolated cases." A review eight years ago of research on the American church concluded that between a quarter and a half of seminarians and priests there were homosexual.
>
> A former Italian MP and gay activist, Franco Grillini, said: "If all the gays in the Catholic Church were to leave it at once— something we would very much like—they would cause it serious operational problems."
>
> Another well-known spokesman for the gay community, Aurelio Mancuso, condemned *Panorama*'s investigation as a "horrible

political and cultural operation," but agreed that if priests in Rome were to follow the advice given to them in yesterday's statement, it would "paralyze" the diocese.

For those at the top of the church, and for many among the faithful, all of this is a headache. The general air of freedom has made victims of abuse by the clergy feel free to speak. It has also made gay priests more self-aware, more assertive, more willing to be openly gay and openly celibate at the same time, or more free to consult their consciences and break the rules of celibacy should they see fit. It has also made other priests, members of the old school as it were, the sort who hire prostitutes, more at risk of getting caught by a press no longer afraid of the Vatican.

There are two ways the church can now go, and it is perhaps a tribute to the extraordinary personality of Karol Wojtyła, who was a master of ambiguities, that during his papacy the church went both of these ways. The first way the church could go emphasizes the spiritual and the mysterious element in Christianity; the second emphasizes the church's interest in control. This latter route was best illustrated by its role in the Cairo Conference on Population and Development in September 1994. The Vatican attended the conference with the aim of preventing any agreement that would imply toleration of abortion, support for artificial methods of contraception and any new definition of the family that did not correspond to the Catholic definition. In attempting to wield influence, and to combat what it viewed as the liberal agenda of the Clinton White House on the issue of abortion, the church forged alliances with states such as Libya and Iran. The Vatican representative told Arab delegates that he supported their wish "to respond to the challenges of the modern world in a way which does not damage what is precious in those traditions," including "the special role of women."

Before the conference, Wojtyła became involved personally, as though he were a head of state (which technically he is, since the Vatican is a state), summoning 120 ambassadors to the Holy See to explain the church's position. Church authorities forced the United States to enter into negotiations with it. The Vatican representative to the conference attacked the draft document, which was to be discussed and agreed on, asserting that it "lacks ethics and a coherent moral vision, promotes contraception and tolerates abortion." At the conference itself, "The Holy See delegation kept up a spirited attack, filibustering on several parts of the bracketed language and delaying the work of the conference," according to Alison McIntosh and Jason Finkle in *Population and Development Review*. Maher Mahran, Egypt's minister for population and the host of the conference, asked: "Does the Vatican rule the world? The world is not here to be dictated to. And let me tell you the delegates here represent more than five billion people in the world, and not only 190 at the Vatican."

This idea that the church should represent not merely the private religious beliefs of its members, but a view of how policy on public matters should be evaluated and carried out all over the world, belongs as much to the legacy of Wojtyła as any strengthening of the church as a locus of an advanced spirituality. As Wojtyła's health declined, it was tempting, as I wrote at the time, to imagine that there was a cardinal in waiting who would resemble Gorbachev or de Klerk, who would move from the ranks of conformity into a position of leadership and would dismantle church teaching on sexuality, clerical celibacy, human reproduction and the rights of women, matters that were bringing the church to its knees, distracting from its spiritual mission.

Even when Joseph Ratzinger was elected pope in April 2005, it was possible to imagine, as he came out onto the balcony of St. Peter's with a benign and humble look on his face and the bearing of a kind but wily old man with a deep inner life, that he was someone with the authority, the intellectual depth and the good sense to carry out these reforms. It was possible to imagine him spending his papacy restoring prayer and the spiritual life to the heart of the Catholic faith, placing much emphasis on the mystery and beauty of the Eucharist and dwelling as much as he could on ideas of redemption, responsibility, solidarity, forgiveness and love in the life of Jesus in the New Testament.

If anyone wonders why this has not happened, it is worth taking a look at Ratzinger's views on homosexuality, which are offered in full in a number of appendices to *The Pope Is Not Gay!* by Angelo Quattrocchi. In 1986, as the Prefect of the Congregation for the Doctrine of the Faith, Ratzinger wrote a letter to the Catholic bishops, which was approved by the pope, on "the Pastoral Care of Homosexuals." He referred to an earlier Vatican declaration on the matter in 1975, which "took note of the distinction commonly drawn between the homosexual condition or tendency and individual homosexual actions" and described the latter as "intrinsically disordered." But in the discussion that followed, according to Ratzinger, "an overly benign interpretation was given to the homosexual condition itself, some going so far as to call it neutral, or even good. Although the particular inclination of the homosexual person is not a sin, it is a more or less strong tendency towards an intrinsic moral evil; and thus the inclination itself must be seen as a moral disorder."

In plainer language, whereas in 1975 having sex if you were gay was "disordered," now doing nothing at all—singing hymns, say, or watching reruns of *Bernadette of Lourdes*—was also "disordered." Just sitting there, you were "disordered." There was no way out, since Ratzinger's catechism of 1992 also declared that "masturbation is an intrinsically and gravely disordered action." Ratzinger went on in his letter of 1986 to wonder whether, since homosexuality "must be seen as an objective disorder," this required the faithful to attack homosexuals. No, he thought, it did not. "It is deplorable," he wrote, "that homosexual persons have been or are the object of violent malice in speech or in action . . . But the proper reaction to crimes committed against homosexual persons should not be to claim that the homosexual condition is not disordered." He continued: "When such a claim is made and when homosexual activity is consequently condoned, or when civil legislation is introduced to protect behavior to which no one has any conceivable right, neither the church nor society at large should be surprised when other distorted notions and practices gain ground, and irrational and violent reactions increase."

Ratzinger does not name these "other distorted notions and practices," but it is not hard to conclude that he may be referring to the sexual abuse of children. It is hard, indeed, to think what else he could possibly mean. He is thus implying that legislation for gay rights has somehow led to an increase in pedophilia. He is careful, however, not to spell this out. This is an interesting moment, the beginning of a culture of denial, a culture in which someone else, somewhere else, had to be blamed.

The "revised statement" of 1992 was mostly a repeat exercise of his letter of 1986 but there were some interesting additions. In Section 12, for example, he wrote:

> Among other rights, all persons have the right to work, to hous-ing etc. Nevertheless, these rights are not absolute. They can be legitimately limited for objectively disordered external conduct. This is sometimes not only licit but obligatory. This would obtain moreover not only in the case of culpable behavior but even in the case of actions of the physically or mentally ill. Thus it is accepted that the state may restrict the exercise of rights, for example, in the case of contagious or mentally ill persons, in order to protect the common good.

Two clauses later, Ratzinger moves from associating homosexuality with disease and madness to pondering the question of coming out, or remaining in the closet. Ratzinger makes clear that he favors the closet.

> The "sexual orientation" of a person is not comparable to race, sex, age etc. also for another reason . . . An individual's sexual

orientation is generally not known to others unless he publicly identifies himself as having this orientation or unless some overt behavior manifests it. As a rule, the majority of homosexually oriented persons who seek to lead chaste lives do not publicize their sexual orientation. Hence the problem of discrimination in terms of employment, housing etc. does not usually arise.

Not publicizing your sexual orientation was something the Vatican supported, perhaps with good reason. However, the idea that "An individual's sexual orientation is generally not known to others unless he publicly identifies himself as having this orientation or unless some overt behavior manifests it" is more complex than Ratzinger might think. An individual may manifest this orientation without intending to, for example. There are ways for people who do not want to identify themselves as homosexual to identify themselves as such while thinking, or hoping, that they are not in fact doing so.

In Częstochowa in August 1991 after morning mass said by the pope, I was wandering around the monastery of Jasna Góra when something caught my eye in the cloisters below. Twelve cardinals and more than two hundred bishops were being disrobed of their splendid and colorful vestments by a group of nuns. A prelate, fresh from the altar, would stand with his arms in the air while two nuns removed his vestments and carried them to a clothes rack to hang up, leaving the prince of the church with his hair tousled, wearing only black. A few years later, on Easter Sunday, as I wandered around the inside of St. Peter's in Rome after mass, I noticed vast numbers of bishops and cardinals, all in their regalia. Since the sun was shining, some of them had the most beautiful seminarians or young priests standing behind them holding yellow umbrellas over their heads. It was a sight for sore eyes.

When I listed the reasons homosexuals might be attracted to the church and might want to become priests, I did not mention the most obvious one: you get to wear funny bright clothes; you get to dress up all the time in what are essentially women's clothes. As part of the training to be an altar boy I had to learn, and still remember, what a priest puts on to say mass: the amice, the alb, the girdle, the stole, the maniple and the chasuble. Watching them robing themselves was like watching Mary, Queen of Scots getting ready for her execution.

Priests prance around in elaborately fashioned costumes. Bishops and cardinals have even more colorful vestments. This "overt behavior" on their part has to be examined carefully. Since it is part of the rule of the church, part of the norm, it has to be emphasized that many of them do not dress up as a matter of choice. Indeed, the vestments in all their glory might make some of them wince. But others seem to enjoy it. Among those who seem to enjoy it is Ratzinger. Quattrocchi draws our attention to the amount of care, since his election, Ratzinger has taken with his accessories, wearing designer sunglasses, for example, or gold cufflinks, and different sorts of funny hats and a pair of red shoes from Prada that would take the eyes out of you. He has also been having fun with his robes. On Ash Wednesday 2006, for example, he wore a robe of "Valentino red"— called after the fashion designer—with "showy gold embroidery" and soon afterwards changed into a blue associated with another fashion designer, Renato Balestra. In March 2007, for a visit to the juvenile prison at Casal del Marmo, he wore an extraordinary tea-rose-colored costume.

Quattrocchi draws conclusions a little too easily from a consideration of the connection between the fury of the pope's attacks on homosexuality and his attire. "The secularist," he writes,

> will inevitably wonder, not particularly maliciously, whether such fury isn't the fruit of a deeply repressed desire for what he condemns. Of an unconscious desire which manifests itself as its opposite . . . Now that he has ascended to the throne, our hero has discovered the dazzling clothes, the trappings of power and wealth, which centuries of pomp have draped on the shoulders of his predecessors. In this way, his true nature, his deepest unspoken inclinations are revealed. In short, he might simply be the most repressed, imploded gay in the world.

Quattrocchi also considers the relationship between the pope and his private secretary. The private secretary is called Georg Gänswein. Gänswein is remarkably handsome, a cross between George Clooney and Hugh Grant, but, in a way, more beautiful than either. In a radio interview Gänswein described a day in his life and the life of Ratzinger, now that he is pope:

> The pope's day begins with the seven o'clock mass, then he says prayers with his breviary, followed by a period of silent

contemplation before our Lord. Then we have breakfast together, and so I begin the day's work by going through the correspondence. Then I exchange ideas with the Holy Father, then I accompany him to the "Second Loggia" for the private midday audiences. Then we have lunch together; after the meal we go for a little walk before taking a nap. In the afternoon I again take care of the correspondence. I take the most important stuff which needs his signature to the Holy Father.

When asked if he felt nervous in the presence of the Holy Father, Gänswein replied that he sometimes did and added:

But it is also true that the fact of meeting each other and being together on a daily basis creates a sense of "familiarity," which makes you feel less nervous. But obviously I know who the Holy Father is and so I know how to behave appropriately. There are always some situations, however, when the heart beats a little stronger than usual.

In his book, Quattrocchi prints many photographs of the pope in his papal clothes, and many of Gänswein looking sultry, like a film star, and a few of the two together, taking a walk or the younger man helping the older one to put on a robe or a hat. He writes:

About ten years before he became pope, when age was beginning to take its toll and was maybe sharpening the secret internal rage, Ratzy [Ratzinger] met Don Giorgio [Gänswein]. And it was a spark of life amid the doctrinal darkness . . . So we can at least imagine how a pure soul becomes inflamed when it meets its soulmate, when a nearly 70-year-old prefect of the Congregation for the Doctrine of the Faith meets a brilliant 40-year-old priest from his native Bavaria who shares the same outlook on the world . . . When we see the photos, which we publish in this book, of Georg putting Ratzy's little hat on for him, handing him his stole, watching his back, looking after him, accompanying him and helping him as he walks, we cannot help being moved.

It seems to me that Quattrocchi is pushing his luck here. In his attacks on homosexuals, Ratzinger was using his full skills as a hard-line Catholic theologian; he was indeed displaying himself as doctrinaire, but he was operating during the papacy of Wojtyła. He could not have issued his declarations without the agreement of the pope. While there is something emphatic and absolute and hateful in his diktats, it should be understood that he has taken this tone on other matters besides homosexuality. He may well have taken it out of conviction and seriousness; to suggest that this most ideological of figures may be homosexual himself simply because he has made so many statements on the matter is unfair to him. And in his way of wearing clothes, he is no different from any other member of the church hierarchy. It is unlikely they all get pleasure from wandering around looking like elderly fashion victims, even if some of them, including Ratzinger, seem to do so. It may depend on who is taking the photographs. And it is natural that Ratzinger would have a private secretary who is also from Bavaria and with whom he appears to share an ideology. It might be a coincidence that he is one of the most handsome men alive.

The problem is that, after all that has been revealed, many of us who were brought up in the church now know that we once listened to sermons about how to conduct our lives from men who were child molesters. And that senior members of the church hierarchy protected these men, believing that the reputation of the church was more important than the safety of children, and that church law was superior to civil law. When they were found out, their sorrow was not fully credible. Thus, when we think of the Catholic Church, we think of secrecy, half-hearted apology, studied concealment.

This makes it difficult for Ratzinger, who is probably the most intelligent and articulate pope for many generations, to be heard properly when he speaks about matters of faith and morals. He wishes to make it clear, from a position that is starkly coherent, that moral values are not relative values, but absolute ones, that we must follow God's will, and that the Catholic Church is in a unique position to tell us in some detail what this entails. However, rather than listening to this message or bowing our heads as he offers us his blessing, because of what has happened, because of a new suspicion that even the most reverent feel about the clergy, we will find ourselves examining Ratzinger's clothes and his accessories, his gestures, and checking behind him for a glimpse of the gorgeous Georg with whom he spends so much of his day.

The Bergoglio Smile:
Pope Francis

London Review of Books · 2021

The trial of Argentina's military leaders took place in Buenos Aires between April and September 1985. The court heard evidence against the nine most senior figures in the regime, including three former presidents—Videla, Viola and Galtieri. Sittings began each day in the early afternoon and often went on until after midnight. The first official inquiry into the extent of torture and disappearances in Argentina, called CONADEP, had been set up by Raúl Alfonsín in December 1983 shortly after his election as president. It reported nine months later, identifying three hundred secret detention centers during the reign of the generals and documenting almost nine thousand deaths and disappearances. Its findings were published as a book, *Nunca Más*.

The coup that brought the military to power in 1976 was led by three men: Jorge Videla from the army, Emilio Massera from the navy and Orlando Ramón Agosti from the air force. Of the three,

Massera was the most dangerous and determined. It was believed that if you were arrested by the army or the air force, you had a roughly one in ten chance of being murdered; if you were taken by the navy you had only a one in ten chance of getting out alive. Videla was named president on March 29, 1976, but in reality power was shared among the three. This meant that no one was ever quite sure who was actually in control, or who to appeal to when things went wrong.

So when Edgardo Sajón, a former government press secretary, was arrested in 1977, his wife went to see one of the generals only to be told that the security forces worked independently from one another and he couldn't help her. Twice she went to see Videla himself, who told her that there was a pact of silence in the military on the disappearances. One official told her that maybe their relationship was the problem and her husband had left her. In the end, as she told the court, she gave up asking questions, since she had her children to think about.

Versions of her experience were repeated many times in the course of the trial. The next witness, however, stood apart. He was General Alejandro Lanusse, president of Argentina between 1971 and 1973. His bearing was dignified, and he brought a sense of his own importance to the witness box. Sajón had been his press secretary, and Lanusse had made a "vehement and long-lasting attempt to find out what happened" to him. He told the court that he had had meetings with four of the military leaders on trial. When he was told there was a small group that acted outside official government channels on security matters, he sent the regime a public telegram demanding information.

He spoke with controlled rage, as a man used to having his orders obeyed. He gave an account of having to identify the body of his cousin, the diplomat Elena Holmberg, found in a river in 1978. Holmberg had been summoned back to Buenos Aires from Paris, with her loyalty to the regime under suspicion. It was believed that she was murdered on Massera's orders. As Lanusse was waiting to see her body, he told the court, he heard a senior officer complain about how long it had taken to find her. A junior officer replied: "How can you worry about one body when you have thrown eight thousand into the Río de la Plata?" The next witness, a former policeman called Carlo Alberto Hours, was able to tell the court how Sajón had died. He gave a graphic description of how they had tied him to a billiard table, wetting his clothes and the surface of the table, before putting electric wires around one of his toes and into his mouth.

The official expectation was that all this explicit and dramatic firsthand evidence would matter, and that the trial would be followed avidly all over Argentina and would establish the enormity of what had transpired before democracy was restored. But everywhere I went in Buenos Aires in those months in 1985 I encountered a similar response. Sometimes it was just a shrug of indifference; at others, it was a firm denial that any of this had ever happened. Some people believed the trial was a waste of resources. Others insisted that I would take a different view had I been in Argentina in 1976 when the generals took over and faced a determined, well-educated and well-funded terrorist group known as the Montoneros, which had emerged as a left-wing splinter from Peronism, with roots in radical Catholic groups. Attending the trial was like being in a bubble. As I began to discover the city, I recognized street names from testimony given in court, places where bodies had been dumped or people arrested. Buenos Aires, for me, even still, is the city where the disappearances happened. But this is not what many people felt in 1985.

Of all those who gave evidence, one figure really stands out. Christian von Wernich was a priest and police chaplain. Later, in 2006, he would be charged with murder and kidnapping as part of the military repression, and in 2007 he would be sentenced to life imprisonment. But appearing before the court in 1985, he was a tall, confident, plausible, well-groomed figure in his forties. He explained that as a police chaplain he had come across a number of young people in detention and had offered them what he called "my spiritual services." They had doubts, they had problems, they had fears, he said with the utmost gravity. When asked about their physical state, he said that he had only considered their spiritual state. He said it with such seriousness that, for a moment, it even sounded true. There was no torture, he said, his voice becoming angry; in all his years as a police chaplain he had never heard of a prisoner being tortured. He would never have tolerated it.

The incredulous laughter broke out when von Wernich said that, having discovered that eight of these young people were going to leave the country, he had counseled them on the perils of living abroad. He spoke to them, he said, about what they might miss if they went to Uruguay or Brazil. It was clear to everyone present that the young people in question were dead. All eight had been named in court. They were last seen in November 1977, having been arrested a year earlier.

During the trial, many odd details emerged about the system the generals oversaw. Evidence was given that the security forces stole from every house they raided. One woman testified that every single object in her apartment was taken, including the light bulbs. The wife of a torturer called Colores couldn't work out how to use a sewing machine taken from a detained woman, so Colores had to appeal to the detainee for advice. Since one prisoner was an electrician, the guards brought him goods to repair, including the cattle prods that they used for torture. After he was released, Julián Alega, who had been tortured badly by both Colores and a man called Julián El Turco, met Colores on the street. He told the court that Colores asked him how he was doing, as though they were old friends, and gave him a telephone number in case he was ever in trouble. He also met El Turco, who proposed that they might go into business together.

The group befriended by von Wernich had been tortured at the beginning of their incarceration, the court was told, but were later held in better conditions than other detainees. When two of the women gave birth, the babies were handed over to the grandparents. This was unusual: most children born in prison were adopted secretly by military families. Towards the end of 1977, the young prisoners who had come to von Wernich's attention were given to believe that they were going to be allowed to leave the country. They asked their parents for money and passports and copies of their degrees. Their parents gave all this material to von Wernich. When time went by and there was no word from the detainees, they appealed to von Wernich, who told them not to give up hope.

In court, von Wernich had a curious way of responding to the most ordinary questions. When asked about a man called Astiz, a notorious torturer, he spoke about what a wonderful name Assisi was and what resonance it had for Catholics. He was asked when precisely the prisoners had departed; he replied that it was in November, because November is the month of the Virgin, and he went on to describe the importance of the Virgin in his own life and the life of the church. In the end, he testified that all eight detainees had left the country, some by air, some by land. He saw them all off, he said, but couldn't remember the name of a single person who had come with them to the airport, though he agreed that there had been a driver and several members of the security forces. No, he couldn't remember what these people looked like or what sort of car it was. There is no record of any of the prisoners leaving Argentina or entering any other country.

On the day after von Wernich gave evidence, I went through the newspapers looking for some comment from the Catholic Church on what he had said. But there was nothing. The church had been mentioned in the trial only because there were chaplains in the detention centers. When I began to ask people where the church was during what became known as the Dirty War, no one had much to tell me.

Twenty-eight years later, in 2013, when Jorge Mario Bergoglio, who had been in Buenos Aires through the reign of the generals, was elected pope, I wondered what his response to the disappearances had been. What was he doing, what was he saying, between 1976 and 1982?

In 1973, at the age of thirty-six, Bergoglio became the youngest provincial in the history of the Jesuits, responsible for both Argentina and Uruguay. At the time of his appointment, the Jesuits were going through a crisis that included a radical drop in the number of novices. In the religious split among Catholics in Latin America, Bergoglio's position was clear: he opposed liberation theology. In Argentina he supported the Iron Guard, a right-wing Peronist group, and was, for a time, spiritual adviser to them. As a novice master, Bergoglio had been a strict disciplinarian. Now he set about imposing discipline on the Jesuits under his control. "He brought in conservative lay professors to replace teachers he considered too progressive," Paul Vallely writes in *Pope Francis: Untying the Knots* (2013). "He tried to make us more like a religious order," one of Bergoglio's students recalled, "wearing surplices and singing the office . . . Bergoglio brought in an arch-conservative, the military chaplain from Moreno Air Base, to teach. He seemed unaware of any of the teachings of Vatican II. It was all St. Thomas Aquinas and the old church Fathers. We didn't study a single book by Gutiérrez, Boff or Paulo Freire" (the main theorists of liberation theology). In his first interview as pope, Bergoglio spoke of these years: "I had to deal with difficult situations, and I made my decisions abruptly and by myself. My authoritarian and quick manner of making decisions led me to have serious problems and to be accused of being ultra-conservative." A Jesuit who lived under Bergoglio's rule is quoted by Jimmy Burns in *Francis: Pope of Good Promise* (2015):

"He exercised his authority with an iron fist as if he was the sole interpreter of St. Ignatius Loyola."

When Jesuit priests visited poor areas, Bergoglio encouraged them to talk about religion rather than social conditions and to have nothing to do with unions or cooperatives. Under orders from his superiors in Rome, Bergoglio had to sell the Universidad del Salvador, one of Argentina's Jesuit universities. He gave it to the Iron Guard. The Iron Guard, Vallely writes, were "an odd bunch . . . who liked to think of themselves as a secret order characterized by obedience, intellectual rigour and ascetic discipline." This decision to hand the university over to them, according to Guillermo Marcó, who was Bergoglio's spokesman for eight years, "is something for which many Jesuits have never forgiven him."

Bergoglio, whose father had emigrated from Italy in 1929, was from a lower class than the normal run of Jesuits and, as Marcantonio Colonna writes in *The Dictator Pope: The Inside Story of the Francis Papacy* (2017), "in the class-conscious society that is Argentina's legacy from its oligarchic past this was always a visible handicap." (Colonna is the pen name of a Catholic writer called Henry Sire.) Before entering the Jesuits, Bergoglio trained as a lab technician. He wouldn't have been fired up by the seminal texts that gave rise to liberation theology.

When the coup took place in 1976, the Jesuits were divided. As the Jesuit historian Jeffrey Klaiber has written, "during these years, the Argentinian province did not march in unison with the rest of the Society of Jesus in Latin America." In *The Catholic Church and Argentina's Dirty War* (2015), Gustavo Morello, another Jesuit, writes: "In contrast to the situations in Chile, Brazil, Guatemala, Peru, Ecuador and El Salvador, in Argentina none of the most important dioceses, nor the Argentine Bishops' Conference as a group, created any framework to protect victims or to document the alleged abuses. Scholars have been perplexed by the public silence of the Argentine hierarchy in those years." Two months after the coup, the bishops issued a statement which, Vallely writes, "called for understanding towards the military government. The document said it was wrong to expect the security agencies to act 'with the chemical purity' they would in peacetime … The moment required, the bishops said, that a measure of freedom be sacrificed."

In 2012, the year before his death, the ex-president Videla gave an interview about his regime's dealings with the church: "My relationship with the church was excellent. It was very cordial, frank and open." During the dictatorship, Admiral Massera played tennis with the papal nuncio, Pio Laghi, once a fortnight. It was arranged for Massera to have an audience with Pope Paul VI on a visit to Rome in 1977. In the same year, he was invited to give a speech and receive an honorary doctorate from the Universidad del Salvador, no longer owned by the Jesuits but still seen as a Jesuit institution. Bergoglio did not attend. Instead, the Jesuits were represented by the rector of the Jesuit seminary in Buenos Aires.

There is no evidence that Bergoglio socialized with anyone much at all in the years of the dictatorship, least of all the leaders of the regime. He knew them, however, and kept avenues of communication with them open. But he spent more energy on keeping recalcitrant Jesuits in line. In 2010 he said:

I knew that something serious was happening and that there were a lot of prisoners, but I realized that it was much more than that only later on. Society as a whole only became fully aware of events during the trial of the military commanders . . . In truth I found it hard to see what was happening until they started to bring people to me.

Part of the justification for not openly denouncing the regime was that it allowed the church to intercede for those detained, but, as Austen Ivereigh, a writer highly sympathetic to Bergoglio, writes in *The Great Reformer: Francis and the Making of a Radical Pope* (2014), "the results were meagre."

The most serious allegation against Bergoglio during the Dirty War was given some attention during the 2005 papal conclave, when he was the main contender against Joseph Ratzinger after the death of John Paul II. It centered on the arrest and torture of two Jesuit priests, Orlando Yorio and Franz Jalics. Bergoglio had known both of them since the early 1960s—they had been his teachers. By the time Bergoglio took over as provincial of Argentina and Uruguay, both men were aligned with what Ivereigh calls "post-conciliar Jesuit chaos," lodging not in a Jesuit house but in a poor area of the city in a community that was, Ivereigh writes, "an avant-garde experiment in non-hierarchical, politically engagé living." In February 1976, Bergoglio told them they would have to dissolve the communities they had established and move to a Jesuit residence. They decided to stay, putting themselves at considerable risk of being treated by the regime as political activists. In May, four women catechists who worked with them were abducted and never seen again. The bishop of the diocese withdrew their licences to say mass. When they appealed to Bergoglio, he said they could say mass in private. A week later, both men were abducted, it was believed by the navy.

They were kept in custody for five months, blindfolded and handcuffed. A judicial inquiry in 2010 concluded that their release was "a consequence of steps taken by the religious order to which the victims belonged and the interest taken in them by leading members of the Catholic church." This included two meetings that Bergoglio had with Massera. The second of these meetings, Bergoglio said, was brief and ugly, ending with Bergoglio saying flatly that he wanted the priests released. He also had two meetings with Videla, the second one occurring only because he asked the priest saying mass for the general to report in sick so that Bergoglio could attend in his place. Videla was more cordial and responsive than Massera.

After the pair were released, Yorio especially began to ask questions about Bergoglio's involvement, claiming that the future pope had visited the building where he and Jalics were being detained. This claim, Jimmy Burns writes, "was never substantiated." Speaking to his authorized biographers in 2013, Bergoglio merely said: "Fortunately, some time later they were released, firstly because they [the regime] couldn't find anything to substantiate their allegations, and second because on the very night I heard they had been arrested, I started seeing what I could do on their behalf." The interesting phrase here is "they couldn't find anything to substantiate their allegations," as though the navy under Massera ever sifted evidence or operated judicially. Yorio claimed, as Ivereigh writes, that Bergoglio "had actually put his name on a list that he gave to his torturers," but again there is no evidence for this. "It is absolutely wrong to say that Jorge Bergoglio delivered these priests," one of the judges insisted at the end of the inquiry in 2010. "We've heard this version, analyzed the evidence presented and concluded that his actions had no legal involvement in this case."

In 1979 Bergoglio was replaced as Jesuit provincial, becoming rector of the seminary. In these years, the Jesuits in Argentina were divided between the Peronists and anti-Peronists, with Bergoglio in the former camp, believing in the need to be close to the people while keeping away from political theory and, in a sort of sanctified Peronism, encouraging the worship of images and devotion to the Virgin. Bergoglio's interest in devotional images was antithetical to Jesuit culture, as one of his colleagues pointed out: "You can't believe it, he introduced Argentine Jesuits to popular religiosity." He encouraged students to go "to the chapel at night and touch images! This was something the poor did, the people of the pueblo, something that the Society of Jesus worldwide doesn't do." Bergoglio also supported Argentinian nationalism. In October 2009, while blessing relatives of soldiers killed in the Falklands War, he told them to "kiss that land which is ours and which seems so far away." Three years later he spoke of the dead soldiers as "sons of the fatherland who went out . . . to claim what belonged to the fatherland."

Just after Bergoglio was elected pope, the superior general of the Jesuits wrote a letter to the members of the order worldwide in which he said that this was a time "not to allow ourselves to be swept away by distractions of the past." The superior general knew, Ivereigh writes, "that there were Jesuits of a certain vintage—both inside Argentina and elsewhere—who mistrusted Bergoglio, saw him as a retrograde, divisive figure, and he knew that this toxicity could damage the Jesuits' relationship with the new pope." The doubts had started early. In 1977 an English Jesuit, Michael Campbell-Johnston, sent to Argentina to report on the order there, wrote that he was appalled that "our institute in Buenos Aires was able to function freely because it never criticized or opposed the government," and, according to Ivereigh, "he berated Bergoglio . . . for being 'out of step with our other social institutes in the continent.'" Between 1988 and 1990, tensions grew within the Argentine Jesuits. Despite the fact that he said little, "Bergoglio was increasingly blamed for stirring this up," Ivereigh writes. In April 1990, Bergoglio was removed from his teaching job and asked to hand over his room key. Those who appeared to be closest to him were sent abroad. He himself was transferred to Córdoba, Argentina's second city, where he spent two years. The new provincial of the Jesuits had been one of his harshest critics. This was a time, Bergoglio later said, "of great interior crisis." It is where his story as a Catholic leader might easily have ended.

In notes he wrote during this exile, there are oblique justifications for what he had done during the Dirty War. He believed that some crises had no human solutions, and that "visceral impotence" imposed "the grace of silence." In a section called "God's War," he observed that there were often times when, in Ivereigh's paraphrase, "God went into battle with the enemy of humankind, and it was a mistake to get involved." In order to return to power, Bergoglio hitched his wagon to the star of Antonio Quarracino, who was appointed archbishop of Buenos Aires in 1990. Quarracino, like Bergoglio a Peronist, disliked the government of Alfonsín, who, as Jimmy Burns writes, was "the first democratically elected Argentine president seriously to challenge the Peronist political dominance and power of the military since 1930." Quarracino opposed moves to liberalize the divorce laws, and in 1994 declared on television that lesbians and gay men should be "locked up in a ghetto"— homosexuality was "a deviation of human nature, like bestiality." Burns writes, "There is no record of Bergoglio having said a word against him. As his auxiliary bishop, Bergoglio professed total loyalty to Quarracino."

By becoming an auxiliary bishop under Quarracino, in 1992, Bergoglio was moving further away from the Jesuits. His vow of obedience to his Jesuit superiors no longer applied. On visits to Rome, he never once stayed in the Jesuit house on Borgo Santo Spirito but found his own lodgings. Once elected pope, Bergoglio wanted the world to know that he was, or had been, sinful. "I don't want to mislead anyone—the truth is that I'm a sinner," he told interviewers.

> From a young age, life pushed me into leadership roles—as soon as
> I was ordained as a priest, I was designated as a master of novices,
> and two and a half years later, leader of the province—and I had
> to learn from my errors along the way, because, to tell the truth,
> I made hundreds of errors. Errors and sins.

There is no evidence that Bergoglio, as one of the six auxiliary bishops, was "pushed" into any role. He remained close to

Quarracino, who was immensely loquacious and liked luxury, by remaining silent and himself eschewing the trappings associated with a prince of the church. "After a short time as a bishop Bergoglio began to distinguish himself from the rest," Guillermo Marcó noted. "He didn't use a chauffeur-driven car, he walked and traveled on public transport . . . He would go and visit individual priests."

Quarracino had many enemies in the church, not least the future archbishop of La Plata, who had powerful friends in the Vatican. But Quarracino had his own associate in the Vatican, a former papal nuncio who was close to John Paul II. A battle began, to choose who would replace Quarracino as archbishop and cardinal, with Bergoglio supported by Quarracino alone. According to one version of what happened—a version supported by both Vallely and Ivereigh—the Curia in the Vatican refused to support Bergoglio's appointment, and blocked Quarracino's access to the pope to make the case for him. "But the wily old cardinal," Vallely writes, "who had been born in Italy, was not defeated. He then wrote a letter of appointment for the pope to sign and went to see the Argentinian ambassador to the Holy See, Francisco Eduardo Trusso, who was an old friend." Trusso, in his next audience, it is alleged, handed the letter to the pope, who duly signed it. Whatever the story, Bergoglio wouldn't have become archbishop of Buenos Aires on Quarracino's death in 1998 had he not had his predecessor's full support (and, possibly, that of Carlos Menem, Argentina's president between 1989 and 1999, to whom Quarracino had made himself an ally).

Bergoglio didn't move into the archbishop's palace, choosing to live in more spartan quarters. On his first Maundy Thursday, instead of going to the cathedral for the washing of the feet, he went to a hospital and washed the feet of AIDS patients. A year later, he caught a bus to wash the feet of prisoners. He allowed these annual foot-washing ceremonies to be photographed. Having kept a low public profile until now, he began to meet an increasing number of journalists—he even invited them for Christmas drinks. In October 1999, at a ceremony to mark the reinterment of a priest murdered for his left-wing views, Bergoglio apologized for the church's position during the dictatorship: "Let us pray for Fr. Carlos's assassins, and the ideologues who lay behind it, but also for the complicit silence of most of society and of the church."

This use of apology and aura of humility that he carried with him to Rome was not something noted previously in Bergoglio, whose meekness, Vallely writes, "was not some natural modesty, bashfulness or self-effacement." It was, rather, an act of will in the spirit of Jesuit self-discipline. "In Pope Francis humility is an intellectual stance and a religious decision. It is a virtue which his will must seek to impose on a personality which has its share of pride and a propensity to dogmatic and domineering behaviour." Slowly, the man who had remained silent during the dictatorship began to "speak out," as Burns writes, "and act in defence of the common good . . . Bergoglio's political as well as spiritual manifesto became that of the Beatitudes, with the poor in spirit, the merciful, those who thirst after justice, the pure in conscience and the peacemakers deserving of blessing or conversion." On Argentina's national day in 1998, Bergoglio preached in the presence of Carlos Menem and his government. "A few are sitting at the table and enriching themselves, the social fabric is being destroyed, the social divide is increasing, and everyone is suffering," he said. "As a result our society is on the road to confrontation." Two months later, he said in another sermon: "The church can't just sit sucking its finger when faced with a frivolous, cold and calculating market economy."

Bergoglio's real confrontation with the Argentinian government began with the election of Néstor Kirchner, in office between 2003 and 2007, and continued after the election of Kirchner's wife, Cristina Fernández, who held power between 2007 and 2015. "The people are not taken in by dishonest and mediocre strategies," Bergoglio said in his first sermon in the presence of the Kirchners. "They have hopes, but they won't be deceived by magical solutions emanating from obscure deals and vested political interests." Soon the Kirchners gave up attending his sermons. Néstor called him "the spiritual leader of the opposition." Quarracino used to take his guitar to the presidential residence and, Burns writes, would "stay up late drinking and socializing with the hedonistic Menem and his entourage." But Bergoglio refused even to visit Néstor Kirchner in Casa Rosada, the seat of government, to pay his respects after the president's election.

Bergoglio was praised for speaking truth to power on behalf of the poor. "Here was the church assuming its proper role as the moral conscience of the community, which had delegated (and could withdraw) its consent to the government to rule on the community's behalf," Ivereigh writes. "It was not to the institution of the church that Bergoglio was demanding that the state defer, but to the ordinary people in a culture imbued with the Gospel, of whose values the church was guardian and protector." This is all very well, but it raises a question about Bergoglio's trajectory. One way of reading his rise to power is to attend to his two-year-long exile in Córdoba between 1990 and 1992. As a Jesuit, Bergoglio would have been skilled in the art of introspection. He could see the ways he had failed. As a novice master and a provincial, he had not been a uniting force. He was austere, a disciplinarian, humorless. And he had neglected to confront a vicious dictatorship. It's possible that during those two years of banishment he decided to change. What he did once he became cardinal archbishop of Buenos Aires was the result of that change. And it happened to lead him to the papacy.

Another scenario is that from the very beginning, from his ordination onwards, Bergoglio sought power, that he was guilty of the very "careerism and the search for promotion" that he would deplore. Recently, he disclosed that while banished to Córdoba he read "all 37 volumes of Ludwig Pastor's *History of the Popes*." But there is perhaps a third and more banal way to see Bergoglio. In this, he is simply a great conformist. His rise, in this version, is not deliberate or calculated. It happened because it was noted that he would not disrupt or act courageously and would not move against the mainstream. He was a quintessential company man.

As he opposed the move to make gay marriage legal in Argentina, Bergoglio let it be known that he himself supported some form of civil union. Nonetheless, he wrote a letter to the four Carmelite monasteries in Buenos Aires in which he spoke of gay marriage as "something that the Devil himself was envious of, because it brings sin into the world by trying to destroy the image of God: men and women with their God-given mandate to grow, multiply and exercise their dominion over the earth." The new law was "a frontal attack on God's law . . . a bid by the father of lies seeking to confuse and deceive the children of God."

He asked the nuns to pray to the Holy Spirit "to protect us from the spell of so much sophistry of those who favor this law, which has confused and deceived even those of goodwill." This was, he wrote, "God's war."

The letter was leaked, and Kirchner responded by saying that it was time for Argentina "definitively to leave behind these obscurantist and discriminatory views." The Mothers of the Plaza de Mayo, a human rights organization, declared that the church's complicity with the dictatorship meant it "lacked the moral authority" to preach on this issue. Even after the Dirty War, Bergoglio had kept his distance from the Mothers and Grandmothers of the Plaza de Mayo. The argument over what should be done about the disappearances—Menem had issued pardons in 1989 and 1990 that were revoked in 2003—continued to rage right through the Kirchners' time in power. Ivereigh weighs in on the subject: "The efforts of the vast, state-funded human rights industry have led to little new information about disappearances . . . while in many ways making it harder for Argentines to come to terms with the 1970s."

This view was not shared by the Kirchners. "At no point," Burns writes, did Cristina Kirchner defend Bergoglio while he was archbishop and cardinal "from those who alleged he had been complicit with the military during the Dirty War." In 2010 he was formally cross-examined: in Burns's words, he "asked for and was granted a special dispensation under Argentine law as a high-ranking official who was not charged of any crime." He was allowed to give evidence in the archbishopric, behind closed doors, without having to appear in court. His evidence, almost three and a half hours of it, can be seen on YouTube.

The video of the hearing is possibly the best view we have of Bergoglio. Most of the time, as he is questioned about the case of Jalics and Yorio, the two abducted Jesuits, he is in full command. His answers are brisk, to the point, without seeming hostile or obviously evasive. His comportment is a far cry from the smiling figure that will emerge in St. Peter's Square little more than two years later. Under pressure, he is steely, distant and formidable, if somewhat impatient, even at moments arrogant. When he is irritated by a question, he has a hard, cold, withering stare. It's easy to see why he would have been selected for early promotion by the Jesuits and then by the cardinal archbishop of Buenos Aires and then by the papal conclave. He exudes authority while keeping a great deal in reserve. Despite his eminent humility, he looks like a prince of the church.

But there are a few moments when he appears less than confident. He said that he first heard about the secret adoption of children born to women in captivity only two decades after the events. When questioned, he quickly revises his statement, saying that he learned about the adoptions at the time of the 1985 trial. But he insisted that he didn't know about it when it was happening.

Estela de la Cuadra, whose pregnant sister, Elena, was kidnapped by the military, said it was inconceivable that Bergoglio didn't know about the stolen babies. Her father had secured a meeting with

Bergoglio at the time. When Bergoglio was asked about that meeting he said: "I don't recall him telling me if his daughter was pregnant." Many of his friends and associates remember how well informed he was in the 1970s. One close friend, the human rights lawyer and judge Alicia Oliveira, stated: "He always seemed to know more than me when we met to exchange information." The Lutheran theologian Lisandro Orlov, who defended Bergoglio's record during the Dirty War, doesn't accept the idea that he knew nothing about the secret adoptions: "None of us who were around in those years can say we didn't know what was going on. He can't sustain the argument that he didn't know about the missing children."

Bergoglio continued his campaign against the Argentine government. He remained, Burns writes, "an ever-present thorn in the side of the Kirchner regime, questioning the legitimacy of its mandate to govern." But he also remained skilled in the use of silence. When a priest called Julio Grassi was found guilty in 2009 of sexually abusing a prepubescent boy, Bergoglio, according to *The Washington Post*, declined to meet the victim. He didn't offer apologies or financial restitution. "He has been totally silent," Ernesto Moreau, a member of Argentina's Permanent Assembly for Human Rights, said. "In that regard, Bergoglio was no different from most of the other bishops in Argentina, or the Vatican itself."

Bergoglio was seventy-six when Pope Benedict retired in 2013. "No runner-up at a conclave," Ivereigh writes, "had ever been elected a pope in the following one." Since Ratzinger's resignation was due to age, it was believed that the conclave would, in any case, elect a much younger pope. On the face of it, it was unlikely that Bergoglio would be elected this time, but as Ivereigh also writes, "Bergoglio was a once-in-a-generation combination of two qualities seldom found together: he had the political genius of a charismatic leader and the prophetic holiness of a desert saint." He had other important qualities too: he was not a theologian, and so might be easy to undermine; he was not homosexual, and so might not have a sense of the amount of secrecy surrounding sex in the Vatican; in fact, he had no intimate knowledge at all of the workings of the Vatican and so might be easy to confuse. Also in his favor: he had been detached from the Jesuits for more than twenty years and would not be controlled by them; he had extensive pastoral experience; he had rearranged and managed the finances of his diocese with skill and prudence; he had openly opposed the government of Argentina on social and economic questions; he had made friends with leaders of other faiths; he had created an aura around himself as a man of humility. And there must have been a few old die-hard cardinals who were not unimpressed at the way he had conducted himself during the Dirty War.

Being elected pope cheered Bergoglio up immensely. He knew that no one wanted a dour old pope. Just as he had adapted to the mood of the moment by becoming humble in 1992 on his return to Buenos Aires as archbishop, now he began to smile and look lively. Immediately after the election, he traveled with the other cardinals by bus rather than in a limousine. He went himself to collect his suitcase from the hotel where he had been staying and to pay the bill. In his first papal sermon, as Ivereigh puts it, he quoted strong stuff from "the radical French convert Léon Bloy, whom he had read with his friends in the Iron Guard in the 1970s: 'Anyone who does not pray to the Lord prays to the Devil.'"

The new pope was shown his palatial quarters by Georg Gänswein. "As Gänswein fumbled with the light-switch," Ivereigh writes, "Francis found himself peering into a gilded cage." He "decided at that moment to remain living in the Santa Marta"—the accommodation where the cardinals had lodged during the conclave. On the same day he personally canceled a dental appointment in Buenos Aires and his newspaper delivery. All this became news, and, combined with his smile and the informality of his "buona sera" when he first appeared on the balcony of St. Peter's, it made Bergoglio a poster boy for informality, humility and good-natured cheerfulness.

One of the subjects that continued to intrigue the Catholic hierarchy was whether members of the faithful who divorce and remarry can receive communion. Bergoglio set up a synod at which this would be discussed. The argument is between a theory and common practice. The theory says that marriage is indissoluble and that those who enter a second relationship are sinful and therefore can't receive communion. The practice is that Catholics all over the world get divorced and remarry and many don't feel sinful. But some of them still look to Rome and want the rule relaxed. This is a divide made in heaven, especially for elderly cardinals who like factions. It can and will go on forever.

Before Bergoglio arrived in Rome, the terms of the debate were set by two Germans, Cardinal Kasper and Ratzinger himself. Kasper insisted that he wasn't asking the church to change its position on the sanctity of marriage, but to change pastoral practice on who should receive communion. "To say we will not admit divorced and remarried people to Holy Communion? That's not a dogma. That's an application of a dogma in a concrete pastoral practice. This can be changed." The other side took the view, Vallely writes, that "this was exactly the wrong time for the debate on communion for the remarried . . . because it would weaken the church's defence of the sanctity of marriage at a time when it was under attack from campaigners for gay marriage."

For many, there was an obvious and simple solution. Anyone at all can walk into a church and, at the appointed time, march up and receive communion. And if the priest in one church recognizes the putative communicant as divorced and remarried and refuses communion, then this recalcitrant person can move his or her business to another church in another part of town. Bergoglio, in his new lightness of spirit, often phoned people out of the blue. One day in 2014 he got a letter from a woman in Argentina who had been refused communion by her parish priest because she had married a divorced man. Bergoglio called her and suggested that she find another priest who would give her the Eucharist. "That had caused a furore," Vallely writes, "with conservatives saying that the pope was undermining church teaching on marriage and also that he should have consulted the woman's priest and bishop before calling her."

Bergoglio could play the anarchist one moment and the next revert to his role as authoritarian. Reforming the governance of the Vatican interested him, as did reining in or retiring the more vocal and inflexible and right-wing cardinals, as did replacing an emphasis on sex with an emphasis on economic justice, as did protesting against the treatment of immigrants, but, Vallely writes, Bergoglio "did not appear to put the same effort or urgency behind the Pontifical Commission for the Protection of Minors that he showed on the Vatican finances. The issue of how to hold bishops to account for their failures in reporting seemed difficult for him to push through a wilfully obstructive curial bureaucracy."

In 2015 Bergoglio showed his inflexible side when he promoted Juan Barros, a Chilean bishop who was accused of covering up a sex abuse scandal and being present while abuse occurred. Barros was to be promoted from the armed forces to the small southern diocese of Osorno. Four lay members of the Commission for the Protection of Minors made their alarm public, one of them, an abuse survivor, saying: "The pope cannot say one thing and then do another." Half of the Chilean parliament, thirty priests and more than a thousand lay people wrote to Bergoglio to condemn the appointment. The cardinal archbishop of Santiago warned Bergoglio against it. At the installation mass, only twelve of the fifty Chilean bishops were in attendance. The ceremony had to be cut short because heckling protesters knocked Barros's miter. "The decision to proceed with the nomination bewildered the Chilean church," Ivereigh writes, "and seemed to contradict two priorities of Francis's pontificate: to give voice to the victims, and to respect the wishes of the local church." Some were unable to believe that Bergoglio was behind the decision but, Ivereigh says, he "was wholly informed . . . The Barros nomination was a reminder that, for all his winning ways, Francis is not a politician weighing a decision in terms of its impact to his standing."

Bergoglio's winning ways were on display again during his visit to Chile in 2018, when he said that the allegations against Barros were "all a calumny" and "The day they bring me proof against Bishop Barros, I'll speak." One of the victims, who alleged he was abused by a priest called Fernando Karadima in the presence of Barros, responded: "As if I could have taken a selfie or picture while Karadima abused me or others and Juan Barros stood there watching it all."

It didn't help that Barros, as a military priest, had presided at Pinochet's funeral in 2006. Nor did it help when it was discovered that Bergoglio, in speaking of the Chilean opposition to Barros, had used the word "zurdos," a term used by Pinochet's regime to describe the left. Nor did it help when emails from two Chilean cardinals were released calling one of the victims "a liar" and "a serpent." In Chile, Bergoglio deplored clerical sex abuse and pledged to support victims, agreeing to a private meeting with some of them. But at the huge papal mass in Santiago he was seen greeting Barros affectionately. The local cardinal noted that Barros's presence was "an undesirable and parallel focus to the Holy Father's visit."

Bergoglio finally realized he was wrong after receiving a devastating report on clerical abuse from his envoy to Chile. His apology was, Ivereigh writes in his second book on Bergoglio, *Wounded Shepherd: Pope Francis and His Struggle to Convert the Catholic Church* (2019), "unprecedented in the depth of its personal contrition." In June 2018, when Ivereigh interviewed him, Bergoglio described the last day of his visit to Chile—the day when he had used the word "calumny"—as "the lowest moment" of his pontificate.

Bergoglio's first foreign trip as pope was to Brazil in July 2013. On the journey back to Rome, in a press conference on the plane, Bergoglio, in what might have been seen as his free spirit mode, responded to a question about homosexuality by saying: "If someone is gay and he searches for the Lord and has goodwill, who am I to judge?" He spoke in Italian, but used the English word "gay."

This might have seemed like a big moment of change for the church, but it's important to look at the context. Towards the end of the press conference, for which neither the pope nor his handlers were given the questions in advance, a Brazilian journalist asked about a priest called Battista Ricca. Ricca was director of the Casa Santa Marta, where Bergoglio was lodging as pope, and served as his clerical representative at the Vatican Bank. An article in *L'Espresso*, written by a veteran Vatican reporter, had claimed that when Ricca was abroad as a diplomat he had been accompanied by his lover, a Swiss army captain. Also, in Montevideo, as Burns writes, Ricca had "been found trapped in the elevator of the nunciature with a gay rent boy known to the police."

"I would like permission to ask a delicate question," the reporter said. "Another image that has been going around the world is that of Monsignor Ricca and the news about his private life. I would like to know, Your Holiness, what you intend to do about this? How are you confronting this issue and how does Your Holiness intend to confront the whole question of the gay lobby?" Bergoglio began by defending his friend: "About Monsignor Ricca: I did what canon law calls for, that is a preliminary investigation. And from this investigation, there was nothing of what had been alleged. We did not find anything of that. This is the response." He then spoke about the need to forgive sin before addressing the final question:

> So much is written about the gay lobby. I still haven't found any-one with an identity card in the Vatican with "gay" on it. They say there are some there. I believe that when you are dealing with such a person, you must distinguish between the fact of a person being gay and the fact of someone forming a lobby, because not all lobbies are good. This one is not good. If someone is gay and he searches for the Lord and has goodwill, who am I to judge?

These remarks are not a new way of formulating church teach-ing so much as Bergoglio's way of trying to please as many people as possible, including the journalists on the plane, his friend Ricca and gay people generally. This could be seen as an aspect of his newfound geniality once he arrived in Rome, but there's another way of looking at it. Bergoglio is a Peronist, and the whole point of Peronism is that it can't be pinned down. The Montoneros, who ran the terrorism campaign in Argentina in the 1970s, were Pero-nists, as were the Iron Guard, the right-wing group with whom Bergoglio was associated. Carlos Menem was a Peronist, as were the Kirchners. Being a Peronist means nothing and everything. It means that you can at times be in agreement with the very things that in other circumstances you don't really favor. You can be both reformer and conservative.

In *The Dictator Pope*, Marcantonio Colonna, who is hostile to Bergoglio, claims that his efforts to please are "classic Peronism . . .

the church has been taken by surprise by Francis because it has not had the key to him: he is Juan Perón in ecclesiastical translation. Those who seek to interpret him otherwise are missing the only relevant criterion." There is another explanation for Bergoglio's remarks. He was defending Ricca because Ricca was known to be close to him. It was possible that the attack on Ricca was a veiled way of attacking him. In that case, what emerged on the plane from Rio was Bergoglio not as soft-hearted old pontiff, but as old-fashioned Peronist street fighter.

Anyone who has spent time in the Vatican will smile wearily at Bergoglio's statement about gay people within its walls: "They say there are some there." Two years ago, Frédéric Martel, a French journalist, published *In the Closet of the Vatican: Power, Homosexuality, Hypocrisy*. (In French, and indeed Polish, the book's title is *Sodoma*.) The many people Martel interviewed for the book in thirty countries included forty-one cardinals, fifty-two bishops and monsignori, and forty-five apostolic nuncios. Christopher Lamb, *The Tablet*'s Rome correspondent, called it "a huge operation, funded by a consortium of publishers, and aimed at revealing church hypocrisy on gay issues . . . The publishers decided to release the book on February 21, 2019, the day of the Vatican summit on clerical sex abuse, thus seeking to capitalize on media attention on the church and sex." Ivereigh called the book "gossipy, rambling, cavalier with sources, and because of Martel's off-the-scale 'gaydar' and his scorn for celibacy, easy for Vatican officials to dismiss. Yet many of his eye-popping stories could not be disputed." Martel, Ivereigh concludes, "showed what

many knew, that 'lace by day, leather by night' was part of clerical culture . . . The hypocrisy had mushroomed above all under
John Paul II, whom conservative Catholics lionized for his moral
clarity." Among the book's early admirers was Steve Bannon, who
wanted to acquire movie rights.

The book sets out to establish that almost everyone who lives in
the Vatican is gay. Martel interviews the rent boys of Rome about
their experience with priests, bishops and cardinals. He also interviews many princes of the church, and when possible and appro-
priate he describes their bathrooms and the high tone of the décor
in their apartments. Some are celibate; some line up handsome
seminarians for their pleasure; some live with their so-called sec-
retaries or chauffeurs or valets; others pester the Swiss Guard. The
Vatican, in Martel's version of things, is a hotbed of sexual joy and
intrigue. "The Vatican has one of the biggest gay communities in
the world, and I doubt whether, even in San Francisco's Castro . . .
there are quite as many gays!"

His book, which is long, is often infuriating. There are many
exclamation marks. Martel can't stop praising himself and his work
and the number of interviews he has done and journeys he has
undertaken. But he can sober up. He interviews the former priest
Francesco Lepore about Casa Santa Marta, where Lepore spent a
year. "Nicknames were given to the gay cardinals, feminizing them,
and that made the whole table laugh . . . A lot of them led a double
life: priest at the Vatican by day; homosexual in bars and clubs at
night." When Martel asked Lepore to estimate the size of the male
homosexual population of the Vatican, he said he believed it to be

"around 80 percent." Martel creates categories of the closet based on rules. One is: "The more pro-gay a cleric is, the less likely he is to be gay; the more homophobic a cleric is, the more likely he is to be homosexual." He quotes a Mexican journalist:

I would say that 50 percent of priests are gay in Mexico, if you want a minimum figure, and 75 percent if one is being more realistic . . . There is a lot of tolerance within the church, so much so that it is not expressed outside it. And, of course, to protect this secret, clerics must attack gays by appearing very homophobic in public. That's the key. Or the trick.

Martel looks into Argentinian political intrigue too. Pio Laghi, the papal nuncio who played tennis with Massera in the 1970s, and who died in 2009, comes up in declassified CIA documents as pleading the case of the dictators to the American ambassador, saying that they were "good men" who wanted to "correct the abuses" of the dictatorship. "According to my sources," Martel writes, "Pio Laghi's homosexuality . . . might have played a part in his closeness to the dictators . . . by making him vulnerable in the eyes of the military, who knew his predilections."

This idea that there are homosexuals in high positions in the church who are afraid of being exposed gives Martel another of his rules of the Catholic closet: "Behind the majority of cases of sexual abuse there are priests and bishops who have protected the aggressors because of their own homosexuality and out of fear that it might be revealed in the event of a scandal." Martel notes that

Bergoglio is not popular among many factions of Vatican homo-sexuals. He interviews Luigi Gioia, a Benedictine monk in Rome:

> For a homosexual, the church appears to be a stable structure . . . when you need to hide, to feel secure, you need to feel that your context doesn't move. You want the structure in which you have taken refuge to be stable and protective, and afterwards you can navigate freely within it. Yet Francis, by wanting to reform it, made the structure unstable for closeted homosexual priests. That's what explains their violent reaction and their hatred of him. They're scared.

He also talks to Francesco Mangiacapra, a male prostitute in Naples, who in 2017 released a dossier on his clerical clients: "Priests are the ideal clientele. They are loyal and they pay well. If I could, I would only work for priests. I always give them priority . . . There are two kinds of client . . . the ones who feel infallible and very strong in their position. Those clients are arrogant and stingy." The second group "are very uncomfortable in their skin. They're very attached to affection, to caresses; they want to kiss you all the time . . . They're like children." Mangiacapra's dossier included the names of thirty-four priests, with photographs, audio recordings and screenshots, and he sent it all to the archbishop of Naples. "I think it's sad for them," Mangiacapra told Martel. "I'm not judging anybody. But what I'm doing is better than what priests do, isn't it? It's morally better, isn't it?"

Martel has a marvelous time being received by various cardinals. At the door of one, he is met by a young man, "the quintessence of Asian beauty"; in the drawing room, he notes all the portraits of the cardinal himself. He understands why the cardinal holds himself in such esteem. "After all, he fought like the very devil to impede the battle against AIDS on five continents, with a certain degree of success, and not everybody can say that." The cardinal is foolish enough to give Martel a tour of his apartment, "his private chapel, his interminable corridor, his ten or so rooms, and even a panoramic terrace with a wonderful view over Catholic Rome. His apartment is at least ten times as big as Pope Francis's." Many photographs of the cardinal are on display: in one he is "on the back of an elephant with a handsome young man"; in another "he is posing insouciantly with a Thai companion."

The sexuality of many senior clergy leaves them open to blackmail. Martel alleges that during the debate about civil unions for gay people in Italy, one cardinal, now dead, with his "legendary homophobia," was vociferously against the change. "He was told, at a tense meeting, that rumors were circulating about his double life and his gay entourage, and that if he mobilized against civil unions, it was likely that gay activists would spread their information this time." Another cardinal known "for the cleverness of his gossip, the gaiety of his heart and his love of lace" similarly calmed down under pressure.

The revelations in Martel's book aren't new to anyone who spends time in the Vatican. They are part of the life there, the air of intrigue that makes clergy who have to go back to their own countries long for Rome. Knowing the codes, reading the signs and being in on the gossip are deeply nourishing for men who are otherwise isolated. Taking Martel's revelations for granted, sighing wearily at the sheer dullness of his breathlessness, or pointing out some errors of fact in the book, are evidence that you are an insider.

The fact that Bergoglio had spent so little time in Rome before he became pope had its advantages. He didn't climb the Vatican ladder while picking up lurid information about the private lives of cardinals. He didn't become part of a whispering circle or feed on innuendo. But his distance from all this also meant that he seemed to believe, at the beginning of his papacy, that there could actually be robust and sincere debate among cardinals and bishops about the private sexual lives of others, including divorced people and homosexuals.

All that winking, nodding, subterfuge and underhand knowledge, all those interlocking networks and double lives, are hardly in line with the transparency and clarity of purpose required by the Heavenly Father, who is invoked regularly by even the most reprobate prelates. Bergoglio's power comes from the fact that he doesn't belong to this world. In April 2019, when a gay man told him that he didn't feel accepted by the church, the pope replied: "Giving more importance to the adjective than the noun—this is not good. We are all human beings and have dignity. There are people that prefer to select or discard people because of an adjective; these people do not have a human heart." Some of these people are members of the Curia. Having read Martel's book, Ivereigh concludes: "Suddenly it was easier to understand Francis's Christmas speeches to the Curia, his tongue-lashing of 'the hypocrites' who 'hide the truth from God, from others, and from themselves,' and his warnings against 'the rigid' who 'present themselves to you as perfect' but who 'lack the spirit of God.'"

It isn't as though Bergoglio, always hard to pin down on any matter, has become a poster pope for gay liberation. Many of his appointments to cardinal—Blase Cupich in Chicago, Joseph Tobin in Newark and Kevin Farrell in Rome—show an urge to get away from the emphasis on abortion, gay rights and divorce, but in a country where signals matter more, such as Ethiopia, he appointed Berhaneyesus Demerew Souraphiel as cardinal, a man who has referred to homosexual behavior as "the pinnacle of immorality" and who, in 2008, endorsed outlawing homosexual activity as part of Ethiopia's constitution.

At eighty-four, as apparent in his latest book, *Let Us Dream: The Path to a Better Future*, written during the pandemic, Bergoglio has come to sound like a gentle soul. In his final years as pope, Ratzinger was the same. It must make Bergoglio smile that there is a group, centered on the influential Princess Gloria von Thurn und Taxis, which, Ivereigh writes, "has busily promoted the emeritus pope"—Ratzinger—"as a pastoral and theological alternative to the Francis papacy." In 2016 Georg Gänswein, still close to Ratzinger, "advanced his 'two popes' theory that the papacy now consisted of 'an expanded ministry, with an active member and a contemplative member,'" Ivereigh writes. When Bergoglio, on a flight back from Armenia, was asked directly, "Are there two popes?" the old steely

Jesuit in him reemerged. He had no trouble putting paid to Gäns-wein, and gently also to Ratzinger himself. This was the tone that Buenos Aires had been familiar with, but it was sweeter now that Bergoglio was in power:

> Benedict is in the monastery praying . . . I've heard, but I don't know if it's true . . . that some have gone there [to him] to complain because of this new pope . . . and he chased them away with the best Bavarian style. This great man of prayer is . . . not the second pope . . . for me, he is the wise grandfather at home.

The Ferns Report

London Review of Books · 2005

Everybody was afraid of Dr. Sherwood. My mother was afraid of him at meetings of Pax Romana, the lay Catholic discussion group in Enniscorthy, because he had a way of glaring at women members when they spoke. He didn't, it seemed, like women speaking. At St. Peter's College he was dean of the seminary, but he had once been dean of discipline of the boarding school, and had a fearsome reputation as a merciless wielder of the strap. I studied him carefully when I first saw him; he was gaunt and unsmiling. Soon, even though he had no business on the lay side, I saw him at work. Four or five of us were hanging around the squash courts after lights-out. When he saw us, he stood quietly at first and watched us; then he picked on the most innocent and vulnerable boy. He called him over and began to interrogate him while pinching one cheek hard and then the other cheek and then pulling his ears with enormous slow ferocity and then moving to his slow-growing sideburns until he had almost lifted our poor friend off the ground. Dr. Sherwood was evil. I made up a song about him with a vile chorus.

Soon he was replaced as dean of the seminary, although he still hovered darkly in corridors. The new dean, Dr. Ledwith, was young and friendly and open and very good-looking. He was also reputed to be really smart. One of my friends knew him from home so he often stopped to talk to us. He was a new breed of priest; he had studied in Europe and America. Many of the teaching priests spent their summers in parishes in America, so they were full of new ideas. Everything was open for discussion, or almost everything. I went to a brilliant lecture by Dr. Ledwith on ideas of paradox within Catholic doctrine. It was whispered that he would one day be a great prince of the church.

I got to know some of the other priests and realized that for some of the three hundred boarders, being friends with a priest meant that you could go up to his rooms and hang out, make phone calls, listen to music, watch TV. I became friends with a few of the priests, but in my last year became especially friendly with a physics teacher, Fr. Collins, because my best mate was one of his brightest students.

All of the teaching priests, except Fr. Collins, had rooms off a corridor in a modern extension. Fr. Collins's rooms were in an older building. It was easy to go up and down to his rooms without being noticed, as the two other priests in his part of the building were often away. His stereo system was amazing. I listened to *Tommy* there and *Jesus Christ Superstar*. He always had a box of sweets. I could ring home on his telephone. On Saturday nights after lights-out, with his full connivance, we could break all the rules and sneak up to his room and watch *The Late Late Show*, a controversial chat show on Irish television. We were often there until after midnight.

After *The Late Late Show*, we would switch over to a British channel to watch a program about new films. One night, without any warning, it showed the naked fight scene between Alan Bates and Oliver Reed in *Women in Love*. I was pretty interested in the clip, but I knew to keep quiet afterwards. Modesty was a primary virtue at the school: there were doors on each shower and we all slept in cubicles. In the debating society everything was open to discussion except homosexuality, which no one would have even thought of mentioning.

I knew that Fr. Collins took a very dim view of homosexuality because he had deeply disapproved when I told a joke about Oscar Wilde at the debating society. And when a friend, who looked slightly effeminate in any case, began to part his hair in the middle, he was told by Fr. Collins that it was better to part it at the side; a middle parting, he said, was a sign of homosexuality. Nonetheless, there were often vague whisperings about Fr. Collins. I knew that he liked my friend, but I never allowed myself to think too much about the implications of that. Nothing ever happened.

The dormitory was overseen by a seminarian whom I liked and respected. He was fair-minded and decent. Through him, I got to know another seminarian called James Doyle. He would stop and talk if we met in the corridor, even though fraternization between seminarians and lay students was frowned on. He had many opinions and enjoyed gossip and had a habit of winding me up so I could never quite tell whether he was serious or not. I liked him.

In the second half of the 1990s these three men—Michael Ledwith, Donal Collins and James Doyle—became part of the pantheon of Irish priests whose names were often mentioned on the news. In 1990 James Doyle pleaded guilty to indecent assault and common assault on a young man and was given a three-month suspended sentence. Four years later, Dr. Ledwith resigned suddenly as president of Maynooth College, Ireland's main seminary. He had been secretary to three synods of world bishops in Rome and had served three full terms on the International Theological Commission, the group of thirty theologians who advise the pope. He had made a private settlement with a young man after allegations of inappropriate sexual behavior. He is no longer involved with the Catholic Church. In 1998 Fr. Collins was sentenced to four years' imprisonment, after pleading guilty to four charges of indecent assault and one charge of gross indecency at St. Peter's College between 1972 and 1984.

These men and others like them became public enemies; they were often filmed leaving courthouses with anoraks over their heads (although it should be emphasized that Dr. Ledwith never faced any charges in court). Part of the reason Doyle was given a suspended sentence was that he promised to leave the Republic of Ireland. He went to England. The country wanted rid of these priests.

Everyone in the country had strong opinions about these men. And so did I. Mine had their roots, I suppose, in the fact that I had known these people and liked them and in the fact that I was gay. The word being used to describe them was "pedophile," which struck me as wrong. They were simply gay; they had believed that their homosexuality, in all its teenage confusion, was a vocation to the priesthood. Whereas other boys, as religious as they were, could not become priests because they were attracted to women, these men had no such problem. No one ever asked them if they were homosexual. Thus they moved blindly and blissfully towards ordination and, eventually, towards causing immense damage to vulnerable young people.

It was easy to ask the question: if heterosexuality were not only forbidden but unmentionable, if blokes married other blokes, and you, as a good closeted heterosexual man, were put in charge of a boarding school of three hundred girls aged between thirteen and eighteen, would you not at one point over a long career make sexual demands on one of the girls? Or hit on one young woman in a seminary of young women aged between eighteen and twenty-five? It was a great argument and I enjoyed making it. I was sure I was right. I am not so sure now.

This is because of the publication of the Ferns Report, written by a tribunal chaired by the former Irish Supreme Court judge Francis Murphy. Ferns is a diocese made up of County Wexford and parts of some of the bordering counties. The tribunal was set up by the Irish government because there seemed to be more clerical offenders in this diocese than in any other, and in reaction to a BBC documentary about abuse there.

The report explains why Fr. Collins's rooms were not close to those of the other teaching priests. In 1966 he had visited the dormitory known as the Attic, which became my dormitory four years later, and, according to the Ferns Report, had performed "examinations of an intimate nature involving the measurement of the length of the boys' penises on the pretext of ascertaining whether or not they were growing normally. The inquiry was told that approximately twenty boys were involved. Fr. Collins has disputed the detail of this account of the alleged abuse."

Dr. Sherwood and another priest, according to the report, soon afterwards approached the bishop's secretary with this news. The bishop sent Collins "to a pastoral ministry" in Kentish Town in north London for two years. The bishop did not inform the diocese of Westminster why the priest was being sent there. The bishop was called Donal Herlihy. I knew him a bit. He had spent many years in Rome and was rather disappointed to be returned to an Irish backwater. It was said of him that he would have made a very great bishop if only he had believed in God. His sermons in the cathedral in Enniscorthy were lofty in tone and content. He loved Catullus and Ovid and Horace and he could not refrain from quoting them to a bewildered congregation. I once sat through a long sermon on the small matter of the "lacrimae rerum." While Bishop Herlihy was very worldly in an Italian way about many issues, his worldliness did not, I think, stretch to a priest under his control wishing to measure the length of twenty boys' penises. He simply would have had no idea what to do.

According to the Ferns Report, the bishop "believed that the problem had been solved" by sending Fr. Collins to England for two years and that it "would be unfair and vindictive to pursue the matter further." The bishop is reported to have said to his secretary: "Hasn't he done his penance?" In 1968 Herlihy ordered Collins back to teaching. This time, however, the bishop instructed that the erring priest should have his lodgings in the old building, at a distance from the dormitories, so that he would not be so easily tempted when night fell.

What is interesting about all of this is that no one at any point considered calling the police. The Catholic Church in Ireland in those years was above the law; it had its own laws. By the time I arrived at St. Peter's in 1970, Fr. Collins had been fully restored to the swing of college life. He prepared students for the Young Scientist Exhibition in Dublin every January, spending time alone with them, traveling to Dublin with them. He was in charge of the darkroom, and taught me and many others how to develop photographs. In 1972 he directed the school play. In 1974 he was put in charge of swimming lessons. The other physics teacher, also a priest, gave his classes and then disappeared each day. There was no law in the school saying that a teaching priest had to have any involvement with students outside the classroom.

Dr. Sherwood continued to haunt the corridors, making a constant nuisance of himself. He must have noticed all of Fr. Collins's activities. Since the priests had three meals a day together, there must have been a moment when Collins alluded in passing to the swimming lessons or the sessions in the darkroom. Did Sherwood catch the eye of one of the other priests and give him a knowing look? Or did they all pretend it was nothing? According to the Ferns Report, one priest who "lived downstairs from Fr. Collins... from 1970 to 1971 and again from 1985 until 1988 . . . was aware of the traffic on the stairs going to his, Fr. Collins's rooms, even after lights out, but stated there was 'not the slightest suspicion of anything untoward.'" The report also states that it received "direct evidence from past pupils and a lay teacher who were in St. Peter's during that time, to the effect that Fr. Collins's continuing inappropriate behaviour with young boys was well known in the school during that period and it is clear that sexual abuse was occurring during that time."

Also, the report states that "at least six priests" working in the college at the time knew why Fr. Collins had been sent to England in 1966. The bishop's vicar-general said in a statement to police in 1995, "It was generally believed that Fr. Collins had a problem with abusing young boys in 1966 and that Bishop Herlihy had sent him away because of it." I presume that he meant the priests only when he said "it was generally believed," because it was not, in my opinion, generally believed by the students, despite the evidence given to the Ferns Report by past pupils; it lay instead in the realm of innuendo, rumor and nudges. It was not generally believed, in my opinion, by the young boys getting swimming lessons or being taught to develop photographs, with the exception of the very few picked on for abuse, most of whom told nobody what was happening until many years later, or by parents, or by the police.

Fr. Collins began to abuse at St. Peter's again in the early 1970s, according to the report. Once more, he measured penises, but this was only for starters. Over a four-year period one boy was masturbated four to six times a year by Collins. In the 1990s ten boys made allegations against him, including that he forced one of them "to engage in mutual masturbation and oral sex" and that he on one occasion attempted anal sex. All of this occurred between

1972 and 1984. In court in 1995, some of his victims spoke about the detrimental effect the abuse has had on their lives.

Collins knew no fear. In 1988 he took time off from his many extracurricular activities to apply to become principal of the school. By this time Bishop Herlihy had gone to his reward, and there was a new bishop, Brendan Comiskey, an outgoing, friendly man who paid serious attention to the press and to public relations. He appointed Donal Collins as principal, despite being warned against doing so, according to the Ferns Report, by two priests.

The first allegation of sexual abuse since 1966 came in 1989, within seven months of Fr. Collins's appointment as principal. In 1991, as more allegations were made, Collins removed himself to Florida, where he sought help and worked in a parish. Bishop Comiskey did not tell the parish in Florida of his history. Although Collins admitted "the broad truth" of the allegations against him to the bishop in 1993, the bishop told the police in 1995 that the priest was continuing to deny the charges.

The first allegations against James Doyle were made to my old friend Dr. Sherwood in 1972. Sherwood's response was, according to the report, "questioning and dismissive." When the president of the college heard the allegations in the same year, however, he suggested that Doyle should join a religious order and not become a diocesan priest. This president was replaced the following year by a president who allowed Doyle to be ordained. When Bishop Herlihy heard a complaint against Fr. Doyle in 1982 he sent him to a psychologist who wrote that it would "seem desirable that he should have a change of role, away from working with young people."

When a new priest, in whose parish James Doyle was a curate, was appointed in 1985, no one informed him of this report. Five years later, Doyle pleaded guilty to indecent assault and received his suspended sentence.

His case is interesting because it was the first prosecution in the courts of a Ferns priest. It is not hard to imagine how much the people of the diocese could have hated James Doyle. Surely he would have been pelted with turnips, which grow plentifully in the area, as he left the court? Instead, people blamed the local newspapers for printing the story, provoking, the Ferns Report says, "a considerable backlash" against one local paper in the Wexford area "as it was felt that Fr. Doyle had been badly treated by the publicity his case had attracted. As the media had already given enough information to disclose the identity of the complainant, this backlash was also directed towards him and his family." Thus in 1990 it was made clear that complaining about these priests to the civil authorities would take considerable courage. Bishop Comiskey told the Ferns Inquiry, "Prior to 1990, the question of reporting child abuse complaints or allegations to the Garda authorities never arose."

The case of Dr. Ledwith is stranger. In 1994 an allegation was made that he had abused a thirteen-year-old boy in 1981, a matter that Ledwith disputes, claiming that he did not meet the boy until after his fifteenth birthday. In any case, Ledwith settled with the boy and his family, paying a sum of money with no admission of liability and with a confidentiality clause. After the boy had had a meeting with Bishop Comiskey, the Diocese of Ferns paid for "intensive counseling" for him and his family. In 1983 and 1984, when Ledwith was vice-president of Maynooth, there were complaints to bishops about him from the seminarians, relating to his "orientation and propensity" rather than any "specific sexual activity." When a senior dean at the seminary continued to make these complaints to the bishops, he was asked to produce a victim. When he could not, he was removed from the seminary.

When the Ferns Report came out, I was eager to read it because I had known these three men. I had believed that the problem lay in their becoming priests. If they had gone to Holland or San Francisco, I believed, they would now be happily married to their boyfriends. But as I read the report, I began to think that this was hardly the issue. Instead, the level of abuse in Ferns and the church's way of handling it seemed an almost intrinsic part of the church's search for power. It is as though when its real authority waned in Ireland in the 1960s, the sexual abuse of those under its control and the urge to keep that abuse secret and the efforts to keep abusers safe from the civil law became some of its new tools.

In 1988 in Monageer, just outside Enniscorthy, for example, Fr. Grennan sexually molested ten girls, aged around twelve or thirteen, while he heard their confessions. Their teacher sent for a social worker, who interviewed seven of the girls; the parents of the other three refused to allow their daughters to be interviewed. The girls, interviewed separately, "described much the same activity in different ways," the social worker wrote.

At confession Fr. Grennan would grasp the child's hands in his hands and pull them towards his private parts. The zip would be described as half down and there was never any allegation of his putting their hands inside of the unzipped area. He would pull the child close and rub his face and mouth around their jaw while asking them questions about their families, etc. He was also described as putting his hands under their skirts and fondling their legs to mid-thigh level only.

While this was going on, the rest of the children were told to keep their eyes closed; they were told that if they opened them, they would be chastised.

When the bishop was told about this, he decided he did not believe it. He did not speak to the social worker or the principal of the school. He agreed that the priest should leave the parish for a while, but then return for the confirmation of the very girls he had been abusing. So Bishop Comiskey and Fr. Grennan stood proudly on the altar waiting for the ten little liars to come up to be confirmed. Two of the families walked out with their daughters. Grennan continued in his role of manager of the school.

Since the social worker was employed by the local health board, the police had to be alerted. They took statements from the seven girls. Before the statements could be typed or copied and a covering report prepared, the policeman who took the statements "was instructed to hand over the files notwithstanding." One of the senior policemen who saw the files judged, without consulting anyone, that prosecution of Fr. Grennan "would only damage the complainants further" and did not send the statements to the director of public prosecutions. The statements, still not copied, disappeared.

The year after I left St. Peter's, Sean Fortune arrived in the seminary. It was alleged to the Ferns Inquiry that he started almost immediately to abuse. He began by fondling boys and masturbating. On one car journey, for example, he asked a boy about a scar on his face and then began masturbating. When he ejaculated, he smeared his sperm on the boy's face, telling him that it would heal his scar. Within a few years the allegations included oral sex, and then he would rape his victims anally, leaving one sixteen-year-old boy "in a mess on the floor, bleeding heavily." He befriended families so he could meet their sons, picking on students and altar boys. One of his alleged victims killed himself in the late 1980s. Fr. Fortune killed himself, while facing multiple charges, in 1999, twenty-six years after he initiated his career as an abuser.

Because the priest in each parish in the so-called Republic of Ireland is automatically manager of the local primary school—of the 3,200 primary schools in the state, 3,000 are still managed by Catholic priests—this gave many of them golden opportunities to take students out of school for special lessons. Canon Martin Clancy liked them young, one as young as eight, another, Ciara, eleven. When she became pregnant at fourteen, she went to England and had the baby. She told no one who the father was. When she was seventeen, Canon Clancy "threatened to have [the baby] taken from her if Ciara told anybody that he was the father." When he died in 1993, Canon Clancy left Ciara three thousand pounds in his will "to be used for your future musical education."

No one was safe from them. One woman who had had an operation on her lower abdomen was visited by a Ferns priest. "He fondled her" and she "could feel his fingers moving around the vaginal area. She said that she attempted to get up when Fr. Gamma"—he could not be named by the report—"pushed the elbow of his arm into her stomach to restrain any movement." Another priest, whom the report calls Fr. Delta, was visited by a young man about to get married seeking a Letter of Freedom. The priest asked the young man to unbutton his trousers to check that "everything down there was in working order." The priest fondled his private parts for approximately ten minutes. Another young man approached a priest to report that Fr. Fortune had abused him. The priest asked the young man to demonstrate what Fortune had done, which included touching his penis, thus beginning to abuse him all over again.

Some of the abuse seemed to take its bearing from a porn movie. In the mid-1960s at St. Peter's, a priest told a boy that there was a researcher from America investigating the development of boys and that he "would be an ideal candidate in terms of age and height." He was told to report to a room where, eventually, he was "blindfolded, stripped and caned. His penis was measured and he thinks, but cannot be certain, that he was masturbated." He is 99 percent certain that all this was carried out by the original priest.

The church, of course, is sorry. Bishop Comiskey has been removed and replaced by Bishop Eamonn Walsh. Two years ago, at an event in Wexford town, I was introduced to Bishop Walsh by a priest from St. Peter's whom I had liked. The new bishop was very skilled at speaking softly. It is his job to clean up the mess that is the Diocese of Ferns. He knows that the way to begin is to apologize and apologize and apologize. If he does it enough, maybe someone will believe that the years of abuse and cover-up were not an imperative but an accident, an aberration.

Bishop Comiskey is blamed for his inaction in many cases covered by the Ferns Report. He has made little comment. Journalists say he is in hiding, but he is not in hiding. He lives around the corner from me in Dublin and I see him sometimes on the street. It would be easy to think as I watch him shuffle away from me that there goes the power of the Irish Catholic church. But that would be a mistake. Its power is slowly and subtly eroding, but it is still strong. No one is afraid of the priests anymore. They have learned a new language and imposed some new rules, but they still appoint the teachers and run the schools. On November 11, in response to criticism of the church's role in education, the taoiseach, Bertie Ahern, said: "The state would not be able to manage the schools without the religious, and the state owes a debt of gratitude to the religious communities." The religious communities still also own many of the hospitals. Their years of fucking and fondling the more vulnerable members of the congregation have ended; their years of apologizing sincerely and unctuously have begun. We must thank the Creator for small mercies.

PART THREE

Putting Religion in Its Place:
Marilynne Robinson

London Review of Books · 2014

Philip Larkin's "Church Going," when I read it first, came as a relief. For once, someone had said something true, or almost true, about religion and its shadowy aftermath. The poem had a lovely assuredness and finality. The self-deprecating voice—resigned and a bit sad—was having an argument with no one. The tone was mild and tolerant, and although it was filled with uncertainty, there was a convincing veneer of pure certainty about the main matter, which is that churches are leftover things, belonging to the sweet foolishness of the past. The future won't be much better, the poem suggested, but we won't have churches, except to visit, of course, and wonder about.

It seems strange that the poem was completed just a decade after Eliot's "Little Gidding": there are light-years between Larkin's melancholy skepticism, his urge to bring religion down to earth, and Eliot's high-toned, abstract, prayerful urge to coax his images into some large, suggestive, mystical space. And yet there are moments in "Little Gidding" that are as precise and worldly as "Church Going." Even when he meets the ghost, Eliot is concerned to make the case for the encounter as something that actually occurred, or that could occur and belongs to experience, perhaps even common experience. His dead leaves "rattled on like tin / Over the asphalt where no other sound was"; they belong to a known, shared, modern world, making the appearance of the spirit less unconvincing:

> I met one walking, loitering and hurried
> As if blown towards me like the metal leaves
> Before the urban dawn wind unresisting.

Eliot is insisting here that the event happened, just as in "Church Going" Larkin makes clear in his very first line that the "nothing going on" in the church he has come to visit is real; if there were something going on, he probably wouldn't enter. He allows "God" into his first stanza, but only as a figure of speech, and jokingly, or at least ironically: there is "a tense, musty, unignorable silence" in the church, which has been "Brewed God knows how long."

The problem for Larkin in telling so much plain truth is that, once he has written six nine-line stanzas, he has difficulty ending his poem. He could perhaps finish with "It pleases me to stand in silence here," the last line of the sixth stanza, but we already know that it pleases him: he has made that much clear from the beginning. His final stanza will have to say something more, just as Eliot will have to find a way to let his poem soar towards some mysterious and totalizing image in the final section, even after the apparent finality of "History is now and England." The last stanza of "Church Going" enacts what any writer has to deal with who has let loose images of God and prayer. Unless the writer is content with mockery or pure old-fashioned nihilism, such images will threaten to have a dialogue of some sort with mystery and the spirit. Larkin's church, once so modestly described, becomes in the final stanza "A serious house on serious earth," "In whose blent air all our compulsions meet, / Are recognized, and robed as destinies." Meet and are recognized—but by whom, by what? And what does Larkin mean by "compulsions"? Does he mean merely human urges and needs? Or, since the word suggests the irrational, does he mean something more? Does he mean, with the help of the words "blent air" (which has a hint of "blessed air"), something beyond the material, approaching the transcendental? And what does he mean by "destinies"? Also, the word "robed" (with "blent" close by) suggests something medieval. And when he invokes a "someone" who will gravitate to this church, to a place "Which, he once heard, was proper to grow wise in, / If only that so many dead lie round," surely he is suggesting that the wisdom here isn't just a worldly wisdom, but may contain something more.

What is the difference, then, between this "someone" of Larkin's with "A hunger in himself to be more serious" and the voice at the end of "Little Gidding" who states: "We shall not cease from exploration"? Poets have it easier than novelists because they don't have to tell us what the "someone" who saw the ghost or visited the church did next, where they slept that night, what they did for a living, or what they said to their wife. Eliot can say "history" and

Larkin can say "destinies" in much the same way an abstract painter can put a single color on a canvas and let it have its tumultuous effect. We poor novelists, on the other hand, have to deal with perspective, context, point of view and banal issues of narrative line and credibility.

If "Little Gidding" and "Church Going" are religious poems, or poems that don't ignore religious feeling, what are religious novels, or novels that don't ignore religious feeling? What are the different implications for their art in Eliot declaring "I am an Anglo-Catholic in religion" and Marilynne Robinson's "I am a mainline Protestant, a.k.a. a liberal Protestant"? In *When I Was a Child I Read Books*, her most recent collection of essays, Robinson wrote: "Relevance was precisely not an issue for me. I looked to Galilee for meaning and to Spokane for orthodonture, and beyond that the world where I was I found entirely sufficient." Surely in the background, as we consider these matters (ignoring, for the moment, the wisdom of looking to Spokane for anything at all), we hear the voice of Virginia Woolf, who wrote to her sister Vanessa in 1928 on hearing from Eliot of his conversion to Christianity:

> I have had a most shameful and distressing interview with poor
> dear Tom Eliot, who may be called dead to us all from this day
> forward. He has become an Anglo-Catholic, believes in God and
> immortality, and goes to church. I was really shocked. A corpse
> would seem to me more credible than he is. I mean, there's some-
> thing obscene in a living person sitting by the fire and believing
> in God.

God represents a real problem for the novelist. The novel is happier in a secular space where people suffer from mortal ailments and failures, where their ambitions are material, their hopes palpable. Changing bread and wine into body and blood could be done in a novel, but it would be hard, and shouldn't be tried twice. Having miracles from on high interfere with choice, chance, destiny or paragraph endings won't help a novel, or not much. Novels like human voices, human will, human failure. They like journeys from one place to another without encounters with fellows such as Moses or Muhammad, not to speak of the Buddha. They like the sadness or fun of the mind at play more than showing how a character's prayers have been answered. Unless of course the prayers haven't been answered at all, and were merely another example of human foolishness, with interesting consequences for the fool and his or her family.

Nonetheless, because I was born in Ireland and brought up Catholic, I have a serious difficulty when it comes to the creation of characters who live entirely in a secular universe and depend on Spokane rather than Galilee for meaning. Irish Catholicism has many mansions, but one of them includes a good bedrock of paganism, or animism. I've never heard the banshee knock on my door in the night to announce that someone in the family would soon die, but I think I would know the sound if I heard it. I don't have a fairy fort in my garden, but if I did I wouldn't allow it to be removed, and if it were removed I would expect bad luck, and soon. (My neighbors have one, and it won't in our lifetime or any foreseeable lifetime be bulldozed, although it is in the way.)

Also, people around me genuinely believe that, at the saying of some words by a priest, the wafer and the wine literally and actually become the body and blood of a man who was, it seems, crucified in the Middle East two thousand years ago. (While growing up, I often wondered at what point in the digestive process the wafer ceases to be the body, but I knew not to raise this troublesome matter.) They believe in eternal life too. (In an essay Robinson ponders the question of the eternal: "The eternal as an idea is much less preposterous than time, and this very fact should seize our attention.") And they believe in an all-seeing God, who knows us and watches us, one who has read our next novel already or at least knows the general outline. ("Calvin says that God takes an aesthetic pleasure in people," Robinson pointed out in a *Paris Review* interview. So he might enjoy invented characters as much as real ones, or even more, especially on his day of rest.)

Since, unlike God, I know nothing much, and, unlike Calvin, don't know how God feels, and generally haven't really a clue what to believe, I have no problem with any of the above beliefs. They might make more sense, indeed, than believing, for example, that nuclear power is safe, or that the United Kingdom shouldn't be split up, or that putting people in prison is a way to prevent crime. My problem isn't about belief itself, however, it's simply a technical one: how do you create a religious or a nonsecular protagonist in a novel without making a dog's dinner out of the book?

Some people, such as Graham Greene, Flannery O'Connor, Chinua Achebe, Georges Bernanos, Kate O'Brien, Maurice Gee, Brian Moore and Andrew O'Hagan have made a big effort. Others, such as James Joyce, have managed to weave religion into a larger fabric, with all the sheer drama of faith and doubt, and have managed also to include the comic possibilities of dogma and ritual to liven up their books. In *Ulysses*, Leopold Bloom, in musing on the use of wine in the mass, comes to the fine conclusion that wine is more "aristocratic" than, for example, ginger ale. It's hard thereafter, at least for me, to witness the sacred consecration without at least smiling at the thought that there wouldn't be much future in a religion that changed bread and ginger ale into the body and blood of Our Lord Jesus Christ. One of the purposes of literature, as Joyce made clear, is to put religion in its place.

Joyce's finding Catholic ritual amusing and Woolf's contempt for Christians are easy to follow and fathom. Having rejected religious faith, they got on with the business of dealing with human consciousness and language and form in the novel without having to genuflect or take the divine into account. We know where we are with them. Part of the result, however, of reading Marilynne Robinson's formidable, serious and combative essays is that knowing where you are—or thinking you do, and being happy with that—comes to seem a sort of illusion and an example of foolishness. "Everything always bears looking into," she writes, "astonishing as that fact is." Or more vehemently:

> I want to overhear passionate arguments about what we are and what we are doing and what we ought to do. I want to feel that art is an utterance made in good faith by one human being to another. I want to believe there are geniuses scheming to astonish

the rest of us, just for the pleasure of it. I miss civilization, and I want it back.

Some of her essays are marvelous, as passionately engaged with the world and as eloquent as the essays of James Baldwin or some of the great nineteenth-century Americans. Part of the pleasure of reading them is Robinson's readiness to do battle using all her intelligence and ardor in support of what is, for most of us, the mystifying and wearying business of religion. It's hard to think of another contemporary novelist who would feel free to refer in passing to "God's otherness," or "this honorable art of preaching." Or to write: "The mystery of Christ's humanity must make us wonder what of mortal memory he carried beyond the grave." Her daring and inspiring defense of the word "soul" singles her out:

> Having read recently that there are more neurons in the human brain than there are stars in the Milky Way, and having read any number of times that the human brain is the most complex object known to exist in the universe, and that the mind is not identical with the brain but is more mysterious still, it seems to me this astonishing nexus of the self, so uniquely elegant and capable, merits a name that would indicate a difference in kind from the ontological run of things, and for my purposes "soul" would do nicely.

But she can also break into a sugary cliché, as when she writes: "God does, after all, so love the world." Or: "The great narrative, to which we as Christians are called to be faithful, begins at the beginning of all things and ends at the end of all things, and within the arc of it civilizations blossom and flourish, wither and perish."

Unlike others who rattle on about God, she is hard to second-guess. That phrase "God's otherness" comes from a sentence so beautifully shaped that I have no interest in whether it is true or not: "Religiosity is a transgression against God's otherness."

With her wide reading and her well-stocked mind, Robinson is also deeply engaged with matters both philosophical and political. Some of her aphorisms are sheer delight, aphorisms such as: "We are not at ease in the world and sooner or later it kills us." Or: "The more tortuous our locutions, the more blood in our streets."

Sometimes she is as interested in surprising herself as she is the reader. She can open the final paragraph of an essay with: "To borrow a question from Jean Genet, what would happen if someone started laughing? What if the next demographically marketed grievance or the next convenience-packaged dread, or the next urgent panacea for the sweet, old haplessness of the body started a wave of laughter that swept over the continent?" And she also can appear to be enjoying herself in the role of a Lady Bracknell of the American Midwest—she lives in Iowa—as she writes against Christians who would make God into "a tribal deity": "I personally would not be surprised to see the secular enter heaven before [them]." ("I know I presume in speaking in such terms," she adds quickly, presumption being, of course, a sin, and, in my opinion, quite a grave one. But this does not stop her later in the same essay offering, without irony, it seems, a further presumptive opinion about the creators of the

French welfare state: "that the secular have an excellent hope of heaven.") And in a similar high tone, she ends another essay with: "We are losing and destroying what means we have had to do justice to one another, to confer benefit upon one another, to assure one another a worthy condition of life. If Jonathan Edwards were here, he would certainly call that a sin. I am hard pressed to think of a better word."

Well, I am not hard pressed, and Jonathan Edwards died in 1758, but I can think of several words. However, I would not, in general, like to get into an argument with Marilynne Robinson.

One of the ways to include religion in a novel is to write about it directly. Another way is to allude to the matter now and then before letting other, more worldly dramas take over. In the early summer of 1926, Ernest Hemingway converted from his family's Congregationalism to Catholicism, but he believed that his Catholicism had begun in 1918 in Italy, when, after being wounded, he was anointed or baptized, or both, by a priest. In a letter to his father in May 1926, he wrote: "Having been to mass this morning I am now due at the bullfight this afternoon. Wish you were along." By the end of that year, he was taking his religious belief seriously enough to write a "Neo-Thomist Poem," which reads:

> The Lord is my shepherd, I shall not
> want him for long.

The following year he and Pauline Pfeiffer, whose family had a private chapel in their house, were married in a Catholic church.

Archibald MacLeish and his wife, Ada, declined to attend because, as Ada wrote, she "was completely disgusted by Ernest's efforts to persuade the Catholic church that he had been baptized by a priest who walked between aisles of wounded men in an Italian hospital... To see this farce solemnized by the Catholic church was more than we could take."

By the end of 1927, Hemingway was in correspondence with a Dominican priest who had written to say: "We need writers of your type to help further the cause for which the Dominican order exists in defence of the Church—the cause of Truth." Hemingway, in reply, wrote:

I have been a Catholic for many years although I fell away badly and did not go to communion for over 8 years. However, I have gone regularly to mass for the last two years and absolutely set my house in order within the year. However I have always had more faith than intelligence or knowledge and I have never wanted to be known as a Catholic writer because I know the importance of setting an example—and I have never set a good example... Also I am a dumb Catholic and I have so much faith that I hate to examine into it—but I am trying to lead a good life and to write well and truly and it is easier to do the first than the second.

While Hemingway was revising *The Sun Also Rises* and writing *A Farewell to Arms* and many of his best short stories, he was attending mass regularly. In *The Sun Also Rises* the protagonist, Jake Barnes, makes clear on a train through France, when the Catholics have taken all the seats for lunch, that he is a Catholic too. On arrival in Pamplona, he sees the cathedral and goes inside and sets out to pray:

> I knelt and started to pray and prayed for everybody I thought of, Brett and Mike and Bill and Robert Cohn and myself, and all the bullfighters, separately for the ones I liked, and lumping all the rest, then I prayed for myself again, and while I was praying for myself I found I was getting sleepy, so I prayed that the bullfights would be good, and that it would be a fine fiesta, and that we would get some fishing. I wondered if there was anything else I might pray for, and I thought I would like to have some money, so I prayed that I would make a lot of money . . . and as all the time I was kneeling with my forehead on the wood in front of me, and was thinking of myself as praying, I was a little ashamed, and regretted that I was such a rotten Catholic, but realized there was nothing I could do about it, at least for a while, and maybe never, but that anyway it was a grand religion, and I only wished I felt religious and maybe I would the next time.

Later, when Jake is asked if he is "really a Catholic," he replies: "Technically." When asked what that means, he replies: "I don't know."

What it meant, perhaps, was that Jake's creator had enough religion in his blood to make dramatic use of it again in 1933 in his story "A Clean, Well-Lighted Place," set in a late-night bar in Spain, when the older waiter prays:

Our nada who art in nada, nada be thy name thy kingdom nada thy will be nada in nada as it is in nada. Give us this nada our daily nada and nada us our nada as we nada our nadas and nada us not into nada but deliver us from nada; pues nada. Hail nothing full of nothing, nothing is with thee.

Joyce would have been proud of Hemingway and his old man. Perhaps it's a feature of Catholics that we like to make jokes about the most sacred things, that blasphemy and mockery are actually signs of faith, a nervous response to its power. This is something that, as far as I can judge, has not caught on among Calvinists, who tend to be more earnest and respectful.

While Hemingway makes a few stray references to God and to the Catholic faith in the rest of his fiction, he had too much else to worry about to make a big deal of it. His characters were more interested in life than in life everlasting, and more concerned with this world than the next, and Hemingway himself had too many of his own demons to worry too intensely about Satan.

Like Hemingway, Henry James had good reasons not to bother too much about religion. His father had spent a lifetime bothering about it, with no clear result. His father's way of raising his children was in direct response to his own upbringing, of whose strictures he gave a resentful account. On Sundays, he wrote, as children they were taught "not to play, not to dance nor to sing, not to read story-books, not to con over our school-lessons for Monday even; not to whistle, not to ride the pony, nor to take a walk in the country, nor a swim in the river; nor, in short, to do anything which nature specially craved." Henry James's vastly rich grandfather, a stern Irish Presbyterian, had even tried to write a will that would police the moral lives of the next generation and punish any of his children who strayed from the straight and narrow by reducing their share of his estate.

Henry James's correspondence has little about religion. Nonetheless, there is an interesting passage in a letter written from Rome to Charles Norton in 1873, when James was thirty, responding to Norton's view that Christianity had, in effect, run its course:

> As to Christianity in its old application being exhausted, civilisation, good & bad alike, seems to be leaving it pretty well out of account. But the religious passion has always struck me as the strongest of men's hearts, & when one thinks of the scanty fare, judged by our usual standards, on which it has always fed, & of the nevertheless powerful current continually setting towards all religious hypotheses, it is hard not to believe that *some* application of the supernatural idea, should not be an essential part of our life ... I don't know how common the feeling is, but I am conscious of making a great allowance to the questions agitated by religion in feeling that conclusions & decisions about them are tolerably idle.

In November 1906, James, having discovered that the medium Mrs. Piper had given his sister-in-law Alice messages purporting to come from James's mother, who was long dead, became interested in the idea that he might hear more. He wrote:

I seem to gather (in another connection) that Mrs. Piper comes out—*has* perhaps actually come out, to England & wish I could learn, dear Alice,—what people or circle she comes *to* & where she is to be, for ever since that message you sent me in the Spring I've had such a desire for the possibility of something further—even to the degree of an obsession.

Living then in the space between believing that discussion of religion was idle and an obsession with news from the dead, James wrote novels about money and secrecy and treachery, sticking to the human element in all its mystery and drama, concentrating on "felt life," as he put it. However, in *The Portrait of a Lady*, there is talk of a ghost at Gardencourt, and by the end of the novel Isabel "apparently had fulfilled the necessary condition" for seeing it because one morning "in the cold, faint dawn, she knew that a spirit was standing by her bed." However, even in their darkest moments, James has neither Catherine Sloper in *Washington Square* nor Isabel Archer in *The Portrait of a Lady* kneel down and pray, or appeal to the Almighty to get them out of the particular fix they were in. It is also significant that James gives his characters a rich freedom, that if "predestination" were to be a mere literary term to use about an author who allows characters no autonomy, but rather seeks to make them tools in the creation of a plot, or illustrations of a theory, or the elaboration of an idea, then James is not guilty of that offense.

But James, while fascinated by style and form, was really more interested in the drama around control and freedom, right and wrong, good and evil. In some of his best novels, he slowly releases an energy that is filled with the pull between light and dark, between ambiguity and clarity, between innocence and cruelty. He is careful, in novels such as *The Portrait of a Lady* and *The Wings of the Dove*, not to release this energy too soon so that the side that is less than good approaches softly and stealthily before emerging lethally.

It is as though there is a conflict going on within his own imagination between an interest in avoiding the dull subject of morality and a desperate concern that without this subject the novel will appear flimsy, playful, not serious enough, not worthy of our full attention. Or there is, indeed, a battle going on between his father's open and sensuous spirit and his grandfather's grim willingness to judge. James begins by not judging at all, only to ambush himself with judgment, as his best novels come to seem like evidence presented in detail, with subtlety and care but also firmness, culminating in a day of judgment that is the final page of the book. Thus, if there were a hereafter, Osmond and Madame Merle in *The Portrait of a Lady*, and Kate Croy and Merton Densher in *The Wings of the Dove*, and, without doubt, Dr. Sloper in *Washington Square*, would present themselves as suitable candidates for a long spell in purgatory, if not a longer time in some deeper, darker, more baleful place where they could be poked regularly by the Devil.

If we accept Marilynne Robinson's definition of the soul, then Henry James had a profound interest in it. He took, in fact, what Robinson calls "this astonishing nexus of the spirit" as his great subject. In the making of Isabel Archer, say, or of Lambert Strether in *The Ambassadors*, James allowed his interests in material and moral matters to wane, and, without ever losing sight of them, he replaced them with a soaring vision of what the questing human spirit could become under certain pressures and in a certain light, and over time. Although the issue of money is never entirely absent, James makes it dissolve in the waters of a yearning soul. He imagines characters who want something from life itself that cannot easily be named without using terms borrowed from religion; it includes beauty and generosity, but it embraces something further—grace, redemption, salvation—terms that are religious. In a letter to Grace Norton who wondered about his use of his cousin Minny Temple in the creation of Isabel Archer, James managed to set out the loftiness of his own ambition: "Poor Minny was essentially incomplete and I have attempted to make my young woman more rounded, more finished. In truth everyone, in life, is incomplete, and it is the work of art that in reproducing them one feels the desire to fill them out, to justify them, as it were."

In both *The Aspern Papers* and *The Golden Bowl*, James tempts us further to look at his characters for more than their material presence or their material desires. In *The Aspern Papers* this occurs in the last two pages when our protagonist returns to the Venetian palace having rejected Miss Tita's offer of marriage the day before. He notices, on seeing her now, "an extraordinary alteration" in her: "She stood in the middle of the room with a face of mildness bent upon me, and her look of forgiveness, of absolution, made her angelic . . . This optical trick gave her a sort of phantasmagoric brightness . . ."

When he says goodbye to her, and she replies that she won't see him again, and does not want to, she smiled strangely, with an infinite gentleness. She had never doubted that I had left her the day before in horror. How could she, since I had not come back before night to contradict, even as a simple form, such an idea? And now she had the force of soul—Miss Tita with force of soul was a new conception—to smile at me in her humiliation.

"The force of soul." James uses the term twice as though it had a clear meaning. It is hard not to wonder if he meant that this force was available to Miss Tita because she had suffered enough, because she had been despised and rejected, that it was always available and could emerge only after darkness and pain, that it was something lurking beneath the veneer of the self in the material world. It is interesting that he used not only the word "soul" but the words "absolution" and "angelic."

There is a scene in chapter 2 of book 5 of *The Golden Bowl* when Maggie Verver's father and husband, stepmother and best friend are playing a game of bridge and Maggie quietly steps outside and begins to observe them through the window. The imagery at first is from the theater, as she watches them perform, but slowly things shift in her perception until, without anything visibly changing in the room, Maggie experiences "the horror of finding evil seated all at its ease where she had only dreamed of good; the horror of the thing hideously *behind*, behind so much trusted, so much pretended, nobleness, cleverness, tenderness."

Just as it is easy, when Marilynne Robinson wishes to use the word "sin" to describe a culture of selfishness and inequality, for us to find more secular terms—"grave injustice" or "plain wrong" come to mind—so too it should be simple to find another, less religious term for "force of soul" in *The Aspern Papers*—"a fierce dignity that came from within" would be one possibility—as we could find another word here in *The Golden Bowl* to replace "evil"—"treachery," for example. But James used his words with care. If he had wanted to use secular terms in these scenes, he would have done so. Instead, he wanted to invoke something deeper and more urgently mysterious, beyond human explanation, extreme. It is interesting that the lexicon he saw fit to raid was a religious one.

In chapter 4 of book 5 of *The Golden Bowl*, tensions increase as Maggie, her father, her husband and her mother-in-law (and old friend) Charlotte Stant circle one another in her father's country house. There is a moment where Maggie and her father listen as Charlotte gives a guided tour of the treasures of the house to neighbors.

So the high voice quavered, aiming truly at effects far over the heads of gaping neighbours; so the speaker, piling it up, sticking at nothing, as less interested judges might have said, seemed to justify the faith with which she was honoured. Maggie meanwhile at the window knew the strangest thing to be happening: she had turned suddenly to crying, or was at least on the point of it—the lighted square before her all blurred and dim. The high voice went on; its quaver was doubtless for conscious ears only, but there were verily thirty seconds during which it sounded, for our young woman, like the shriek of a soul in pain.

James is desperately in need here. He wishes to render in the gravest possible light what is in outline a comedy of manners verging on a farce. Charlotte Stant must not be seen as merely an adulterer and a liar and the prince her corrupted accomplice; any novelist could do that. Charlotte has to be presented as involved in something beyond badness, slowly inhabiting some distant and poisonous and other moral realm. But what other realm is there? James's Presbyterian grandfather would not have had any trouble with the last twenty-two words as quoted above. He would have felt that, despite all the wanderings and the big dinners, all the grandeur and the intense worldliness, his errant grandson had come home. He would have only wondered at the arrival in the next chapter of a Catholic priest, Fr. Mitchell, the "good holy hungry man" as James describes him, "a trusted and overworked London friend and adviser, who had taken for a week or two the light neighbouring service, local rites flourishing under Maggie's munificence..." Thus we learn that not only is Maggie good and innocent, but she is of course married to an Italian, a Catholic, and thus herself enjoys the rites of the unreformed church, including, we learn, the sacrament of confession. In having Fr. Mitchell at her table Maggie allows an actual religious figure into the secular house of fiction to match James, who has already exalted this dwelling with his use of the religious terms that his novel repels and then strangely, at one of its greatest moments, comes to require.

Marilynne Robinson's first novel, *Housekeeping*, published in 1980, has an undertone of a story from the Old Testament mixed with a novel by William Faulkner. It's a narrative of misfortune and pestilence, an account of survival in a rugged landscape against all the odds, told in a tone that is fearless, poetic, elaborate in its cadences but also, at times, sharp and precise, and at other times comic. It begins with no nonsense and plenty of command: "My name is Ruth. I grew up with my younger sister, Lucille, under the care of my grandmother, Mrs. Sylvia Foster, and when she died, of her sisters-in-law, Misses Lily and Nona Foster, and when they fled, of her daughter, Mrs. Sylvia Fisher." It's clear from "and when they fled," from the number of carers and the formal, distant way they are named that this won't be a story of domestic harmony and bliss.

The next image adds to the sense of dislocation: we are told that before the narrator's grandfather Edmund Foster "put us down in this unlikely place," he grew up "in the Middle West, in a house dug out of the ground, with windows just at earth level and just at eye level, so that from without, the house was a mere mound, no more a human stronghold than a grave." "This unlikely place" is called Fingerbone. Ruth says that it "was never an impressive town. It was chastened by an outsize landscape and extravagant weather, and chastened again by an awareness that the whole of human history had occurred else-where." The extravagant weather brings a flood, which "flattened scores of headstones" and makes the house where Ruth and her sister Lucille live almost uninhabitable. The town isn't helped by the flood either: "Much of what Fingerbone had hoarded up was defaced or destroyed outright, but perhaps because the hoard was not much to begin with, the loss was not overwhelming." The loss, of course, comes as a gain to the narrative, which has tremendous fun describing flood damage: "The afternoon was loud with the giant miseries of the lake, and the sun shone on, and the flood was the almost flawless mirror of a cloudless sky, fat with brimming and very calm." Some of the sentences seem overblown: "Every spirit passing through the world fingers the tangible and mars the mutable, and finally has come to look and not to buy." But the world being described is rooted enough to survive Robinson's high rhetorical flight, and we breathe a sigh of relief when she ends the paragraph that contains the sentence I just quoted with: "But then suddenly the lake and the river broke open and the water slid away from the land, and Fingerbone was left stripped and blackened and warped and awash in mud."

America here is desolation, an unpromising Promised Land waiting for redemption. The language of the novel moves from terse description to sentences that have distinct references to scripture, not just the general tone of the Bible but images and stories from the Old Testament and the New. When two apple trees die, Robinson invokes Lazarus, as well as the parting of the waters: "One spring there were no leaves, but they stood there as if expectantly . . . miming their perished fruitfulness. Every winter the orchard is flooded with snow, and every spring the waters are parted, death is undone, and every Lazarus rises, except these two."

Later, when Ruth is on a boat with her aunt, she witnesses the dawn. Writers should always be careful with the dawn—it's tempting to be overblown—but Robinson manages two reasonable sentences: "To the east the mountains were eclipsed. To the west they stood in balmy light." And then she moves into what we know from her essays as her area of interest: "Dawn and its excesses always reminded me of heaven . . ." She is too intelligent to expect her readers to connect the dawn and heaven, so she ends the sentence with a twist: "a place where I have always known I would not be comfortable."

But she is ready, too, to take risks. There is an extraordinary passage, for example, that describes the grandmother's death: "It was as if, drowning in air, she had leaped toward ether." Ruth then imagines her grandmother as she "burst through the spume" of life, as though she had been rescued from a disaster. "And my grandmother would scan the shores to see how nearly the state of grace resembled the state of Idaho, and to search the growing crowds for familiar faces."

Later, there is a description of the lake using further images from the Old Testament:

> One can imagine that, at the apex of the Flood, when the globe was a ball of water, came the day of divine relenting, when Noah's wife must have opened the shutters upon a morning designed to reflect an enormous good nature ... Looking out at the lake one could believe that the Flood had never ended. If one is lost on the water, any hill is Ararat.

In the first few pages of chapter 10 Robinson turns up further the great hot tap of her biblical prose to muse on God's response to events of the Old Testament. Cain and Abel get a look-in, as do Rachel, King David, Absalom and Eve. This is, in all its fervid rhythm, as good as it gets. The second paragraph begins:

> Cain killed Abel, and the blood cried out from the ground—a story so sad that even God took notice of it. Maybe it was not

the sadness of the story, since worse things have happened every minute since that day, but its novelty that he found striking. In the newness of the world God was a young man, and grew indignant over the slightest things.

Robinson's application of high images from religion and high tones from the Bible to the low world—forlorn, inhospitable and backward America—is startling and fascinating. The power of *Housekeeping* comes from the confidence with which she merges this heightened, numinous world with the ordinary, the detailed, the credible. The problem with casting such a glowing spell on our poor, sad universe, however, is that, as with a novel that changes the bread and wine into the body and blood, it shouldn't be attempted twice. The danger for Robinson, having managed such a successful piece of high-voltage fiction, is the same as the danger for Hemingway once he had created a low-voltage style, or indeed for James in his opaque late style: the danger of self-parody and the seeping presence of the reader's irony, the reader's restlessness. While Robinson gets away by the skin of her teeth with comparing the state of Idaho with the state of grace, she wouldn't were she to find another state of the union and try the comparison a second time. ("Let's go through Georgia fast so we won't have to look at it much," Flannery O'Connor has one of her characters say.)

Robinson didn't publish her second novel, *Gilead*, until twenty-four years after *Housekeeping*. She wrote it, she told *The Paris Review*, in eighteen months. It would be impossible for a future biographer, even if there are diaries and letters, to chart what happened to her sensibility over the years between the two books. Certainly, there is evidence of a tonal softening, a freeing up of the processes of imagining, a peeling away of protection that causes her now to insist less on a high-voltage style and concentrate instead on character. *Gilead* and the novels that have come since—*Home* (2008), *Lila* (2014) and *Jack* (2020) depend more on sympathy and ambiguity. Robinson has learned to cast a gentler gaze on the world, but the gaze is still filled with depth and wonder. The Christian God, apparent in *Housekeeping*, also lives in the body of these novels, but Robinson has come up with the inspired idea of allowing the souls of the novels, so to speak, to be fully human.

One of the best novels about religion in America is Willa Cather's *Death Comes for the Archbishop*, published in 1927. Some of the power of the book arises from the dramatizing of the relationship over forty years between two Catholic priests as they attempt to make a Catholic diocese out of New Mexico. It is easy to see how much duller the book could be were one of the priests left out. Its plot would be predictable, no matter how much conscience the priest could muster, or how many prayers he said, or ghastly setbacks he suffered. In Cather's novel, the drama arises from the differences between Fr. Latour and Fr. Vaillant, as a sort of Catholic Don Quixote and his optimistic, energetic sidekick. Fr. Vaillant, "wherever he went . . . soon made friends that took the place of country and family." But Fr. Latour, "who was at ease in any society and always the flower of courtesy, could not form new ties. It had always been so. He was like that even as a boy: gracious to everyone but known to a very few." These differences, then, make their way into the very texture of the novel, which becomes the story of a friendship as much as the account of the conversion of New Mexico to the rigors and regulations of the One True Faith.

But the drama arises too, as it does in Marilynne Robinson's work, between the world as it is, as we see it, and the fabled shadow cast by the Bible. For both novelists the very landscape of North America, and how it came to be peopled after Columbus, suggest, in ways both direct and surprising, various books from the Old Testament. As Fr. Latour, in Cather's novel, moves between Laguna and Acoma in New Mexico, trying to spread and organize the faith, he sees "great rock mesas" that resemble "vast cathedrals." As he moves into the mesa plain he notices that it "had an appearance of great antiquity, and of incompleteness; as if, with all the material for world-making assembled, the Creator had desisted, gone away and left everything on the point of being brought together . . ."

Later, when he sees a rock whose summit had once been inhabited, he thinks of the Testament both Old and New. "Christ himself had used that comparison for the disciple to whom He gave the keys of his Church. And the Hebrews of the Old Testament, always being carried captive into foreign lands—their rock was an idea of God, the only thing their conquerors could not take from them." Soon, as he goes along, he thinks "that the first Creation morning must have looked like this." It would be hard to write this, I think, in Germany or South Sudan, as you traveled through the landscape, or even in County Cork, not to mention the Home Counties. It seems America lends itself to this sort of writing, indeed this sort of belief. This would come to have significant political implications, but in the small matter of art, it would also be a gift to an American novelist interested in religion.

Gilead, *Home*, *Lila* and *Jack* dramatize the lives of a small number of characters who appear in all of the books, focusing closely on one or two of them in each novel. Although there are references to the wider community in the small Iowa town of Gilead, Robinson hasn't attempted to create a *Middlemarch*, or a panoramic view of the society. Instead, the books concentrate fiercely, and indeed lovingly, on just two households, those of Reverend John Ames and his lifelong friend Reverend Robert Boughton, with flashbacks in *Lila* into the eponymous heroine's life before she came to Gilead and married Ames and had a son with him and an account in *Jack* of the eponymous protagonist's time away from home. *Gilead* takes a strand from *Middlemarch* and turns it around. Ames, like Casaubon, is old, dry, bookish and alone when he marries Lila. The novel, however, is told from his tender point of view, narrated as death approaches to be read by his young son when he grows up. It begins gently:

> I told you last night that I might be gone sometime, and you said, Where, and I said, To be with the Good Lord, and you said, Why, and I said, Because I'm old, and you said, I don't think you're old. And you put your hand in my hand and you said, You aren't very old, as if that settled it.

Ames's tone is both wise and engaged, without the stuffiness we associate with poor old Casaubon. He writes about his father and his grandfather, about strange things he witnessed, and about religion. Religion fills his life; Robinson doesn't have to remind us cumbersomely that he has been a Congregationalist minister; she allows Ames's belief in the scriptures to offer an energy to the rhythm of his thinking. Here he is describing a photograph of his grandfather:

> It shows a wild-haired, one-eyed, scrawny old fellow with a crooked beard, like a paintbrush left to dry with lacquer in it, staring down the camera as if it had accused him of something terrible very suddenly, and he is still thinking how to reply and keeping the question at bay with the sheer ferocity of that stare. Of course there is guilt enough in the best life to account for a look like that.

That last sentence has a melancholy acceptance of the fact that we live the aftermath of the Fall, that we're sinful, but it doesn't make too much of the notion; it doesn't feel like something the author thought of and then gave to Ames because she felt she should. It's intrinsic to the way he sees the world—not as an afterthought or an imposed thought but as an easy thought.

Making religious thought easy is part of the genius of *Gilead*. Ames has been preaching all his life; he is interested in what truth sounds like and in finding further images for it. Robinson has found a meditative tone for him that can allow in anything at all, including casual observations of each day and serious speculation about the afterlife. The tone is helped by a faint urgency mixed with sweetness and regret as Ames realizes he may not have much longer to live. Unlike the narrators, say, of Joan Didion's *A Book of Common Prayer* or J. M. Coetzee's *Age of Iron*, who are also both close to death and whose tone grows heightened and sharp and staccato in the face of extinction, Ames remains calm. But he shares with those narrators a particular eloquence, which the reader is made to feel has been given to him now in the light of his old age, and a more poetic tone than he might have used earlier in his life. But it is the memory of life rather than the thought of death that animates Ames. And his life has been enriched by his friendship and discussions about theology with Robert Boughton, whose family becomes the focus of Robinson's third novel.

In *Home*, Boughton is old too, and widowed, when his daughter, Glory, and eventually his wayward son, Jack, come home. Just as Robinson is prepared to take great risks in placing religious belief at the very center of a character's being—not as something that will animate the plot, but as something as ordinary and fundamental to a novel as money or love—she now takes the risk of making Glory very dull indeed and her daily routines and concerns in her father's house as tedious to herself as they almost are to the reader. Glory is, at one level, one of fiction's least interesting creations. Yet she slowly exudes an inner power, a light, almost like the woman in a Vermeer painting or an early Velázquez painting or a Margaret Laurence novel. Her presence becomes persistent; every detail of her consciousness is etched into the prose. All she really does is regret her life, look after her father, read a bit and listen to the radio, and worry about her brother. And yet that is enough to give the novel a bedrock of closely observed drama. In both *Gilead* and *Home*, Robinson has a way of making nothing much matter, of filling things with gravity and grace, and then offering them depth. She has a seriousness about her characters that helps defeat their solemnity and helps to distract us from what is almost an aimlessness, a looseness, in the plotting of the novels.

The real drama in *Home* arises when Jack returns. In *Gilead*, we saw his return from the point of view of John Ames. Jack casts a shadow over Ames's general serenity:

> Glory has come to tell me Jack Boughton is home. He is having supper in his father's house this very night. He will come by to pay his respects, she said, in the next day or two. I am grateful for the warning. I will use the time to prepare myself. Boughton named him for me because he thought he might not have another son and I most likely would not have any child at all.

While Jack, who has been in trouble with the law, becomes a sort of fixation for Ames, as Ladislaw does for Casaubon in *Middlemarch*, the context is as much religious, or mysterious, as it is sexual. Ames writes to his son:

> My impulse is strong to warn you against Jack Boughton. Your mother and you. You may know by now what a fallible man I am, and how little I can trust my feelings on this subject. And you know, from living out years I cannot foresee, whether you must forgive me for warning you, or forgive me for failing to warn you, or indeed if none of it turned out to matter at all. This is a grave question for me.

That paragraph would itself amount to a warning. Perhaps I can say to your mother only that much. He is not a man of the highest character. Be wary of him.

Ames muses over Jack's antics as a child, his slyness, his loneliness, his sadness and the small mean thefts he committed.

Then he started doing the things that got his name in the newspaper, stealing liquor and joyriding, and so on. I've known young fellows who spent time in jail or got themselves sent off to the navy for behavior that wasn't any worse. But his family was so well respected that he got away with it all. That is to say, he was allowed to go right on disgracing his family.

It emerges that Jack fathered a child out of wedlock and the child died. Ames writes: "I have never felt he was fond of me," while noting later that Jack's own family "really loved him" and his siblings "would stand up for him no matter what."

Jack has been away for twenty years, had not even come home for his mother's funeral. Finally returned, he is damaged, unsettled, unsettling. He waits for letters that don't come; he leaves the house for no reason; his sister doesn't know what's on his mind. He is a nuisance, and yet oddly innocent and uneasy and endearing. Robinson charts all this with patience and skill and, at times, amusement. The scene in which the Boughtons invite Reverend Ames and his young wife and son to Sunday dinner is worthy of James in its use of minute movement and flickering change of atmosphere, and close also to

Alan Hollinghurst's work in the way it mixes comedy of manners with sheer social tension. There is a marvelous moment when Jack, at the piano, plays some hymns and then begins to sing, "I want a Sunday kind of love, a love that lasts past Saturday night," only to find that Lila also seems to know the words. They are interrupted by Reverend Boughton, who, for a moment, sounds like Reverend Chasuble in *The Importance of Being Earnest*: "I thought we might enjoy something a little more in keeping with the Sabbath."

The tension between Jack and everyone else in *Home* increases when he, for no good reason, attends a service led by Reverend Ames, only to find that the sermon concerns the abandonment of children by their fathers, which Jack believes to be an open reference to his own behavior. When he gets home he says to his sister: "Ah, little sister, these old fellows play rough. They look so harmless, and the next thing you know, you're counting broken bones again . . . I left through the chancel. I had half a mind to pull my jacket up over my head." As Jack, despite doing nothing to make anyone like him, continues to bask in the love of his sister and his father, a reader might feel that this is a retelling of the story of the Prodigal Son. But slowly we realize that Robinson, with infinite subtlety and care, is dealing with a stranger and more dramatic subject: the matter of predestination.

In a riveting scene, Jack abruptly asks Reverend Ames: "Do you think some people are intentionally and irretrievably consigned to perdition?" When Ames prevaricates, Jack softly returns to the question: "I would like your help with this, Reverend." Slowly, the reader begins to wonder if Jack thinks that he might be one of the damned, and if this has been on the mind of Reverend Ames. Since this scene occurs on page 230 of the book, we already know Jack in all his awkward frailty and uncertainty: he isn't a cipher, someone who can be reduced to a theory. Once the theory is named, however, it is haunting and deadly serious. As well as predestination, Jack needs to know what he should believe about the sins of fathers; he needs to know if a man who is sinful can cause the death of his own child by his own sinful nature.

Robinson manages to dramatize and almost normalize this most difficult subject. As the scene proceeds, the question isn't some abstract theological matter best left to Calvinists: the question is tearing Jack apart, and it's also affecting the reader of the novel. Despite being told that his father is tired, Jack persists with the discussion. Robinson attempts to make us offer Jack our complete sympathy. He is a man who may believe that he is predestined for damnation; or he may be, indeed, genuinely and really among the damned. It doesn't matter for a moment whether we think this kind of speculation is sheer nonsense or not. Because Jack in all his weakness has been created for us with such tenderness, it matters what he thinks and believes—not what we think. "I'm the amateur here," Jack says.

> If I had your history with the question I'd be sick of it, too, no doubt. Well I do have a history with it. I've wondered from time to time if I might not be an instance of predestination. A sort of proof. If I may not experience predestination in my own person. That would be interesting, if the consequences were not so painful.

For other people. If it did not seem as though I spread a contagion of some kind. Of misfortune. Is that possible?

In the background of *Home*, a real America is simmering. There is a mention of polio, there are discussions about the atom bomb, about Eisenhower, about race riots in the South, which Reverend Boughton thinks should be of no interest to the people of Gilead. Jack takes a different view on this subject, and in a moving, unexpected and convincing end to the book Robinson makes clear why this is so. Although *Home* makes reference to the story of the bad thief in the New Testament, and although Glory comes in the end to see Jack as the suffering Christ, Robinson remains more concerned with the texture of this world than the tone of the next. Despite her interest in religion, the predicaments dramatized in the book—including the religious ones—are rendered mostly in human terms. She manages to make this seem like amplitude rather than restraint.

In Robinson's novel *Lila*, the tone is both more otherworldly and also more oddly venal. In *Gilead* and *Home*, the two reverend gentlemen are stable, decent and kind, almost noble. Now, with the character of Lila, Robinson is interested, as with Jack, in a wayward nature, in someone who has lived apart from the grace of Gilead. But while Jack is wilful and smart, Lila has an unusual, almost feral innocence. Robinson is concerned here with the tension carried by someone who appears lost in the world, a sort of waif, yet who carries a glow, sometimes too much glow for a novel to bear—a striving for sanctity, the aura of someone destined for another world.

Lila first came to the town, Ames tells us in *Gilead*, in 1947, sheltering from the rain in his church at Pentecost, on a day when the sermon was about light, or indeed, about Light.

> I do enjoy remembering that morning. I was sixty-seven, to be exact, which did not seem old to me. I wish I could give you the memory I have of your mother that day. I wish I could leave you certain of the images in my mind, because they are so beautiful that I hate to think they will be extinguished when I am.

Before she sought refuge in Gilead, Lila was wandering Middle America with a tribe of the poverty-stricken. The novel moves between her life now, a life of comfort and ease as a wife and mother, and her life before, when she was looked after by a woman called Doll. Robinson deals with hunger and violence and carnality, but she also wishes to dramatize religious questions. This time, because of Lila's inexperience, her poverty, her life of deprivation, it requires a leap of faith for the reader to follow Lila fully as she discusses divine grace with Reverend Ames while lying in bed with him.

> But he seemed to be telling her that . . . souls could be lost forever because of things they did not know, or understand, or believe. He didn't like to say it, he had to try different words for it. So she knew he thought it might be true. Doll probably didn't know she had an immortal soul . . . If Doll was going to be lost for ever, Lila wanted to be right there with her, holding to the skirt of her dress.

This question of what happens to the unsaved continues to pre-occupy her. Since none of the people she had known were baptized, could it be that they wouldn't go to heaven? Robinson manages, some of the time, to make Lila's concern with this credible and dramatic. "I've been tramping around with the heathens," she says. "They're just as good as anybody, so far as I can see. They sure don't deserve no hellfire." At other times, however, Robinson gives poor Lila too many weighty things to say and inquire about. In one scene, when she is out walking with her husband and he asks her what is on her mind, she replies: "Nothing, really. Existence." Later, as he talks about his thoughts on religion, she says: "Near as I can tell, you were wanting to reconcile things by saying they can't be reconciled. I guess I know what you mean by reconcile."

It's possible that Robinson, having put so much concrete detail and credible fact into *Gilead* and *Home*, felt that she deserved some freedom, and wished to make Lila a soul as much as a body. She gives her body enough in the novel's backstory, including a spell working in a whorehouse, and much wandering and hunger, but perhaps that's not enough for Robinson's grave and unearthly ambitions as a novelist. Some of the soulful scenes, however, ring true, such as the scenes where Lila and her aging husband fall in love and want each other, and the scenes where Lila's spirit is more and more unsettled. Some of the writing has echoes of the lyricism of *Housekeeping*:

> There was night everywhere and snow, under a big moon. Beyond
> the few lights of Gilead the great white nowhere that the wind
> had all to itself, the frozen ponds and stricken cornfields and the

ragtag sheds and shacks. The wind would be clapping shut and prying open everything that was meant to keep it out, bothering where it could, tired of its huge loneliness.

But all the time, as she creates this unlikely coupling between the old preacher and the waif, to which she has devoted two full novels, Robinson may have been building up to the exquisite scene after the birth of their child when Boughton falteringly attempts to baptize it in water from melted snow. Since they aren't sure this worked, they have to repeat the effort, or the sacrament, when the baby is two weeks old. As Lila speaks to the child, Robinson lets us see why religion, despite everything, can be a godsend to a novelist, as much as it is to her characters. "But when you were just two weeks old," Lila says,

we took you to the church to be christened for sure, because Boughton kept on worrying until it was done. Your father said it was intention that mattered, and that didn't matter either, because a newborn child is as pure as the snow. Boughton said if they did not act on the intention when circumstances allowed them to, then the seriousness of the intention was questionable.

The two old men then argue about intention, quoting Calvin for their own purposes, as though they had all the time in the world.

Issues of Truth and Invention: Francis Stuart

London Review of Books · 2001

In March 1992 I received a printed invitation from the Irish novelist Francis Stuart to a party in Dublin commemorating a party he had given in Berlin on St. Patrick's Day 1941. I wondered, when I read it, why Francis had sent this. Over the years he had invited me to several events, but he had never had invitations printed. I wondered if it was clear to him, as it was to me, that the invitation was a direct provocation. He was almost ninety years old; a good deal of mystery and controversy still surrounded him, his political opinions, his novels and, especially, the fact that he had spent the war years in Germany and broadcast from there to Ireland.

He lived at that time in Dundrum in the suburbs of Dublin and he had settled, it seemed, into an extremely mellow and happy old age. He still wrote novels and followed public events, but he exuded a sort of dreaminess, loving cats and rabbits, remaining quiet-spoken and smiling and charming and hospitable. He preferred silence to small talk and solitude to gossip, but sometimes when he spoke, especially about public life, there was a steely anger in his tone, a dislike for the liberal editorial policies of *The Irish Times*, for example, and a hatred for political leaders and politics generally. In his manner he was serene: in his opinions he was not. He was the exact opposite of every member of his generation I had known.

I met him first in 1972 when I was seventeen and in my first week at University College Dublin. He shared a platform with the American poet James Tate. While Tate read from his work, Stuart spoke about his difficulty in publishing his novel *Black List, Section H*, which had finally come out from an American university press. He did not look like a seventy-year-old man. He was tall, his frame was thin but strong, his hair was gray in a crew cut. His accent sounded foreign. His position that night was that of outlaw, of someone who spoke dark and difficult truths that were not acceptable to those who controlled publication. But he was connected at the same time to the higher reaches of Irish grandeur: he had been married to Iseult Gonne, Maud Gonne's daughter, and had been a friend of Yeats's. I found myself sitting beside him in the student bar and it was astonishing and fascinating to hear someone talk with familiarity and slight contempt about Maud Gonne, and then withdraw into himself, become silent and vague and uncomfortable, refusing to deal in colorful anecdotes or fond reminiscences.

Black List, Section H had been published the previous year by Southern Illinois University Press. It was the only book by Francis Stuart in any Dublin bookshop. Because it had come from America, it cost much more than a normal hardback. Slowly, over the next year or so, I met people who had read it and talked about it in hushed and reverent tones as something special and strange and haunting. And slowly, too, an argument developed about Stuart. For some, the writing was too awkward; for others, the insistence on outlaw status was too labored; for others, the years in Germany placed Stuart outside the pale.

I read the book myself in the spring of 1975. I began it sometime on a Saturday and put it down only to go to a student party. I remember that I came back at four in the morning to the damp basement flat where I lived and picked the book up again and read it until I had finished it, at some point on the Sunday morning. Neither before nor since have I read anything that overwhelmed me in the same way. I shared nothing with H, the narrator who was so close in his biographical details to Stuart himself. I was not from a Northern Unionist background; I had not fought in the Irish Civil War; I did not marry Iseult Gonne in 1920 when I was seventeen; I did not know Yeats or hang around with Liam O'Flaherty; I did not go to Germany in 1940.

These, however, were merely the outlines of Stuart's life and that of his narrator, H, who used the real names of figures like Yeats and O'Flaherty to make you believe in him. What hit me hard in that first reading of *Black List, Section H* was Stuart's ability to deal with the notion of a damaged self, someone who was clearly weak, clearly wrong and who felt nothing but contempt for the world around him. I had come across these anti-heroic attitudes in other books, but this was an Irish self, and a man I had met, who seemed willing to dramatize his own moral awkwardness and his own dark search for an opening in the forest where these qualities could be, however tentatively, recognized and healed.

It was apparent to me even then that most people who read the book would not feel what I felt. It continued to provoke argument, and the argument in its favor was hard to win. The book was not well written, for example, and the contempt in it certainly implied a contempt for liberal and democratic values as well as for many people. And H's account of himself mixed self-love and self-indulgence; and there was something oddly forced about H's outlaw status. None of this mattered to me, and none of this mattered to other people I met over the years who had also been hit by the wave of complex emotion that came from the book.

Francis Stuart was born in Australia in 1902. His parents were both Ulster Protestants, and after his father's suicide when he was four months old, his mother brought him back to Ireland. He was sent to various English schools, including Rugby. In 1920 he married Iseult Gonne, who was seven years older than him, and was Maud Gonne's daughter with the right-wing (and fiercely anti-Semitic) French politician Lucien Millevoye. (Iseult had had an affair with Ezra Pound before Francis married her; in 1917 Yeats had proposed marriage to her.) Stuart published poetry that Yeats admired. He fought on the Republican side in the Irish Civil War and was interned. He published his first book of poetry in 1923 and lived in County Wicklow with Iseult Gonne, traveling frequently to Dublin and London; they had two children. Between 1931 and 1939 he published eleven novels, an autobiography and a book called *Racing for Pleasure and Profit in Ireland and Elsewhere.*

Stories of the demise of his marriage begin quite early. In July 1920 Maud Gonne wrote to Yeats that Stuart's "conduct towards Iseult is shocking. While they were staying with me in Dublin he struck her and one day knocked her down. He threw her out of her own room with such violence that she fell on the landing." The failure of their life together is dramatized in many of Stuart's later books.

In 1940 Stuart went alone to Germany, where he taught at Berlin University and between 1942 and 1944 broadcast to Ireland. After the war he was arrested by the Allies, along with Madeleine Meissner, who later became his wife. The couple eventually made their way to Paris and then London and then to Ireland in 1958. Stuart wrote a number of novels that dealt with his experience of the war: *The Pillar of Cloud* (1948), *Redemption* (1949), *The Flowering Cross* (1950), *Victors and Vanquished* (1958) and *Black List, Section H* (1971).

When Stuart returned to Ireland, Madeleine and he lived first in a cottage in County Meath, then moved in 1971 to Dundrum. Stuart published nothing in the 1960s and they lived in relative obscurity. His seventieth birthday in 1972 was marked by a Festschrift edited by W. J. McCormack and this book set the tone for Irish writing about Stuart over the next twenty-five years. "Despite the outbreak of war," McCormack wrote, "Stuart decided that he should be where Europe was then focused, that somebody should bear witness. In addition, he felt that in wartime Germany he would at last be cut off from conventional demands on his feelings and that in isolation he might begin to find himself." He discussed Stuart's novels of the 1930s and their treatment of violence and war and isolation and said, "Perhaps no other artist in the English language was so aptly prepared by his earlier psychic life for the experience of wartime Germany, for the shades of humanity who populated Europe."

In the 1970s Stuart wrote book reviews for the weekly Dublin newspaper *Hibernia*. He made himself available to younger writers and journalists and was kind and oddly wise and encouraging. Although he never openly sought either success or popularity as a novelist, he became a respected figure in literary Dublin. For example, in 1980, when Neil Jordan, at that time the most promising young writer in the country, published his first novel, it seemed natural that Stuart would launch the book. In the early 1980s Penguin reissued *Black List, Section H.*

For me and many others who visited the Stuarts in these years, there was a special aura around both of them, Madeleine as much as Francis. That they were religious and interested in mysticism may explain part of it, but the fact that they were old and made clear their loathing for Ireland's pieties is also significant. They were warm and engaged with the world and with each other. Many of us came away from their house inspired and cheered up.

Some of the stories were funny. When Stuart spoke to Fintan O'Toole about his friendship with the poet Paul Potts, and his admiration for him, Fintan thought he was talking about the dictator Pol Pot. He imagined Stuart in Paris befriending the future mass murderer and now, after all the years, talking casually and fondly of him.

Some of the stories were not so funny. I once asked Stuart about his friendship with members of the UDA—these were the bad years of the UDA's rule in Belfast—which I had heard about but supposed to be untrue. He nodded and said that yes, he had been traveling to Belfast to see the UDA and had become friendly with one of the younger members and had met Andy Tyrie, the leader, and come to admire him in certain ways. Stuart would leave a silence at such moments, and if there were a rabbit or a cat close by, he would stroke it. I knew that he was also sending books to IRA prisoners and writing letters to them. I was puzzled by his refusal to make moral judgments of a conventional kind.

When you talked to him and to Madeleine, you knew, or could imagine, that they had been through experiences in the war and after the war that had marked them deeply. And those experiences had included their own involvement in the German side of the war and implication in its activities. I knew they both lived in the shadowy spaces between knowledge and forgiveness; their response to this was not simple, and I never fully understood it, and I still don't.

Once—I was working as a journalist then—I came to see Stuart because another friend of his, on the Republican side, had been found guilty of the murder of a policeman. I believed the evidence to have been very scanty and the conviction unsafe. (It was, many years later, overturned.) I thought Stuart would be concerned about this, but he was not. He was pretty sure, he said, that his friend was guilty. His friend, however, was a wonderful man, and killing the policeman was part of his bravery and courage and seriousness, Stuart said. Madeleine then spoke about the man's girlfriend and the great love between them and what would happen now. I remember her eyes lighting up and I remember the words vividly as she said: "He is the love of her life."

Always, there was the strangeness of what they had been doing in Germany. In *Black List, Section H*, the narrator went to Germany not because he admired Hitler or the Nazis, but because he sought his own crucifixion there, sought to be where there was darkness and destruction. If the book had any politics, it was a hatred of the hypocrisy that could preach democracy and then bomb Dresden. The attitudes in it seemed to take their bearing from Stuart's reading of Dostoyevsky while interned. The narrator of *Black List, Section H* and the old man who lived with his German wife in Dundrum were, ostensibly, both apolitical. Only once in all those years did Stuart say anything that made me wonder about that. It was late at night in a Dublin restaurant, it must have been 1981 or 1982, and Stuart turned to me and asked if I did not believe that democracy was merely a system in which scum could come to the top. For once, I was able to argue with him—there was nothing oblique or ambiguous about his position. As usual, he spoke calmly and gently, smiling all the while.

By this time, he was writing a column for *In Dublin* magazine, of which I was features editor. The columns were short and sharp in their blanket attacks on the establishment—church, state, consumers all. They proposed a sort of anarchism and mysticism. The interesting thing, of course, was that the writer was an elderly man whose name carried with it an uncertain stigma.

In 1983 Robert Fisk published *In Time of War: Ireland, Ulster and the Price of Neutrality 1939–45* and this seemed to settle the argument about what Stuart had been doing in Germany. Fisk's account of the episode was based on transcripts of Stuart's broadcasts in the Northern Irish Public Record Office and an interview with Stuart. In the interview, Francis spoke about Hitler: "I felt that somehow the system in Europe needed completely destroying and for me Hitler was a kind of Samson pulling everything down." He regarded Hitler, he said, as a "super-dissident." Fisk wrote that Stuart accepted the lectureship in Berlin "partly because his marriage to Iseult Gonne was breaking up and also because the new job was well paid."

"Although Stuart was drawn towards the Nazis," Fisk went on, "because he 'had the idea that the war might end in everything collapsing, and this was always my dream,' he was also a political innocent, contemplating a visit to Moscow until advised against it by some White Russian friends, and realizing only after a year that Hitler—far from being a dissident—was an ultra-conservative." According to Fisk, however, his broadcasts "could have left no one in any doubt that the system of government he was expounding was the National Socialist one . . . But Stuart's broadcasts were unexceptionable compared to most of the material about Ireland which emanated from Germany." Fisk mentioned the "poisonous" anti-Semitic tone of other broadcasters to Ireland. He did not, however, include Stuart in their company.

A few strange passages from the transcripts are quoted in Fisk's book, such as this one on the German defeat at Stalingrad: "This has moved Germany more than any other event of the war, for while such victories as the fall of Paris might be attributed to the perfection of the German war machine, this is an affair of human beings, a triumph of flesh and blood." Or another on St. Patrick's Day 1943:

"One day we will have a great hurley match, or a great race meeting to celebrate peace and we will hold it outside Belfast to celebrate the return of the Six Counties." Or: "It is of no importance at all that the Tricolour should fly from the City Hall in Belfast instead of the Union Jack if Belfast workers are to find it as hard to live and support their families as before. Such freedom is merely an illusion and such nationalism a farce and a danger."

Stuart told Fisk that he had refused to make anti-Russian broadcasts: that as a result "his telephone began to ring at odd hours of the night and anonymous voices at the other end of the line threatened him with 'being sent to a camp.'" Stuart added that he hated the "insufferable attitude of Germans when they were on top" and "if I had really asked myself in a sober way in 1940 whether I wanted a German domination of all Europe, I don't think I would have desired that." He also said that when he returned to Ireland "I hardly ever met anyone who heard me. I don't think anyone really listened."

Fisk also wrote about the Görtz affair. Hermann Görtz was a German agent selected for a mission to Ireland. He "was given two objectives in Ireland; to gain the IRA's help during a possible German invasion of Britain and their assistance in cutting off Eire's connections with the United Kingdom." Görtz was introduced to Stuart, who gave him Iseult's address in County Wicklow and told him that he could contact her in an emergency. When he parachuted into Ireland in May 1940, Görtz made his way to Iseult's house. She was later arrested for harboring him briefly and held for a month before being found not guilty.

By the time Fisk's book came out I was no longer seeing much of Francis and Madeleine. In 1982 we had printed a letter about Stuart's column that accused him of having been a Nazi supporter. On the morning *In Dublin* appeared, Francis phoned me and we had a short, friendly conversation about the letter, which, foolishly, we had not consulted him about. Since our conversation had been so amicable, I was rather surprised to get a solicitor's letter and rather more surprised when it became clear that Francis intended to sue the magazine. We settled with him, but it was obvious to me that he had wanted a court case. I thought at the time that he had wanted his name cleared of Nazi and anti-Semitic connections once and for all, but I am no longer sure about that.

In 1981, with the encouragement of the government, the Irish Arts Council set up an organization called Aosdána. This consisted of 150 writers, artists and composers. Once the original group had been chosen by the council, new members would be elected by the existing members, and, with certain restrictions, members whose incomes fell below about £12,000 a year would receive a stipend for the rest of their working lives. The scheme also included an honors system where a limited number of members would be elected a saoi, or "wise person." Samuel Beckett was one; so was Seamus Heaney. Since Francis Stuart was one of the original members of Aosdána, he was entitled to be nominated, and this was where the trouble began.

When it was proposed that Stuart be made a saoi, there was some informal debate between members of Aosdána over whether honoring him involved more than honoring his work. At first, he was defeated, but in 1996 he was made a saoi and the honor, symbolized by a collar of gold, was conferred on him by President Mary Robinson, who spoke about his "awkward" presence in Irish literary life. I am a member of Aosdána and I was among those who voted for him.

In October 1997 Channel 4 in the UK made a program about Irish anti-Semitism in which Stuart was interviewed. He told the interviewer: "The Jew was always the worm that got into the rose and sickened it. Yes, but of course I take that as praise. I mean all those so-called healthy roses, they need exposing—many of them are sick."

> INTERVIEWER: Are you ashamed that you helped Nazi Germany now?
>
> STUART: Sorry?
>
> INTERVIEWER: Are you ashamed, yes, are you sorry?
>
> STUART: Did I help them by broadcasting, you mean?
>
> INTERVIEWER: Yeah.
>
> STUART: No, I'm not sorry.
>
> INTERVIEWER: But knowing what you do know, as the person you are now, which is the only way you can answer—
>
> STUART: That's right.
>
> INTERVIEWER: Now, what would your answer be, and would you broadcast again?
>
> STUART: No, probably not.
>
> INTERVIEWER: Do you have any regrets in your life generally?
>
> STUART: Non, non, je ne regrette rien, rien du tout.

The *Irish Times* columnist Kevin Myers was watching this program and would have much to say about it: "Honouring such a man with the highest artistic accolade this state has to offer is at best to be morally neutral about the barbarous cause he served. It is to follow the fascist chic ethic that art counts above all else," he wrote in October 1997. Two months later he returned to the subject:

> Francis Stuart offered his services to the Third Reich after the outbreak of the Second World War. There would be no controversy had he repented for doing so. Has he repented, clearly and unambiguously? Specifically and precisely: he has not . . . By honouring this man who unrepentantly served the Third Reich, Aosdána has disgraced itself, which is its right, and the country which pays for it, which is not.

Also watching the program was the poet Máire Mhac an tSaoi, another member of Aosdána. Just as Francis Stuart was connected to the higher echelons of Irish grandeur, Máire Mhac an tSaoi has her own elevated coordinates. She is married to Conor Cruise O'Brien. Her father, Seán MacEntee, fought in the Irish War of Independence and was a minister in most of Éamon de Valera's governments. Her uncle was a cardinal. Every schoolchild of my generation knew her poems, written in Irish, by heart. She is a formidable presence at any gathering. She proposed a motion whereby Aosdána would condemn what Stuart had said and call on him to resign from the organization.

In the lead-up to the meeting of Aosdána many people came to Stuart's defense, including a number of journalists on *The Irish Times*. Nuala O'Faolain referred to the "spiritual excitement" of reading *Redemption* and later *Black List, Section H* and wrote that she was amazed "that so many people are so comfortable with their own righteousness. How can they know that they would not have made the broadcasts in Berlin during the war, in the circumstances described in *Black List, Section H*?" Fintan O'Toole, another columnist on the paper, wrote:

> Stuart was undeniably a Nazi collaborator. And he did, in his broadcasts to Ireland from Hitler's Germany, use coded anti-Semitic phrases . . . None of that was, is, or ever will be excusable . . . But Stuart was, in the overall scheme of things, a very minor figure. If we want to talk about Irish guilt regarding Nazism and the Holocaust, there are more obvious places to begin . . . The difference between Francis Stuart and all of these other collaborators is that he, at least, engaged with the consequences of his actions. Other writers who had been drawn to right-wing totalitarianism and then became disillusioned with it—W. B. Yeats and T. S. Eliot, for example—took refuge in an artistic flight from reality. Stuart's work, after the war, became more real. He moved towards, not away from, the terrain of his shame.

Other commentators, including Conor Cruise O'Brien, took the opposite view.

I could not attend the meeting of Aosdána that discussed Máire Mhac an tSaoi's motion, but I wrote a piece about the controversy in the *Sunday Independent* in Dublin. "Coming from a Unionist background," I said,

Stuart (and indeed H) would become a Republican, even though the politics meant nothing to him; and later in the 1930s when liberal opinion (and indeed most other opinion) considered Hitler's Germany to be a place of evil, he would go there, he would live there during the war, he would broadcast to Ireland, and he would know what the consequences were going to be. And all this, his novel *Black List, Section H* makes clear, had nothing to do with politics, with anti-Semitism or fascism, or Nazism, but arose from something rooted in his psyche—the need to betray and be seen to betray.

By this time, *Black List, Section H* had been reissued once more as a Penguin Classic, and my piece in the *Sunday Independent* was fueled by the acknowledgment by the main players in the anti-Stuart camp that they had not read the book. I had done the introduction to the Penguin edition, in which I wrote that in the experience of reading the book there was a feeling "that nothing had been invented. Not only the names were real, but the places, the gestures, the emotions and moments of truth were described and evoked with a sense of absolute truth and total honesty."

Máire Mhac an tSaoi's motion was defeated and she resigned from Aosdána. Stuart did not attend the meeting. A fax supporting the motion was sent by the Jewish Representative Council of Ireland. Stuart initiated libel proceedings against Kevin Myers and *The Irish Times* and the case was settled—in Stuart's favor—in June 1999. The settlement included the statement: "*The Irish Times* accepts that Mr Stuart has never expressed anti-Semitism in his writings or otherwise and regrets the publication of an impression to the contrary. *The Irish Times* has agreed to pay a sum of money in respect of the costs of Mr Stuart's action."

In January 1998, six weeks after the Aosdána meeting, Stuart gave an interview to Irish television in which he tried to explain his use of the phrase "the worm in the rose": "the rose of our consumer society," he said—"which to my mind is a very horrible society." Asked if he regretted the Holocaust, he said: "Well, of course I regret it." Asked if he ever supported it, he replied: "Never." Asked if he regretted his support for the Nazis, he said: "I never supported that regime and I'm intensely sorry for the hurt I caused so many people by appearing to. As I did understandably appear to support it." The war, he said, "was probably by that time the greatest war in history. I have always believed that the sort of writer I am should be at the heart of where things are most intense and that I should report it, unbiased as I hoped to do, primarily for my own people." Asked about Hitler, he replied: "Hitler came to power in Germany after the Versailles Treaty, when things were very, very . . . I know people who were there in a terrible state then and he did a lot for Germany until, until . . ." He appeared lost for words and then: "I think that certain people are possessed, as it's called in the Old Testament. I think of Hitler as becoming possessed by the spirit of evil."

Around this time, a book called *Hitler's Irish Voices: The Story of German Radio's Wartime Irish Service* by David O'Donoghue appeared and made clear that Stuart had had a meeting with the IRA leadership late in 1939 before he went to Berlin and that he had operated as a messenger for the IRA, which was interested in obtaining German assistance for its campaign. (Stuart's brother-in-law Seán MacBride—Maud Gonne's son by the Irish revolutionary John MacBride—had been chief of staff of the IRA from 1936 to 1937; Stuart had also maintained informal contact with some of his old colleagues from the Civil War, those who had not followed de Valera and joined Fianna Fáil, which entered the Dáil in 1926 and took power in 1932.) O'Donoghue's book gave the most complete account of Stuart's broadcasts thus far. He confirmed Fisk's assertion that there was no anti-Russian propaganda in them. He also confirmed that there was no direct or specific anti-Semitic content. Stuart's broadcasts as reported in O'Donoghue's book supported Irish neutrality, and attacked the British. On two occasions, the broadcasts, which were monitored by the Irish security forces, annoyed the Irish government and caused a diplomatic complaint and this may have been the reason Stuart's Irish passport was not renewed in 1942. On one occasion, when Stuart called on troops from Northern Ireland to go over to the other side, he was himself crossing a line that could have caused him much trouble after the war. O'Donoghue notes that Francis and Madeleine (who had also worked for German radio's foreign service) deliberately allowed themselves to be arrested by the French rather than the British after the war.

This, then, was the evidence against Francis Stuart. I wish sometimes that I had been able to go to the Aosdána meeting and speak against Máire Mhac an tSaoi's motion.

I believe that in his postwar work, in his three best novels, Stuart had placed himself in a peculiar position. He was able to write those books only because of his own foolishness and treachery. His material was gathered in the most outrageous place in the most outrageous way. The novels do not, in Allen Tate's phrase about Ezra Pound, reach us pure, but to refuse to praise them or honor them, or indeed honor their author for writing them, is to confuse crafted, self-conscious novels, written in the postwar period, with their author's life during the war. The novels are dramas of guilt and innocence that do not incite us to join any party or hate anybody, but instead to consider how one strange figure ended up in Germany and broadcast for Hitler (*Black List, Section H*), how three wounded figures dealt with the postwar desolation (*The Pillar of Cloud*) and how one strange figure brings disruption and the possibility of transcendence back to Ireland from the European war (*Redemption*).

I cannot accept that writers should be good people. I believe that part of the purpose of writing is to speak up for the damned and I can hardly object when a novelist takes this seriously enough (or is led by other motives) to place himself outside the pale of the saved, no matter how much I might disapprove of his actions and disagree with his politics. I wish that after the war others who had collaborated or expressed anti-Semitic views had also written novels that explored, or even refused to recognize, their own foolishness and badness. I wish that the business of evil were explored more often and more seriously in fiction. Thus I cannot complain when Francis Stuart is honored by his fellow artists. It is not a simple matter; it does not come to us pure. But I cannot regret voting for him.

There is, however, another matter. No one in Aosdána, as far as I am aware, had lost family in the war. All of us were part of the legacy of Irish neutrality, and all of us, debating the issue of Francis Stuart, were living in a sort of backwater, protected from the terrible pain and anger suffered by the families of those killed by the Nazis. What hung in the balance was a fundamental question: had Stuart's name been so dishonored by what he did in the war that nothing he could write would be enough to justify offering him the highest honor an artist can have in Ireland? I believed and I still believe that the honor was justified, but I'm not sure I would believe this if I had lost family or friends in the war.

Brendan Barrington is a young American living in Dublin. Like Stuart and Máire Mhac an tSaoi, he has connections in the upper echelons of Irish life. His Irish father is a member of a family of distinguished public servants that includes a Supreme Court judge and Brendan Bracken, minister for information in Churchill's War Cabinet. Barrington is an editor at the Lilliput Press. He has gone into the Military Archives in Dublin and transcribed Stuart's war broadcasts; he has read all the novels and written an introduction to the transcripts that deals with Stuart's politics and his controversial place in Irish intellectual life.

In *The Wartime Broadcasts of Francis Stuart*, Barrington writes:

Stuart's allegiances to the anti-Treaty side in the Irish Civil War and to the Third Reich in the Second World War have usually been explained as arising from non-political forces in his psyche: a sense of adventure, a compulsion to betray, a mystical desire to suffer.

These forces were undoubtedly present but they existed along-side a political consciousness that was far more highly developed, and also rather more discriminating and conventional, than has generally been recognized. The wartime broadcasts . . . are concerned primarily with politics, and could not have been written by someone as politically naive, or gormless, or blindly revolutionary as Stuart has usually been depicted as being.

Barrington examines Stuart's claim in 1996 that he had "spoken and written several million words in my life. No one could ever point to a sentence of mine that was or is anti-Semitic." He finds the following in a pamphlet Stuart wrote for the IRA in 1924 when he was twenty-two:

> Austria, in 1921, had been ruined by the war, and was far, far poorer than Ireland is today, for besides having no money she was over-burdened with innumerable debts. At that time Vienna was full of Jews, who controlled the banks and the factories and even a large part of the Government; the Austrians themselves seemed about to be driven out of their own city.

Ireland should overcome the British influence, he suggested, as Austria had overcome the Jewish influence.

This is the only direct and unambiguous anti-Semitic statement published by Stuart that has ever been found, but having trawled through the fiction Stuart published in the 1930s, Barrington finds a definable set of attitudes towards Jews, expressed both by characters in the novels and directly by the author in his creation of Jewish stereotypes. There are no prizes, for example, for guessing the racial identity of Ike Salaman in *The Great Squire* (1939):

> His keen swarthy face glowed with the cold passion that con-sumed him as he bent over the grey parchment. Figures. How secretly beautiful they were! What delight in getting them to dance to one's own tune! Ah, that was the real happiness: this secret mathematical dance of figures, in rows, in spidery waltzes, in formal gavottes, to that thin maddening tune that he had long dreamed of but only heard for the first time today, the clink and clank of a great number of sovereigns.

It would be impossible to say there isn't anti-Semitism here; and the same is true of the broadcasts quoted by Fisk, where, as Fintan O'Toole has pointed out, it is easy to find stock references to international financiers and bankers and easy to see that Stuart means Jews.

Casual and less than casual anti-Semitism survives in all types of writing from the 1930s. The problem with Stuart is that he wrote the stuff about Jews in Vienna in 1924, then put the stereotypes into his novels in the 1930s, then made anti-Semitic comments in letters to his wife from Germany in 1939 (these are quoted in Geoffrey Elborn's 1990 biography), then went to Germany in 1940 and lectured at Berlin University and then included easily detectable, if indirect, anti-Semitic references in his broadcasts. "There is no evidence that anti-Semitism was a motivating force in Francis Stuart's decision to live, teach and broadcast in Nazi Germany," Barrington writes. "At the same time it is difficult to avoid the conclusion that some strain of anti-Semitism was a necessary enabling factor in that decision."

It can be argued, then, putting it more mildly, that Stuart was not sufficiently repelled by German anti-Semitism to decide not to go to live in Berlin. It can also be argued, however, that Stuart was attracted to Hitler's Germany partly because of its anti-Semitism. The truth maybe lies somewhere between the two. The evidence against him makes me, as someone who has written about his work and enjoyed his company, very uncomfortable.

Just as the tone of the IRA pamphlet in 1924 is harder and nastier than any tone Stuart would later use in his account of himself, the tone of his letters to *The Irish Times* in December 1938, which Barrington also quotes, is very far from his later version of himself. In the first letter Stuart opposed admitting refugees from nondemocratic countries into Ireland. In his second letter he wrote:

> When democracy has found some solution to the pressing problems observable in the countries where it is practised, which I would define as, among others: unemployment, slums, the tyranny of money, and the appallingly low level of general culture, then let it sit in judgement on other forms of government. But, in my belief, our bureaucratic democracies can never of their nature find such a solution, being themselves largely responsible for these evils.

Barrington has done us all a favor in unearthing this letter and the 1924 pamphlet. The main thrust of his argument is that the hero of *Black List, Section H* is not Francis Stuart, that the man who went to Germany and the mind that created the novel were different, and that a great number of Irish writers and commentators, including myself, have been fooled by the novel. "It would appear that Stuart had not forgotten the broadcasts, but had reimagined them," Barrington writes:

> What is unfortunate—although not surprising, in light of the enormous personal affection that the elderly Stuart inspired—is that so many writers and scholars have been enthusiastic participants in this reimagining, creating a myth of Stuart that is far more palatable to contemporary sensibilities than the literary and political persona of the man who wrote and delivered the talks printed herein.

In 1976 Stuart gave an interview about the broadcasts: "These broadcasts didn't usually deal with politics; they dealt very often with literature, both English and Irish, and even with other literature." This is not true. They hardly ever mentioned literature, and it is an interesting example of Stuart's "reimagining" of what he did in these years.

Barrington's case, then, is that the holy fool, the awkward, apolitical and damaged figure of H in the novel is an invention, a fictional disguise for a more political and nastier self. His point "is not that there is anything intrinsically remarkable about deviations between an autobiographical novel and the life on which it is based, but simply that we cannot and should not look to Stuart's fiction to supply a reliable account of his life."

Barrington's quotations from the 1924 pamphlet and the 1938 letters to *The Irish Times* prepare you for a series of broadcasts in a similarly strident tone. And his point about the distinction between Stuart and H makes you expect a skilled rhetorician in front of the microphone. Instead, you get the sort of dullness that perhaps only someone who has done a lot of hackwork could properly recognize. These broadcasts could well have been written by the holy fool who is H in the novel, but now he has a deadline and, for the most part, a few tired and platitudinous opinions. Even at the time, some of these talks must have seemed absurd. And it is easy to imagine Stuart leaving the studio filled with shame at his own ineptitude, once more, like H, aware of his own awkwardness and inability to exercise his intelligence and putting the whole thing out of his mind for another week.

The most absurd, perhaps, was on August 12, 1942, when he managed to compare Hitler with Gandhi. But the broadcasts are also full of the most terrible sentimentality about Irish people, their spiritual qualities, their struggle for freedom, their decency and open-mindedness, their rural life, their sport. Stuart's efforts at a folksy, common touch must have made him cringe as much as his listeners. His efforts at patriotism were ridiculous. ("If a committee of six average Irishmen, let us say a farmer or two, a National University student, a Civic Guard and an IRA man, were formed into a committee with sovereign powers to settle all the present problems of the world, they would make a far better job of it than Churchill and Roosevelt and company.") Only once did he make a reference to neutral Ireland that made any sense: "When I hear a report on the debate in the Dáil, as I did the other evening, on whether pubs should be open on Sundays at 1 or 1:30, I'm reminded more vividly than ever how peaceful life is in the twenty-six counties of Ireland."

Two things stand out, however, that give weight to Barrington's thesis. There is an astonishingly fierce anti-Englishness in the broadcasts and constant reference to a united Ireland and the problem of partition. This is to remind us that Stuart fought on the Republican side in the Civil War and was interned. He was one of a sizable number of people who fought in Ireland between 1918 and 1923 who never settled down afterwards, never held a job (Stuart's first job was in Berlin in 1940) and roamed American cities, or stayed in Ireland and took to drink, or kept the IRA flame alight. They remained locked into the ideology of the cause for which they fought or became totally disillusioned. Stuart seems to have done both. The tone of his broadcasts about partition and England, his call for Allied troops from Northern Ireland to defect, lead me to change my view that he had an apolitical nature, as does the content of the broadcast of December 16, 1942: "Like most Irishmen I have no use for secondhand opinions," Stuart begins. His reaction to the jokes and jeers about Hitler was to

wonder what Hitler really was. Anyone who is the butt of these small city-made mentalities seemed to me to be probably someone of consequence. I began to find out something about Hitler and the new Germany and then, of course, I was completely fired by enthusiasm, for here was someone who was freeing life from the money standards that dominated it almost everywhere I had ever been, not excluding my own country; here was someone who had the vision and courage to deny financiers, politicians and bankers the right to rule. Nor did the word dictator frighten me—I saw that as it was. Our lives were dominated by a group of financial dictators and it seemed to me at least preferable to be ruled by one man whose sincerity for the welfare of his people could not be doubted than by a gang whose only concern was the market price of various commodities in the world markets.

What was Stuart going to do now that the war was over? His first instinct was to deny his role. In April 1946, he turned to Basil Liddell Hart, who had praised one of his prewar novels: "Your help would be especially valuable. As you know . . . I was deeply opposed to Nazism and state tyranny, and my experience during the war only deepened this opposition. It is not only the hardship of detention here, but also the hold-up in that work which I believe I could do now, that is hard to bear with patience." When, in October 1946, he was rearrested by the French, Madeleine wrote to Liddell Hart: "Please, please dear sir help him! Francis Stuart has such a fine and rare soul, the influence of which humanity has great need." In the earlier letter to Liddell Hart, Stuart had written: "What we have gone through . . . has, I think, fitted me to write a novel which will have the breadth and maturity which *The Angel of Pity* lacked."

The Pillar of Cloud, finished in October 1947, was written during a time when he and Madeleine had to report weekly to French security. Victor Gollancz, his old publisher, agreed to bring out the book. It is set in the world Francis and Madeleine inhabited after the war.

(The first chapter is called "Hunger and Cold.") Surrounding our Irish hero, Dominic Malone, are a number of people who have been imprisoned during the war, and are broken and damaged presences in the book. Dominic remains under suspicion and is called in for further interrogation about his own activities. He is questioned not about broadcasts but about his visits to various prisoner-of-war camps in Germany during the war, but "only against one charge was he vitally concerned to defend himself. That he had ever, in any way, in thought or deed, sided with the captors against the captives, with the executioners against the victims." During his interrogation the French are puzzled about the reason the Irishman desperately sought to be imprisoned by the Germans towards the end of the war. "It was not very difficult to have myself suspected and finally taken and put into a camp . . . I was not there long but I had time to see that in such places a new world was taking shape; in the hearts of the tormented a new world was born."

A novel by any of us is a set of lies, a set of organized, premeditated fantasies. There is no such thing as an honest novel. Between *The Pillar of Cloud* (1948) and *Black List, Section H*, published in 1971, but finished much earlier, Francis created versions of himself and versions of the war and its aftermath that redeemed him, inasmuch as they could, from the ordinary guilt or blame that might attach to collaboration. It must have been a relief to write them. In those years after the war when they were virtual prisoners and were cold and hungry, Francis and Madeleine found enormous comfort in each other. ("I needed a war and hunger and cold and imprisonment. I needed all these things before my eyes were opened enough to see a good woman," Dominic says.) In *The Pillar of Cloud* there is an astonishing air of tenderness in the moments the weak and wounded sisters Lisette and Halka share with Dominic. The writing about hunger and the search for food is brilliant. But the real world of guilt and accusation is not allowed to enter. Captain Renier, the French interrogator, is an anarchist and wants to discuss the possibilities for world change rather than accuse Dominic of collaboration.

Stuart needed to believe that he had gained something spiritual, some new insight into the human condition, during and after the war. In his fiction he worked at trying to rescue himself, heal himself, re-create his past. At the same time he wrote letters to figures like Liddell Hart denying everything, he gave interviews in which he made inaccurate statements about the broadcasts, he even tampered with his diaries. But he mainly used his novels to save the situation in which he found himself.

In these novels he set about spiriting away what really happened and offered images of the criminal who is less guilty than those who would seek to capture him.

During this time, Stuart was still married to Iseult Gonne, who sent him food parcels and encouraged him to come home. After a certain point he was free to leave, but Madeleine was not free to leave with him. In 1948 Seán MacBride became minister for external affairs in Ireland, and for this, and several other reasons, the Irish state could not offer hospitality to Madeleine. Things were not helped when Stuart let it be known that he was prepared to return to Iseult, but intended to bring Madeleine with him.

By the time Madeleine finally managed to make her way to Paris in the summer of 1949, Stuart's second postwar novel had appeared. (Madeleine, in a short memoir, published in 1984, wrote of Victor Gollancz: "This was an immense joy to us and Gollancz was so enthusiastic that he even sent the most wonderful telegram which we could hardly grasp. We were overwhelmed, especially when we considered that Gollancz was a Jew who could have resented Francis's stay in Germany during the war.") In *Redemption*, Francis began to imagine what would happen if a figure who had been imprisoned at the end of the war, and who had fallen in love with a German woman, returned to an Ireland in which his first wife still lived, an Ireland that had remained undisturbed by the war.

Ezra Arrigho, the returnee, becomes involved with a priest (who plays something of the same role as the interrogator in *The Pillar of Cloud*), the priest's sister and the local fishmonger. When the fishmonger murders a woman and when, a little later, Ezra's German lover arrives in the town, it is decided that they will all—the priest, his sister, Ezra, his lover and the murderer—move into a flat above the fishmonger's. "Isn't it time we forgave each other?" the priest asks. "Perhaps this is our last chance to lead a new life and if we don't take it there won't be another. And your wife, Ezra, let her take her place in it too. Let her forgive you and Margareta and come and live with us too."

In chapter 14, Ezra's estranged wife, Nancy, and his aunt talk about him—these scenes caused particular offense to Iseult Gonne, her mother and her mother's friends. "There was always a kind of heartlessness about him," Nancy says. "He'd use people and then drop them." "Like he used you," the aunt replies. The portrait of the aunt in the book is unpleasant; the portrait of Nancy for the most part renders her lonely and pathetic and sexually frigid. When Ezra meets her he says: "Isn't there something horrible about the thought of all the married couples shut up together in houses and flats everywhere, all the watertight little families bound together more by fear and suspicion of the rest of the world than by love of each other?" Ezra asks his wife to "abandon everything, and come out with me now and we'll find a corner for you and get a basin and hang up a mirror—there are beds enough." He brings her to the house, where she sees the sleeping German lover. "I'd go mad in a place like this," she says and leaves. But before she goes there is one of those moments in which Stuart had come to specialize. Nancy is looking at her husband's lover:

> The face of the sleeping girl that, without asking, she had known was Margareta had touched her with a pang of pity. Like that, asleep, people had another aspect than when they were awake and active. Awake, she was probably that designing little creature that she had expected, but there, looking at her asleep in the shadows, there had been a moment of recognition. Nancy had, in spite of her sense of wrong, seen in the sleeping face, not the feared stranger, but something almost familiar—a defenselessness, was it?—like her own.

"The daring and delicate experiment," the community over the fish shop, is harboring a murderer and this allows Stuart to dramatize ideas of guilt and innocence. When the policeman tells the priest that the murderer stuck a "cold knife into her heart," the priest replies: "That knife was not so cold as your justice. And it struck quickly. Agony is a mysterious concoction of many things, of fear and of time in the first place. In Annie's agony there was very little time. But in his there will be weeks and months of which each hour will be endless." When Margareta hears what Kavanagh has done, she says: "Who needs us most, we will love most. It can never be otherwise." In a strange ceremony on the night before Kavanagh is arrested, Fr. Mellows marries his sister to him.

These two novels are closer to parables than pieces of social realism. They use aspects of Stuart's experience, but merely as a way of exploring the states of consciousness and ideas of good and evil that preoccupied him, for good reason, in the postwar years. He imagined himself not only as innocent, but as a victim, and not only as a victim, but as someone who had come to understand something fundamental about suffering. The images in the final chapter of each book are particularly solemn and almost sacramental in their ideas of communion and community; the writing is suddenly beautiful and clear, as though Stuart had in his imagination created a new space for himself. "The dark must have its hour, and there was no good trying to stem it when it came, with complacent words. It could not be held back as the sea could not be held back. It was like the sea, the cold unfathomable sea, balancing and counteracting the dry land and the teeming, human dry-land activity." What impelled Stuart in these novels is a paradigm for what pushes us all towards writing novels: the dramatic revelation of matters that are hidden and dark and difficult. The impulse was urgent and raw, and the glow of pure feeling is intense.

Stuart wrote six more novels between *Redemption* (1949) and *Black List, Section H*. In 1960 Victor Gollancz turned down a seventh. He wrote to Ethel Mannin (who had known Stuart well between the wars, visited him in Germany after the war and put him up when he came to London with Madeleine): "I am terribly sorry about Francis Stuart as it has of course been obvious for some time that no one except myself would publish him." The Stuarts had moved to London in 1951, where Madeleine worked as a cleaner and Francis, intermittently, as a night security officer at the Geological Museum. When Iseult died in 1954, Francis and Madeleine married.

Slowly, Stuart's war activities became a rumor, a matter of conjecture; his novels with their interest in mysticism and victimhood, on the other hand, won him fame among a small number of readers. His war rhetoric was lodged in the archives: his novels, written in a different style, were open to the public. He and Madeleine had suffered at the end of the war, and those few years had soldered their relationship. Rather than collaborators, they felt like survivors.

In 1958 Francis published *Victors and Vanquished* and Barrington is right to see it as significant. Here, the hero "is an exact replica of Stuart in almost every respect, except that he refuses to carry the IRA message to Germany, refuses to get involved in collaborationist schemes while in Germany and refuses to make propaganda broadcasts; he spends most of his energy looking after a Jewish family, a wholly imagined (and deeply unconvincing) plotline."

Yet there are moments of illumination in the novel, and careful examinations of what preoccupied Stuart most after the war—his own reasons for going to Berlin in 1940. Here he allows a Jewish friend to question Luke, his protagonist, not about his support for Hitler but about another matter that may have kept Stuart awake at night in the years after Iseult's death: his leaving her and their two children in Ireland. "It's not a matter of whether you met with weariness or ecstasies; it's that your wife was your destiny and you had to learn to be one with it. Then, as that happened, your heart would have widened to embrace the difficulties and pain, and you yourself would have been changed, whether she was or no, and you would have come to some peace." Later, when his Jewish friend tells him, "It's a disease that spreads, this hardening of hearts, and it seems to me you didn't guard yourself against it," our Irish hero answers: "I know you're right, that's the worst of it."

There is one short scene in *Victors and Vanquished* that I found surprising and affecting. In Berlin, Luke dreams that he goes back to Ireland and visits his wife and talks to her and she doesn't fully recognize him. He goes upstairs and fails to see his daughter. The dream leaves him oppressed and uneasy. Immediately on reading it, of course, I fell into the trap of believing the dream, or the sense of longing behind it, to be true, part of what happened to Stuart, that his escape from Ireland brought with it complex feelings rather than mere relief. The passage has the feeling of a difficult truth being told, of something yielding in Stuart's version of his own past. On the other hand, he may well have made it up, or allowed something he felt for a moment as he wrote the book to become something his protagonist had felt during the war.

Issues of truth and invention become more intense when we reread *Black List, Section H* in the light of the broadcasts and Barrington's introduction.

This book remains a study in drift. H is a gambler, an unsettled figure, in need of spiritual healing, unable and unwilling to connect with the social, political or sexual world around him. But it is also a desperate attempt, through the medium of fiction, to explain H's drift to Germany, to give it meaning, to make it seem part of a plan. When H reaches Berlin, having had an argument about treachery with a man called Stroud in London, he sees the boarded-up shops and he thinks about the Jews, such as Gollancz, who had been his friends:

> Was his being here a betrayal of them? The message that reached his conscience from his deepest nature, from what he felt were the genes on which his being was constructed, suggested that he had to experience, in his own probably small degree, some of what they suffered, and, on one level, even more, because he could not claim their innocence. He had long suspected that his destiny bound him to them in a manner more obscure than that of their present defenders such as Stroud. He also realized that he would go to certain lengths in association with their persecutors, in violent reaction against the mores of home, thus ensuring that his condemnation would not, unlike theirs, arouse any sympathy.

Stuart wrote this twenty years after the event. It suggests that he genuinely believed that he had gained a great deal from his outlaw status after the war, that the feeling of being beyond the liberal pale gave him strength and insight and inspiration. Nonetheless, there is something preposterous about this passage; as an explanation for taking a job in Berlin in 1940, it is outrageously forced.

H is a self that Stuart imagined, even though he gave him many of his own attributes—his own hatred for authority and the established order, his own friends and associates, and the same itinerary. He did not include in H's makeup the man who wrote the pamphlet in 1924, the man who wrote the letters to *The Irish Times* in 1938, the man who broadcast his admiration for Hitler in 1942, the man who made constant and easy-to-decipher references to international finance. He made him a mixture of a muddled drifter and searcher for truth. Those of us who believed that H and Stuart were one and the same person were wrong to do so.

After *Black List, Section H*, Stuart wrote another six novels, some autobiographical pieces and some poems. His interest in being an outlaw, in being loathed by well-meaning liberal people, was not a joke or something made up. Anyone who knew him in his last years will attest that he meant it. And this perhaps explains his efforts to sue *In Dublin* and Kevin Myers and *The Irish Times* and to send out provocative invitations. He longed for the dock. He longed to be accused in front of everybody and despised in public. He longed for public disapproval as much as he longed for (and won) the love and support of a small group of friends. He also, in his own contradictory way, longed for fame as a novelist and man of letters.

In the late 1980s when two biographers were vying with each other for his attentions, Francis remarked to a friend that he had led "a not uninteresting life." He meant, I think, his connection with Yeats, his part in the Irish Civil War and his life in Germany. But the fifty years after the Second World War, when he grappled with the truth and fiction of what he had been through, seeing what he did and then evading, avoiding and denying it, are the years that are really interesting. He was, in the end, an artist, and he created memorable images of both destruction and the possibility of healing and comfort, of treachery and close communion, of his own hurt self and a self that he invented.

After Madeleine died in 1986, Stuart married the Irish painter Finola Graham. He became weaker as he went into his nineties, but managed still to write and give readings and travel. Eventually, he moved from the house in Dundrum into a home, and then to a private house in County Clare, where he was looked after until his death in 2000. Towards the end, he threw away his reading glasses and delighted in the freedom of not having to read, but he continued to write in old-fashioned copybooks. He told a visitor that he had a recurring dream that he went to a ticket office and asked for a ticket to his father, who had killed himself almost a century earlier. He managed to combine, in the years I knew him, a steely interest in causing as much trouble as he could and an extraordinary and feline serenity. His legacy is likely to remain difficult.

Snail Slow:
John McGahern

London Review of Books · 2022

The first letter in *The Letters of John McGahern* (ed. Frank Shovlin)—five lines written to his father in April 1943 when John McGahern was eight years old—could take an entire book to gloss:

> Dear Daddy,
>
> Thanks very much for the pictures. I had great fun reading them. Come to see us soon. We got two goats. Uncle Pat does not like them. Will you bring over my bicycle please and games. We are all well. I was gugering for Uncle Pat Thursday.
>
> Goodbye from Sean to Daddy

At the time, McGahern and his siblings were living in Aughawillan, County Leitrim, with their mother. Their father, a sergeant in the Gardaí, lived some distance away and visited occasionally.

He appears in McGahern's early novels—*The Barracks* (1963), *The Dark* (1965)—and in some of his best short stories. "Gugering," Frank Shovlin explains in a footnote, "is the act of dropping seed potatoes into holes in the ground." Uncle Pat, he suggests, is a model for the fictional character "the Shah" in McGahern's final novel, *That They May Face the Rising Sun* (2002). There, McGahern offers a portrait of this bachelor uncle: "he was intensely aware of every other presence, exercising his imagination on their behalf as well as on his own . . . Since he was a boy he had been in business of some kind but had never learned to read or write. He had to rely on pure instinct to know the people he could trust." Just as the word "gugering" belonged to a world that was disappearing, the Shah is someone whose manners and habits are part of a time that has almost passed.

The figure at the center of *That They May Face the Rising Sun*, however, is Joe Ruttledge, who has come home from London to live in this isolated place. He is both insider and outsider, watching and noticing just as a novelist does. His house resembles the one McGahern lived in, and some of the novel's characters are lightly fictionalized versions of neighbors and friends. "It was a little strange to be so public again," McGahern wrote after the book appeared. "People were talking about the characters in the book as though they were real people. That was even stranger." After the sudden death of a neighbor's brother, Ruttledge and another character have to lay out the body and prepare it for the wake: "They closed the ears and the nostrils with the cotton wool, and when they turned him over to close the rectum, dentures fell from his mouth. The rectum absorbed almost all the cotton wool. The act was as intimate and warm as the act of sex." In 1981, in a letter to his French translator, Alain Delahaye, McGahern describes laying out the brother of a neighbor in the company of a chemist from Dublin who kept adjusting the mouth: "I knew this pursuit of perfection could go on all night. The murmurs outside the door were rising, people restless to start drinking, which they couldn't do decently until they had viewed the Departed."

After the funeral, Ruttledge has a conversation with the undertaker, Jimmy Joe McKiernan, a version of John Joe McGirl, a former IRA leader and a local undertaker and auctioneer in County Leitrim. McKiernan, in the novel, has overseen Ruttledge's purchase of his small house and farm. McGirl must have done as much for McGahern, who mentions him in a letter to a friend as "the one I dealt with, more interested in machine guns than in coffins." In the novel, when McKiernan asks, "You don't seem to have any interest in our cause?" Ruttledge replies: "No. I don't like violence." It is tempting to read the argument about Northern Ireland that follows as one that must have taken place, since so much else in the novel can be traced to facts. I know it didn't happen only because I once asked McGahern about it; with some satisfaction, he assured me that it was pure fiction.

Despite the autobiographical elements in his fiction, McGahern wasn't especially interested in exploring his own psyche. He rowed in familiar waters because the cadences in the prose and the resonant images came more naturally to him. And it was cadence and image that energized him, not self-revelation. In a letter from 1960, before he had published anything, he wrote: "The common notion that you can make art out of your life, refinement of pleasure etc, is pure moonshine as far as I see it. There must be some morality. You might as well call the philanderer a lover."

One day in the mid-1990s, after lunch in McGahern's house overlooking a lake in County Leitrim, the house from which many of these letters were sent, the house at the center of *That They May Face the Rising Sun*, McGahern handed me a sheaf of typed pages and indicated that I could take them with me. They contained a story, perhaps his best piece of fiction, called "The Country Funeral." In it McGahern writes about Philly, home from the oil fields, and his "delight in the rounds of celebration blinding him to the poor fact that it is not generally light but shadow that we cast." The story treats "light" and "shadow" and "poor fact" not as events taken from life, but as suggestive and potent words that move the narrative out of its own particular time, beyond its own ordinary occasion. By the end, Philly sits alone in his dead uncle's house, thinking: "Tomorrow he'd lie in the earth on the top of Killeelan Hill. A man is born. He dies. Where he himself stood now on the path between these two points could not be known . . . He must be already well out past halfway."

The second letter in the selection of McGahern's letters is from 1957, when McGahern was working as a teacher in Dublin. "I hope to go home about Wednesday," he writes to a friend. A footnote explains: "Home, at this point, was still the garda barracks in Cootehall, Co. Roscommon," where McGahern and his siblings were brought up by their father after their mother died in 1944. Over the next few years McGahern would explore the many levels of darkness and violence in this "home." In the meantime, though, he was a young writer in Dublin, gleefully attacking his elders. On Sean O'Faolain: "I have had no contact with him except through his work and it has always seemed phoney to me." On the novelist Kate O'Brien: "I find literary people bore me to almost the point of violence." On Austin Clarke, the reigning high priest of Irish poetry: "a sentimentalist gone sour."

Among McGahern's circle was the painter Patrick Swift, who in 1960 was in London, co-editing a magazine called *X*. The following year Swift published an extract from McGahern's unpublished first novel. It was spotted by Charles Monteith at Faber, who went on to oversee the publication of many of McGahern's books. When Swift read the first part of another novel—to be called *The Barracks*—he wrote: "It's a real advance. Very exciting. I still think the first book worth preserving but this is clearly a finer job, sharper and keener." Faber published *The Barracks* in 1963.

By then, McGahern's father had retired and moved to Grevisk in County Roscommon with his second wife. "It is constantly tense," McGahern wrote to a friend about the atmosphere in the house. "Egotism both greedy and afraid, once savage, wasting away as a kill-joy, gnawing at its own loneliness and despair." McGahern told Monteith: "My father says that [*The Barracks*] is an immoral disgrace and has called here from the country with that priest of my adolescence. I am afraid I am just living on my nerves. I would wish the next days out of my life." The novel tells the story of Elizabeth Reegan, the second wife of a sergeant, who is slowly dying of cancer in a police barracks in the Irish midlands. It would not have been lost on McGahern's father that the disease that killed John McGahern's mother had been given to his stepmother. But the book's offense arose more from the frank and unsparing way it dealt with the privacy of family life and its intimate domestic spaces.

"I am afraid my family are not reconciled and won't," McGahern wrote to one of Monteith's colleagues at Faber. "I am not wanted at home this Easter. It's strange how one learns to be alone. It was such a nightmare house to grow up in too." Three weeks later, he wrote to Monteith describing a family meeting in which

> I was formally expelled from my home and poor inheritance . . . It was then I realized that the old blackguard [his father] was enjoying himself as never before in his life. He made speeches. "If he can write, why can't he write about South America or some of those exotic places, and he'd make more money" . . . The local bumpkins say they'll "dip" me if I ever show my face again in Cootehall. The priest in Ballinamore removed the book from the County Leitrim library where my aunt lives as unfit for parochial consumption. It's such an absurd country, but from a safe distance I am as well to enjoy it quietly too.

Later that year, McGahern wrote to Monteith again: "Images of old horror started to come at me without warning and with horrible violence, atmospheres of evil. For weeks I lived in a state of pure panic. They'd always come suddenly. And the only time I was free of them was strangely when I was working with them."

As Faber prepared *The Barracks* for publication, Monteith wrote to McGahern to discuss the use of the word "fucking" in the book's dialogue. Having warned about the loss of sales to libraries in the English provinces, he suggested that "the retention of this word would of course almost certainly lead to your novel being banned in the Irish Republic." McGahern replied: "I have gone through the 'fuckings.' I could eliminate all Reegan's, indeed every one except three or four in Chapter 3, the doctor's dialogue, used to shock Elizabeth's awareness into a harsh despairing world of a particular consciousness. I don't know how I can really leave out these without harming the work."

Despite Faber's concerns, *The Barracks* wasn't banned in Ireland, but it seemed more than possible that McGahern's next novel, *The Dark*, would fall foul of the censor. In May 1964, McGahern wrote to Monteith to say that a *Guardian* journalist had told him "the novel should make a very interesting test case with the censorship here, they're growing very self-conscious about it and might let it through . . . And if they did ban it, it would attract outside attention." Monteith expressed his worry about a description in the novel "of the father in bed with the boy where the father uses the boy to excite himself sexually and eventually has an orgasm." He believed that if the scene were to remain, "an Irish banning would be a near certainty," and worried further about a possible libel action. "I remember you telling me how violently your father reacted to the publication of *The Barracks*; and I wonder if there's any possibility that he might identify himself—or be identified by his friends—with Mahoney [in *The Dark*]." McGahern replied:

I had actually started to change the passage you mentioned . . . I was very disturbed by the possibility of the legal business, it'd be for me the last horror, I'd rather not publish. It'd never occurred to me and I think it extremely unlikely . . . But what I will do is I will quietly investigate the position, in my own family first.

Two of McGahern's sisters read the manuscript and

felt practically certain that there would be no trouble. They said that there is only a spiritual resemblance between the man and the character . . . the house was a great deal worse than the house of the book. One of my sisters was temporarily paralysed by a beating . . . my father would never dare risk this becoming public.

In December 1964 Monteith sent a memo to a colleague at Faber: "I'm sure it would be wise, wouldn't it, not to distribute review copies of *The Dark* too widely or too far in advance to some of the Irish papers . . . We want to avoid a ban if possible—which is, I fear, probably inevitable." In New York, the editor at Macmillan who had published the U.S. edition of *The Barracks* wrote to Faber and McGahern: "It is a most unpleasant book with details that make the skin creep . . . John is young and no great harm would be done, if he did put this manuscript away, forgot it completely, and went on to his next book."

McGahern, on a year's leave from teaching in Dublin, was writing from Helsinki, where he had married the Finnish theater producer Annikki Laaksi in a civil ceremony. Laaksi remembered being taken to meet McGahern's father: "The moment I entered the McGahern family house . . . I sensed the horror and the violence. It was stifling. I could hardly breathe and I refused to stay a second night in the place." By May 1965 *The Dark* had been banned. "It's disturbing but there's nothing to do," McGahern told a friend. The book was seized by Irish customs before the censorship board even saw it. "I was more disturbed than I could have known by the seizing," McGahern told Monteith. "It was fortunate that the reviews were favourable, or I'd have no protection, I don't know what'll happen as it is if I go back." At the end of July he wrote to Brian Friel:

The Appeal Board have now rejected the Faber plea to revoke the ban. So I may get sacked [from his job as a teacher]. I intend to return as if nothing had happened and I have no other plans. I am anxious to live in Dublin for some more years if I can. If that's not possible I think I'll go to London.

The Irish censorship laws were a godsend to amateur moralists and general busybodies. The censorship board didn't read every book that was published but waited until a member of the public or a customs or police officer complained about a book or a passage in it. Although enthusiasm for banning books was waning by the time *The Dark* appeared, novels by Edna O'Brien, Maurice Leitch, Brian Moore and J. P. Donleavy were banned in the same period, as was *Catch-22*. (*Ulysses*, oddly enough, never was. And while the original Irish version of Brian Merriman's eighteenth-century poem "The Midnight Court" was freely in circulation, Frank O'Connor's

1945 translation into English was banned. The censorship laws were reformed somewhat in 1967.)

Since the board didn't have to explain its decisions, there is no way of knowing precisely why *The Dark* was taken out of circulation. It would not have helped that the word "fuck" is spelled out (as F-U-C-K) on the very first page in a scene where the father strips his young son naked before threatening him with a strap. It might not have helped either that the boy in question learns to masturbate. But there is another scene likely to have caused the board to sit up straight. Although McGahern wrote to Monteith to say that he had introduced "vagueness" into the scene in chapter 3 in which the father and son share a bed, it's clear that some sort of sex takes place between them. The chapter opens: "The worst was to have to sleep with him the nights he wanted love." By the morning, there was "shame and embarrassment and loathing, the dirty rags of intimacy." McGahern adds: "There were worse things in these nights than words." The father's hands "drew him closer. They began to move in caress on the back, shoving up the nightshirt, downwards lightly to the thighs and heavily up again, the voice echoing rhythmically the movement of the hands."

That autumn, when McGahern returned to the school where he had been teaching, he was told that he was fired, and that the instructions to remove him had come from the archbishop of Dublin. Like most Irish schools, it was effectively controlled and managed by the Catholic Church. When McGahern approached the teachers' union, they said they were willing to fight the sacking on the basis of the novel, but would not defend his civil marriage.

McGahern wrote to Michael McLaverty: "The union is a paper tiger, the church has all the power." One of the union officials asked him what had come over him to marry a foreigner when there were thousands of Irish women "with their tongues hanging out for a husband." McGahern could easily have become an important presence in the debate about censorship and liberalism, or indeed sex abuse, in Ireland. Instead, he went to London, worked as a temporary teacher, and stayed silent.

McGahern was thirty when he began his period of exile. He found London bleak. "Remorseless fog, blue where it can't be penetrated, utterly depressing," he wrote to a friend in January 1966. "In Dublin there's always an expectation of some change or there'll be some crack in the sky, to little virtue certainly, but not here. I always want to laugh when I see a sun or moon over London, it seems always they've come to the wrong place." He found writing "snail slow" and his next novel, *The Leavetaking*, would not appear until 1974. "The trouble I have with the work," he wrote to his U.S. editor, "is that it must be all the time as disciplined and as explosively accurate as verse, or it's nothing: one has to live in a continual thread-the-needle hell."

His marriage was also under strain. In July 1968 he noted drily: "Anu [his wife] spends most of her time with a friend at a sociological conference, to end the system of oppression and being oppressed." The previous year, McGahern had begun corresponding with Madeline Green, an American photographer he had met in New York who was now living in London. "I'm not calm enough to write," he told Green as his marriage fell apart. "It's insanity all the time in the house now." Soon he was telling his editor not to use his home address because "if the letters appear personal . . . Anu uses them against me; and she almost always gets and opens letters first . . . I don't want to go into it here, it seems close to illness, the whole business." The couple divorced in 1969.

In November 1970 McGahern and Green moved into a house in Cleggan, on the County Galway coast. McGahern didn't inform his father even of Green's existence. By the end of the month, though, Mary Kenny, a journalist in Dublin, had been told of the arrival in Cleggan of the notorious writer by "a second cousin of hers who owns a village bar," and she published it all in a national newspaper. McGahern and Green were married in 1973. Over the next few years, they lived in Achill in County Mayo, in Paris, in upstate New York, where McGahern taught at Colgate University, and in Newcastle, where he was writer in residence at the university. In 1974 they bought a small house and some land in a remote part of Leitrim. This was where McGahern lived for the rest of his life.

As he grew older, McGahern did not become more tolerant of other writers. Of the poet John Montague, he wrote: "I see him and his work increasingly as a very frail, and sincere, fraud." In 1975 he wrote to Seamus Heaney about being "caught" on a train by the poet Padraic Fiacc: "It was like being doused in soft warm shit." The following year, he wrote to Madeline about an event he had done, attended, he said, by "Shit Silkin," i.e., the poet Jon Silkin. When *The Barracks* was adapted for the stage by the playwright Hugh Leonard, McGahern wrote to his U.S. editor: "The tart's name is Hugh Leonard, did Stephen D. once, and several cheap hits."

During these years, McGahern was writing his fourth novel, *The Pornographer*, in which the protagonist, a young man called Michael, makes a colonel and a woman called Mavis get up to all kinds of tricks. In 1978 McGahern wrote to Madeline to say that he "had managed to get half of the Colonel & Mavis scene done this morning. I'll be glad to finish with it." Shovlin offers a useful footnote: "McGahern found [the sex scenes] difficult to write and had relied on Madeline to purchase pornography on his behalf when they lived in Newcastle upon Tyne."

At the time *The Pornographer* came out, I had little interest in McGahern's work. I found too much Irish misery in it, too much fear and violence and repressed sexuality, too much rural life and Catholicism. Perhaps my aversion was made more intense by the fact that I recognized this world. I had been brought up in it; I was still living in it. But *The Pornographer* was a departure from his previous work. It had the same slow cadences and relentless bleakness as *The Barracks*, but the Dublin it described was a damp, unforgiving place, stripped of any easy Irishness; it could have been any run-down European city, and the protagonist could have been at the center of an existential novel. Six years before it was published, McGahern wrote to Monteith: "I have noticed that all my serious mistakes have been made when I have copied life too closely." In *The Pornographer*, he found a useful metaphor for the act of writing fiction, but, more important, he created a character lost in a city, obsessed with sex and death, writing scenes that soared above the mere facts of McGahern's own life. (Even so, we do find elements from the novel in these letters, including a reference in 1960 to an aunt being treated for cancer in a Dublin hospital, and letters about a love affair in 1962 that led to the birth of a child.)

After the novel appeared, a Dublin journalist, according to a footnote here, "asked McGahern if the character of Maloney, the eccentric editor in *The Pornographer*, was based on him. [This] led to a temporary cooling of relations between the two." "Read the book," McGahern replied. "The character alluded to isn't a caricature of anybody. Very little of him exists in 'real life.' Of the characters I have drawn, with the possible exception of Elizabeth Reegan [in *The Barracks*], he is the person I like best."

McGahern's world was self-enclosed. From unpromising material, and in a tone that was simple and spare, he could evoke a scene or an undramatic moment with astonishing precision. After *The Pornographer*, I began to reassess his earlier work, and grew to love *The Barracks*, with special reverence for the battle between light and darkness in a small domestic setting at the very start of the book:

Mrs. Reegan darned an old woollen sock as the February night came on, her head bent, catching the threads on the needle by the light of the fire, the daylight gone without her noticing. A boy of twelve and two dark-haired girls were close about her at the fire. They'd grown uneasy, in the way children can indoors in the failing light. The bright golds and scarlets of the religious pictures on the walls had faded, their glass glittered now in the sudden flashes of firelight, and as it deepened the dusk turned reddish from the Sacred Heart lamp that burned before the small wickerwork crib of Bethlehem on the mantelpiece. Only the cups and saucers laid ready on the table for their father's tea were white and brilliant. The wind and rain rattling at the window-panes seemed to grow part of the spell of silence and increasing darkness, the spell of the long darning needle flashing in the woman's hand, and it was with a visible strain that the boy managed at last to break their fear of the coming night.

McGahern's third collection of stories, *High Ground*, appeared in 1985. By now he had begun to relax his sentences and to allow public life in Ireland, and the changing social world around him, into his fiction:

> The tide that emptied the countryside more than any other since the famine has turned. Hardly anyone now goes to England. Some who went came home to claim inheritances, and stayed, old men waiting at the ends of lanes on Sunday evenings for the minibus to take them to the church bingo. Most houses have a car and color television. The bicycles and horses, carts and traps and sidecars, have gone from the roads. A big yellow bus brings the budding scholars to school in the town, and it is no longer uncommon to go on to university.

Around the same time I wrote a piece about McGahern for a Dublin magazine. Having watched him appear as a shy and uncomfortable man in a television interview with Mary Holland, I was surprised when I went to Galway, where he was speaking to a university audience, to see that he was confident and funny on stage. He read amusing bits from books that I had thought, up to then, were drooping with melancholy. Soon afterwards, I went to see him in Leitrim. This involved getting a train from Dublin to a small station on the Sligo line called Dromod and being met by McGahern and transported along narrow roads to a lane that led to a lake and a further lane that followed the contours of the lake to a small one-story house.

All the malice that is in the letters was also in the conversation. He made it sound natural. So many men of his generation in Ireland, including writers, were cautious and circumspect and tremendously boring. It was a relief to be in McGahern's company. In person, he could make harsh judgments, but he could also have wondrous responses to anything that appealed to him. This mixture of tones can often be found in the same letter, as when he writes to Alain Delahaye from America in 1984:

Then we drove south to visit Madeline's mother . . . She lived alone with an aged cat, feeding birds and wild animals. She's a terrible person, almost worse than Madeline's father. It may be luck that we have no children . . . [Yves] Bonnefoy spoke here last week. A nice man . . . read in French, poem by poem, very plainly and beautifully. Questions followed. Many of the questions were irrelevant or stupid but Bonnefoy handled them beautifully. He seemed to me to speak out of an enlightened commonsense. He'd plainly lived for long in that solitary place where poetry happens, and spoke clearly of its simple, unchanging laws. It was a relief after the glittering nonsense that often travels on the same passport round here. There were forty to fifty people. Seven hundred cheered a drunken [James] Dickey some months before. I didn't go to the reception.

McGahern was amused by many things and people. There was no telephone in the house in Leitrim on my first visit ("I'm uneasy on the phone," he wrote in 1998. "I think it comes from having to 'mind' the phone when I was a boy in my father's police station") and I noticed no television. I realized that he had no interest in music as he was tone-deaf. But most of all, he had no interest in Dublin. His capital was the town of Enniskillen in Northern Ireland. After that, Paris, where Madeline owned a flat. After that, Colgate University in upstate New York. ("There is so much wealth," he wrote in 1983. "The trees, the cut grass, white houses, the tanned beautiful young people in their energetic indolence. They continually wave to me. I feel like some stranded idiot, half believing that it's real . . . The people are pleasant but sometimes the very force of the friendliness can be numbing, the ruthless practicality it hides.")

McGahern disliked some of the books I mentioned to him, or had no interest in them. He had not read any of the writers who were all the rage at the time. He wanted to talk about ones who still mattered to him, including early Joyce, Proust, Yeats, Rilke, some Forrest Reid, Patrick Kavanagh, Philip Larkin ("His work will outwear his own time and all its fashionable gases," he wrote to Monteith after Larkin's death) and, later, Alice McDermott's *Charming Billy*, the stories of Alistair MacLeod and John Williams's *Stoner*, of which he was an early champion.

McGahern's letters would usually come when I had sent him a book I had published or an article I had written or when I had news that might interest him. The handwriting was emphatically that of a schoolmaster, each letter clearly made. The tone could be that of a schoolmaster too.

The selection includes a letter from 1991 in which McGahern responds to a researcher who is writing a thesis about his work. "I think the difficulty of dealing with letters," he writes to her, "is that they are never quite honest. Often out of sympathy or diffidence or kindness or affection or self-interest we quite rightly hide our true feelings." He goes on to explain the way his frank epistolary style caused the end of his relationship with Michael McLaverty:

> I was dismayed when he sent me *The Brightening Day* [in 1965]. I wished it had never been published as I saw it could only damage the work. I am sure I tried to put it as gently as I could, but there was no way I could give him the support he so much wanted for such a book . . . and that ended what was always a tentative, cautious relationship. He did not want to see me when I came to give a lecture in Belfast, it must have been 1967 or 1968.

In November 1986, as he worked on his novel *Amongst Women*, McGahern wrote to Delahaye: "I know it will be my last novel." Three years later, he and Madeline came to dinner at my house in Dublin. On the way out, he pointed to an envelope he had left on a table. It contained the flat proofs of *Amongst Women*. When I wrote to him to say how much I admired the book, he replied that "it was a pure pig to write. There were times when I thought it had me beaten and that I was finished as a writer. Many times in those four or five years it took to write." On publication, he wrote to Delahaye: "There will be no peace till it is over. Already journalists have been here and more are on the way." When the book was shortlisted for the Booker Prize, McGahern wrote to the playwright Thomas Kilroy: "Horseracing is fun . . . but not when you're the horse."

In 2002 McGahern was diagnosed with cancer. He wrote to a producer at the BBC:

> I am out of hospital, tending the cattle, going for the odd walk, drinking the occasional glass of wine—waiting to be called for chemotherapy, one hour a week in Dublin for 24 weeks. I had so resigned myself to a worse fate that I cannot believe it, as if it is unlucky to think I may be all right for a time.

A year later, he told a friend that a liver scan had shown "my condition is terminal." He could be treated with drugs, but "they are all containments and not a cure, of course, but they said I could have a number of years. They were so blunt and straight about everything that I sort of believe them."

In these last years, with access to his father's letters to his mother, he wrote *Memoir*. In February 2006, a month before he died, he replied to questions from a graduate student about the process of charting the past in that book:

Memory is uncertain. I had many letters that I was able to check. These showed me that I had often arranged things in different sequences in my mind. My sisters read the manuscript in draft, and naturally had different versions, or slightly different versions, of the same event, and they recovered two important scenes that I had blanked out. My aim at all times was to get as close as possible to the facts.

The facts were already known to the readers of his novels. Heaney considered the repetitions in McGahern's work in a review of *The Leavetaking*:

> McGahern's imagination is ruminant. It chews the cud of the past, digests and redigests it, interrogates it for its meaning, savours it for its bittersweet recurrence. This is the way to understand the compulsive return to certain landscapes and themes in his work. *The Leavetaking*, for example, plaits the cable of its story from strands drawn out of *The Barracks* . . . yet it would be a misunderstanding of his art to imply . . . that McGahern is "repeating himself." He is rather retrieving himself, achieving a new self.

In this last book, then, McGahern sought to retrieve himself once more, alert to the uncertainty of memory, and helped, as he said, by family and documents. Helped also, perhaps, by the fact that he had written the story as fiction thirty years earlier in *The Leavetaking*. It is as if a precise set of memories actually became more solid and vivid and indisputable by virtue of having been set down in the earlier book.

"I want you to promise not to cry if I go away," the mother asks the boy in *The Leavetaking*. In *Memoir*, this becomes: "I don't want you to be too upset if I have to go away." In *The Leavetaking*, a neighbor asks about the mother: "Say if she doesn't get better what'll you do?" This becomes in *Memoir*: "What would you do if she didn't get better?" In *The Leavetaking*, the father asks: "Could you say shit or piss before women?" In *Memoir*: "Could you say shit or piss in front of women?"

The connection between the memories in *The Leavetaking* and in *Memoir* occur most intensely in the pages that deal with the emptying out of the house where the mother is dying, the hammering loose of the iron beds, and then the news of her death coming to the son, who has been taken to his father's house. In *The Leavetaking*, this news is announced by the father: "The children's mother died at a quarter past three today. May the Lord have mercy on her soul." In the memoir, the time is different: "The children's mother died at a quarter to three. May the Lord have mercy on her soul." In the novel and in *Memoir*, the narrator, who does not go to the funeral, imagines it as he watches the clock. In the novel: "A wren flitted from branch to branch under the leaves." In the memoir: "I had only a wren for company, flitting from branch to bare branch under the thick covering of leaves." This last detail—the wren—seems an integral part of the novel, another detail that serves to distract from the knowledge that the mother's funeral is going on in the narrator's absence. In the memoir, however, it is hard not to wonder about the wren. Could you be sure you remembered a single bird sixty years after the event?

I did not raise these questions with McGahern. The few times I saw him in the last year of his life there was too much else to talk about. The hospital and the staff intrigued him, as did the shape of the day as a patient. He made it all sound local, the hospital as a village or a parish. And he remained in a state halfway between wonder and indignation on recalling that, having been diagnosed with cancer, he was asked if he needed to see a counselor to help him absorb the news.

It was late at night in the house in Leitrim when he told that story. McGahern went to a sideboard and poured more whiskey. He turned around. "A counselor!" He shook his head at the very thought. "What would a counselor tell you? You would want to be an awful fool not to know that we only bloom once."

These were the exact words. I made sure to remember them. McGahern spoke them as though he had written them, relishing the pattern in the sound, putting hard emphasis on "bloom" and letting "once" die away with a short breath after it. I remember the expression on his face even better than his voice, the look of immense sadness at the thought that he would soon die and that there was nothing that could be done about it, and then a smile, almost triumphant, and then a look of pure satisfaction that something true had finally been said. He had found the right words for it. And then he changed the subject.

EPILOGUE

Alone in Venice

London Review of Books · 2020

S uddenly, there was nothing to complain about. No cruise ships went up the Giudecca Canal. There were no tourists clogging up the narrow streets. Piazza San Marco was often completely deserted. On some bridges a few gondoliers stood around, but there was no one to hire them. Instead, dogs and their owners walked the streets, with no one pushing them out of the way. People greeted one another familiarly. They had the city back.

Suddenly, the intimate spaces were free. In San Polo, I could spend time in the side room that houses Giandomenico Tiepolo's Stations of the Cross. I would never have that room to myself again. In the Scuola di San Giorgio degli Schiavoni, where the Carpaccios are, the woman at the door was almost glad to see me. It was as if she were putting on a play that was about to fold. I sat for a while contemplating St. Augustine in his sumptuously lit study. I liked that he threw books on the floor. No one came to the small gallery in the hour I stayed there.

It was late October. The days were foggy. By lunchtime, a pale sun fought to break through, and, for about an hour before it did, an unearthly and sickly yellow light clung to everything. And then there was sunshine. One day, however, the fog licked its tongue over Venice all afternoon as well. At twilight, a strange, dark blueness descended. I got a vaporetto from San Zaccaria to San Stae and there was no other traffic, none at all, on the Grand Canal. After dark, as I walked from Piazza San Marco to Campo Santa Margherita, the restaurants were open, but hardly anyone was inside or even at the outside tables. When I bought ice cream, the little cup was put into a paper bag and I was warned not to eat it on the street. Even pulling your mask down for a second to sample ice cream was not allowed. Soon the restaurants would be ordered to close at six o'clock.

One morning, I managed to gain early access to San Rocco. As I stood in front of Tintoretto's Crucifixion in the side room upstairs, I wondered if my eyes were more alert than usual because of the early hour. The different tones in the huge painting almost shone out. I could trace varying shades of pink, each one catching the light in a different way, or note the yellow tunic of the figure I supposed to be St. John with what felt like fresh, or better, vision. I wondered if the new emptiness that had fallen on the city had somehow added clarity to the art.

Since I had been given this new gift of sudden acute vision in San Rocco, I thought that I should go and look at Tintoretto's other versions of the Crucifixion in Venice. Maybe I would be able to see these better too, even if they were not as epic as the one in San Rocco. I made a few doomed efforts to get inside the church of San

Cassiano, but it was always closed. Then one morning, on finding the side door open, I pushed it and went in. There was some sort of ceremony going on, with five or six people in attendance. It might have been a wedding, but it was hard to think who was marrying whom. Maybe a middle-aged black-haired woman was tying the knot with the little fellow beside her. I sought to sneak by them to get a look at the Tintoretto Crucifixion at the side of the main altar.

Even in shadow, this painting is startling. The three crucified figures are on the right-hand side, facing left. The painting is dominated by dark clouds. In the background, silhouetted against a brightness on the horizon are about two dozen looming lances and pikes. Most of the colors are somber, except some textured pink in the garments. Because the painting is dark, I kept peering at it, trying to see it better. When I turned on the little light, I drew attention to my presence, and a young woman told me that I must leave. I let her know by a process of shrugging that I would depart in my own time. This caused her to make clear, as the light flipped off, that I should not turn it on again. What was strange was that the electric glow took all the mystery out of the painting, in which ominous cloud hits against embattled light, in which the viewpoint is oblique, in which shadow does more work than light. Seeing it in shadow satisfied the eye more than looking at it when illuminated.

This was true also of another Tintoretto Crucifixion, the one towards the back of the Gesuati, a church overlooking the Giudecca Canal. It was a rainy afternoon; some scarce light came in from the entrance, the main door having been left open. I sat for a while and tried to get my eyes used to the watery grayness because there was no artificial light available to focus on paintings. This Crucifixion was easier to see than the one in San Cassiano because the central image, taking up the whole top half of the painting, was Jesus on the cross, with radiant light painted behind him. This image lacked the complexity of the two other Crucifixions. More interesting than the hanging Jesus were the mourning figures below him. Most of the light, such as it was, focused on them. Intricate and intense work had been done on their faces and robes. They were huddled together; the robes appeared to be all made of the same material, with the same few colors, thus adding to the idea of them as a mass, a shocked cluster rather than a set of individuals. They faced away from the hanging savior; only two outliers looked up at the cross.

Slowly, as I tried to disentangle each face and set of robes, I found that I could see the painting as well as I wanted to, even though the light was dismal. A day later, at the Accademia, I felt that it was too easy to see the large Tintoretto Crucifixion that had formerly been in the church of San Severo. The light was too modern, the colors were too clean, the seat in the middle of the large, high room too comfortable. I shouldn't complain. The pose of the good thief—hanging off rather than on his cross—could not have been more intriguing. But I couldn't understand why the lighting in San Rocco had been more satisfying and comforting than the lighting here, and why the daylight of early winter in the Gesuati was far more helpful than the crude electric light in San Cassiano.

At the Accademia, I turned from Tintoretto's Crucifixion to look at Veronese's Annunciation. The Virgin, who is almost cowering in the corner, looks frightened in this painting, and the angel is overbearing and hovering over one side of the room. The center of the painting is empty, just interior domestic space, with some lovely tiling, an archway leading to what could be a little temple, with trees around it, and the pink and blue sky. Veronese made an image of pure harmony and then disrupted it at the edges with the presence of the angel and the frightened woman. For once, I was glad that I could see this drama in a gallery space and that the painting has been cleaned and restored. That meant that the glass vase on the balustrade to the right, which picks up the light in two inspired white daubs of paint and breaks the symmetry, could be clearly seen.

Suddenly, I discovered that there was a man in the next room, and he had just coughed loudly. He was sitting on the bench looking at a gallery guide and had his mask around his chin. For one glistening moment, my inner little fascist emerged. I stood in the doorway until I caught his eye. I thought he might be Italian. I signaled to him that he should put on his mask. Ruefully, he did so. While I felt the glow that only self-satisfaction can bring, he will hate me for the rest of his days.

During my time wandering from church to church, a friend gave me a book called *From Darkness to Light: Writers in Museums 1798–1898*, edited by Rosella Mamoli Zorzi and Katherine Manthorne. Writers, it seems, have been grumbling about the lighting of paintings in Venice for some time. These include John Ruskin and Henry James, who, Mamoli Zorzi writes, "fell in love with the paintings in San Rocco despite not being able to see them properly." Ruskin wrote that the three halls in San Rocco were "so badly lighted, in consequence of the admirable arrangements of the Renaissance architect, that it is only in the early morning that some of the pictures can be seen at all, nor can they ever be seen but imperfectly."

In 1869 Henry James wrote to his brother that Tintoretto in Venice was "at a vast disadvantage inasmuch as with hardly an exception his pictures are atrociously hung & lighted." "It may be said as a general thing that you never see the Tintoret," he wrote in an essay of 1882. "The churches of Venice are rich in pictures, and many a masterpiece lurks in the unaccommodating gloom of side-chapels and sacristies . . . some of them indeed, hidden behind the altar, suffer in a darkness that can never be explored." James had it in for San Giorgio degli Schiavoni, where I got to spend time on my own looking at Carpaccio's St. Augustine: "The place is small and incommodious, the pictures are out of sight and ill-lighted, the custodian is rapacious, the visitors are mutually intolerable, but the shabby little chapel is a palace of art."

Mamoli Zorzi writes about this business of loving a painting more the less you can really see it: "We are facing an aesthetics of darkness." She goes on:

> Darkness remains a constant element in the second half of the nineteenth century; it is interrupted only by candles. Even in the 1880s and 1890s, when gaslight was already in use and was on the brink of being supplanted by electric light, candles appear to have been the only source of light in the churches and in the Scuola Grande di San Rocco. They were lit only during ceremonies, and snuffed out immediately afterwards for fear of fires.

James believed that Tintoretto's Crucifixion was, Mamoli Zorzi writes, "the only picture which could be seen well in the Scuola Grande di San Rocco" and continued: "It is true that in looking at this huge composition you look at many pictures; it has not only a multitude of figures but a wealth of episodes . . . Surely no single picture in the world contains so much of human life; there is everything in it, including the most exquisite beauty."

In his introduction to *The Tragic Muse,* James wrote again that the painting showed "without loss of authority half a dozen actions separately taking place."

In his essay "Light at the Scuola Grande di San Rocco," Demetrio Sonaglioni writes, "There is no evidence that gas or oil were ever used inside the Scuola." And it was not until 1937 that electric light was installed there. The system was created by the designer Mariano Fortuny, who used "diffusing lamps with indirect light." In 2014 these were replaced by an LED system. That is why I felt that I could see the San Rocco Crucifixion, without it being overlit or overcleaned.

All this business of light and shade kept me distracted until, once more on a vaporetto on the Grand Canal, I saw a motorboat that doubled as a water hearse and plonked in the middle of it a coffin. It was like a moment that Thomas Mann might have conjured up and it made me plan to go to the Lido and take a look at the Grand Hotel des Bains, now a shell, where he set *Death in Venice.* More than sixty years after the story was written, Katia Mann, Thomas's widow, in a book called *Unwritten Memories,* left an account of their trip to Venice in 1911:

In the dining room, on the very first day, we saw the Polish family, which looked exactly the way my husband described them: the girls were dressed rather stiffly and severely, and the very charming, beautiful boy of about thirteen was wearing a sailor suit with an open collar and very pretty lacings. He caught my husband's attention immediately. The boy was tremendously attractive, and my husband was always watching him with his companions on the beach. He didn't pursue him through all Venice—that he didn't do—but the boy did fascinate him, and he thought of him often.

At Cook's, when they went to book a sleeping car, an "honest English clerk" said: "If I were you, I wouldn't make the sleeping car reservations for a week from now, but for tomorrow, because, you know, several cases of cholera have broken out; naturally it's being kept secret and hushed up. We don't know how far it will spread. You must have noticed, though, that many guests in the hotel have already left."

The best part of the Lido is the journey there from Venice, and even better is the journey back, especially if it is close to sundown. It's all pretty ordinary over there: I did not see or feel any literary ghosts, least of all those of Tadzio or his Teutonic admirer. It was a sunny afternoon on a disused beach. There was one swimmer, and there were a few men fishing at the end of a modest breakwater. Sand was piled up to prevent the Adriatic from encroaching too near the road on which the old Hotel des Bains stood, its gates padlocked.

I wonder if I am alone in still liking *Death in Venice*, even in Helen Lowe-Porter's translation. It has become common not to approve of her translations of Mann. This dislike may be exacerbated by the knowledge that she is the great-grandmother of Boris Johnson. Mann's story has many small details—losing the luggage, the appearance of the old roué, the dishonest gondolier—that tally with Katia's memory. Mann's putting death and pestilence beside all the desire bubbling away in his protagonist Aschenbach satisfied some set of deep longings in his own nature. He loved disease and he could not stop thinking about sex; he was especially content, his diaries tell us, when dreaming about young men.

It is fascinating to watch him spread his own heightened fear of the exotic, feverish world beyond Europe as if mentioning the very names of the places would inflame the blood:

> For the past several years Asiatic cholera had shown a strong tendency to spread. Its source was the hot, moist swamps of the delta of the Ganges, where it bred in the mephitic air of that primeval island-jungle, among whose bamboo thickets the tiger crouches, where life of every sort flourishes in rankest abundance, and only man avoids the spot. Thence the pestilence had spread throughout Hindustan, raging with great violence; moved eastwards to China, westwards to Afghanistan and Persia; following the great caravan routes, it brought terror to Astrakhan, terror to Moscow.

In the light of all this mephitic terror, it was a relief to have my temperature taken the next day when I returned to the Accademia. I had another plague on my mind, almost as a way of keeping away the one raging outside and perhaps even inside the gallery, although it was mainly empty. This plague happened in Venice in the last months of Titian's life and is vividly evoked in "The Plague and the Pity," the last chapter of Sheila Hale's biography of the painter.

Between August 1575 and the following February, there were 3,696 plague deaths in Venice, about 2 percent of the population. Most of the cases were "in the slums and the crowded ghetto," Hale writes. Soon, however, the authorities relaxed, lifting the ban on crowds, manufacturing and trade. But then fatalities rose again. The doge invited two medical experts to explain that "the infection was not plague but a famine fever that affected only the undernourished poor." A few days later, these experts were proved wrong when "the contagion spread like wildfire into the houses of rich and poor alike." "Doctors," Hale writes, "circulating the city in gondolas followed by barbers and Jesuit priests, took pulses, lanced boils, applied leeches and spread the contagion by marking the doors of contaminated houses with the infected blood of their patients." By the time the plague ended, it had done away with a quarter of the population of Venice.

Titian stayed in the city during the pestilence. He was at least eighty-six; he might have been even older. He must have labored on a number of paintings, but he definitely worked on one—the Pietà in the Accademia. Hale sees this as a quintessential piece of late work: "It is a commemoration of his artistic life, a dialogue with the paintings, sculptures and architecture that had nourished his genius, a final declaration of the capacity of paint to represent and improve upon stone sculpture, and a testament to his devotion to Christ and his mother Mary." Titian put a tiny portrait of himself and his son, a sort of token, under the lion in the right-hand corner. He died of fever in the middle of the plague. There is an account of a "long and elaborate" funeral service, but it did not take place. He was carried through the plague-ridden city to the Frari and buried there. Soon afterwards, his son died of the plague.

The Pietà, then, is Titian's plague painting, just as *Death in Venice* is Mann's cholera story. The image Titian made is not, as other Pietàs are, an image of peace and resolution; the mother is not resignedly holding her son whose suffering is over. Rather, it is a painting filled with shock and panic. Something atrocious has just occurred. Maybe Titian made this great last painting as a way of keeping the noise outside at bay. In his studio, as the doctors of Venice were busy, he created his own mourners so that the public ones might keep away from him. Maybe he worked on making his stone in the painting embody real stone, the backdrop like a piece of sculpture, as a way of defying all the fuss out in the street.

One of the subjects to muse on as old age begins is how unfair life is. Venice is a good place for such thoughts. One day I walked down to Riva dei Sette Martiri, which is where I stayed first in the city. I had a coffee and looked out over the misty water. I came to this very spot first in 1977, which is forty-three years ago. If I have the chance to come and sit here in forty-three years' time, I will be 108. I realize that this is a most banal and useless subject for contemplation. But what else is there to think about?

There was quietness to ponder; maybe that was enough. When I stood outside the Accademia, the only sound came from a stray boat on one of the lesser canals and a vaporetto on the Grand Canal, a dutiful, useful ghost, taking the small population of Venice from one place to another while the hordes that normally come to the city remained crouched in their homes, fearful, socially distant. Once they come back, we can all start complaining again. Until they do, we will wear our masks and whisper about small mercies and think about light and shade.

Text Permissions

Cancer: My Part in Its Downfall
London Review of Books, Vol. 41, No. 8, April 18, 2019

A Guest at the Feast
Penguin Short, 2011

A Brush with the Law
The Dublin Review, Autumn 2007

The Paradoxical Pope
The New Yorker, October 9, 1995

Among the Flutterers
London Review of Books, Vol. 32, No. 16, August 19, 2010

The Bergoglio Smile: Pope Francis
London Review of Books, Vol. 43, No. 2, January 21, 2021

The Ferns Report

London Review of Books, Vol. 27, No. 23, December 1, 2005

Putting Religion in Its Place: Marilynne Robinson

London Review of Books, Vol. 36, No. 20, October 23, 2014

Issues of Truth and Invention: Francis Stuart

London Review of Books, Vol. 23, No. 1, January 4, 2001

Snail Slow: John McGahern

London Review of Books, Vol. 44, No. 2, January 27, 2022

Alone in Venice

London Review of Books, Vol. 42, No. 22, November 19, 2020

Acknowledgments

I am grateful to the *London Review of Books*, where many of these pieces first appeared, especially to Mary-Kay Wilmers, Alice Spawls and Daniel Soar. Also, to Brendan Barrington at *The Dublin Review*, where "A Brush with the Law," delivered as a lecture to the Burren Law School, was first published. Also, to *The New Yorker*, where "The Paradoxical Pope" first appeared. And to my agent Peter Straus, as well as Mary Mount at Penguin and Nan Graham at Scribner. And to Catriona Crowe, Hedi El Kholti, Ed Mulhall and Angela Rohan.

About the Author

Colm Tóibín is the author of ten novels, including *The Magician*, winner of the Rathbones Folio Prize; *The Master*, winner of the *Los Angeles Times* Book Prize; *Brooklyn*, winner of the Costa Book Award; *The Testament of Mary* and *Nora Webster*, as well as two story collections and several books of criticism. He is the Irene and Sidney B. Silverman Professor of the Humanities at Columbia University and has been named as the Laureate for Irish Fiction for 2022–2024 by the Arts Council of Ireland. Three times shortlisted for the Booker Prize, Tóibín lives in Dublin and New York.